**W9-ARN-824**

# SELF-COMPASSION

# *Self-* Compassion

### Stop Beating Yourself Up and Leave Insecurity Behind

## KRISTIN NEFF, PH.D.

*wm*

**WILLIAM MORROW**
*An Imprint of* HarperCollins*Publishers*

This book contains advice and information relating to health care. It is not intended to replace medical advice and should be used to supplement rather than replace regular care by your doctor. It is recommended that you seek your physician's advice before embarking on any medical program or treatment. All efforts have been made to assure the accuracy of the information contained in this book as of the date of publication. The publisher and the author disclaim liability for any medical outcomes that may occur as a result of applying the methods suggested in this book.

FIRST EDITION

*Designed by Jamie Lynn Kerner*

---

Library of Congress Cataloging-in-Publication Data

Neff, Kristin.
  Self-compassion : stop beating yourself up and leave insecurity behind / by Kristin Neff. — 1st ed.
      p. cm.
  Summary: "A book that teaches readers how to silence self-criticism and re-place it with self-compassion in order to fulfill our highest potential and live happier, more fulfilled lives"—Provided by publisher.
  ISBN 978-0-06-173351-2
  1. Self-acceptance. 2. Compassion. 3. Security (Psychology) I. Title.
BF575.S37N44    2011
158.1—dc22
                                                                2010047190

---

13 14 15  OV/RRD  20 19 18 17 16 15 14

*To Rupert and Rowan*
*For the joy, wonder, love, and inspiration they give me*

# CONTENTS

|  | Acknowledgments | ix |
|---|---|---|
| *Part One* | Why Self-Compassion? | 1 |
| 1 | Discovering Self-Compassion | 3 |
| 2 | Ending the Madness | 18 |
| *Part Two* | The Core Components of Self-Compassion | 39 |
| 3 | Being Kind to Ourselves | 41 |
| 4 | We're All in This Together | 61 |
| 5 | Being Mindful of What Is | 80 |
| *Part Three* | The Benefits of Self-Compassion | 107 |
| 6 | Emotional Resilience | 109 |
| 7 | Opting Out of the Self-Esteem Game | 135 |
| 8 | Motivation and Personal Growth | 159 |
| *Part Four* | Self-Compassion in Relation to Others | 185 |
| 9 | Compassion for Others | 187 |
| 10 | Self-Compassionate Parenting | 207 |
| 11 | Love and Sex | 221 |
| *Part Five* | The Joy of Self-Compassion | 243 |
| 12 | The Butterfly Emerges | 245 |
| 13 | Self-Appreciation | 267 |
|  | Notes | 285 |
|  | Index | 299 |

# ACKNOWLEDGMENTS

First and foremost, I have to thank my husband, Rupert, for encouraging me to write this book, for helping me to craft the proposal and book itself, and for being my main editor. He taught me how to drop the academic-speak and write in plain English, and I couldn't ask for a more brilliant or eloquent mentor. Thanks also to my friend and agent, Elizabeth Sheinkman, who believed in me and somehow managed to make my dream a reality. Thanks to all the kind and supportive people at HarperCollins, who have taken a chance on me and made this book happen.

With great gratitude I'd like to acknowledge the various teachers who have helped me understand the meaning and value of self-compassion. My long-term teacher Rodney Smith has contributed greatly to my knowledge of the dharma and has been a compassionate and wise guide over the years. Many others have had a major impact on me, either from the meditation retreats they've led and/or the books they've written: Sharon Salzberg, Howie Cohen, Guy Armstrong, Thich Nhat Hahn, Joseph Goldstein, Jack Kornfield, Pema Chodran, Tara Brach, Tara Bennett-Goleman, Ram Dass, Eckhart Tolle, Leigh Brasington, Shinzen Young, Steve Armstrong, Kamala Masters, and Jon Kabat-Zinn, to name but a few.

I must also thank Paul Gilbert for his brilliant thinking and research on compassion, and for his encouragement of my work. My partner in crime, Christopher Germer, has been a wonderful friend as well as an amazing colleague, and I hope we continue to teach and write about self-compassion together for years to come. I'd like to thank Mark Leary, who gave me my first break by publishing the initial theoretical and empirical articles I wrote on self-compassion. He's also a brilliant researcher and I'm grateful that studying self-compassion has caught his interest. There are many others who have played an essential role in making this book possible, too many to mention here.

Finally, I'd like to thank my mother and father, who each in their own way opened my mind and heart to spirituality when I was a young child, so that my personality formed around the desire to awaken.

*Part One*

# WHY SELF-COMPASSION?

*Chapter One*

# DISCOVERING SELF-COMPASSION

*This kind of compulsive concern with "I, me, and mine" isn't the same as loving ourselves . . . Loving ourselves points us to capacities of resilience, compassion, and understanding within that are simply part of being alive.*
—SHARON SALZBERG, *The Force of Kindness*

IN THIS INCREDIBLY COMPETITIVE SOCIETY OF OURS, HOW MANY OF us truly feel good about ourselves? It seems such a fleeting thing—feeling good—especially as we need to feel *special and above average* to feel worthy. Anything less seems like a failure. I remember once as a freshman in college, after spending hours getting ready for a big party, I complained to my boyfriend that my hair, makeup, and outfit were woefully inadequate. He tried to reassure me by saying, "Don't worry, you look fine."

"*Fine?* Oh great, I always wanted to look *fine . . .*"

The desire to feel special is understandable. The problem is that by definition, it's impossible for *everyone* to be above average at the same time. Although there are some ways in which we excel, there is always someone smarter, prettier, more successful. How do we cope with this? Not very well. To see ourselves positively, we tend to inflate our own egos and put others down so that we can feel good in comparison. But this strategy comes at a price—it holds us back from reaching our full potential in life.

## Distorting Mirrors

If I have to feel better than you to feel good about myself, then how clearly am I really going to see you, or myself for that matter? Let's say I had a stressful day at work and am grumpy and irritable with my husband when he gets home later that evening (purely hypothetical, of course). If I'm highly invested in having a positive self-image and don't want to risk viewing myself in a negative light, I'm going to slant my interpretation of what transpires to make sure that any friction between us is seen as my husband's fault, not my own.

> "GOOD, YOU'RE HOME. DID YOU PICK UP THE GROCERIES LIKE I ASKED?"
>
> "I JUST WALKED THOUGH THE DOOR, HOW ABOUT 'NICE TO SEE YOU, DEAR, HOW WAS YOUR DAY?'"
>
> "WELL, IF *you* WEREN'T SO FORGETFUL, MAYBE I WOULDN'T HAVE TO ALWAYS HOUND YOU."
>
> "AS A MATTER OF FACT, I DID PICK UP THE GROCERIES."
>
> "OH . . . WELL, UM . . . IT'S THE EXCEPTION THAT PROVES THE RULE. I WISH YOU WEREN'T SO UNRELIABLE."

Not exactly a recipe for happiness.

Why is it so hard to admit when we step out of line, are rude, or act impatient? Because our ego feels so much better when we project our flaws and shortcomings on to someone else. *It's your fault, not mine.* Just think about all the arguments and fights that grow out of this simple dynamic. Each person blames the other for saying or doing something wrong, justifying their own actions as if their life depended on it, while both know, in their heart of hearts, that it takes two to tango. How much time do we waste like this? Wouldn't it be so much better if we could just fess up and play fair?

But change is easier said than done. It's almost impossible to notice those aspects of ourselves that cause problems relating to others, or that keep us from reaching our full potential, if we can't see ourselves clearly. How can we grow if we can't acknowledge our own weaknesses? We might *temporarily* feel better about ourselves by ignoring our flaws, or by believing our issues and difficulties are somebody else's fault, but in the long run we only harm ourselves by getting stuck in endless cycles of stagnation and conflict.

## The Costs of Self-Judgment

Continually feeding our need for positive self-evaluation is a bit like stuffing ourselves with candy. We get a brief sugar high, then a crash. And right after the crash comes a pendulum swing to despair as we realize that—however much we'd like to—we can't always blame our problems on someone else. We can't always feel special and above average. The result is often devastating. We look in the mirror and don't like what we see (both literally and figuratively), and the shame starts to set in. Most of us are incredibly hard on ourselves when we finally admit some flaw or shortcoming. "I'm not good enough. I'm worthless." It's not surprising that we hide the truth from ourselves when honesty is met with such harsh condemnation.

In areas where it is hard to fool ourselves—when comparing our weight to those of magazine models, for instance, or our bank accounts to those of the rich and successful—we cause ourselves incredible amounts of emotional pain. We lose faith in ourselves, start doubting our potential, and become hopeless. Of course, this sorry state just yields more self-condemnation for being such a do-nothing loser, and down, down we go.

Even if we do manage to get our act together, the goalposts for what counts as "good enough" seem always to remain frustratingly out of reach. We must be smart *and* fit *and* fashionable *and* interesting *and* successful *and* sexy. Oh, and spiritual, too. And no matter how well we do, someone else always seems to be doing it better. The result of this line of thinking is sobering: millions of people need to take pharmaceuticals every day just to cope with daily life. Insecurity, anxiety, and depression are incredibly common in our society, and much of this is due to self-judgment, to beating ourselves up when we feel we aren't winning in the game of life.

## Another Way

So what's the answer? *To stop judging and evaluating ourselves altogether.* To stop trying to label ourselves as "good" or "bad" and simply accept ourselves with an open heart. To treat ourselves with the same kindness, caring, and compassion we would show to a good friend, or even a stranger for that matter. Sadly, however, there's almost no one whom we treat as badly as ourselves.

When I first came across the idea of self-compassion, it changed my life almost immediately. It was during my last year in the Human Development doctoral program at the University of California at Berkeley, as I was putting the finishing touches on my dissertation. I was going through a really difficult time following the breakup of my first marriage, and I was full of shame and self-loathing. I thought signing up for meditation classes at a local Buddhist center might help. I had been interested in Eastern spirituality from the time I was a small child, having been raised by an open-minded mother just outside of Los Angeles. But I had never taken meditation seriously. I had also never examined Buddhist philosophy, as my exposure to Eastern thought had been more along California New Age lines. As part of my exploration, I read Sharon Salzberg's classic book *Lovingkindness* and was never the same again.

I had known that Buddhists talk a lot about the importance of compassion, but I had never considered that having compassion for *yourself* might be as important as having compassion for others. From the Buddhist point of view, you have to care about yourself before you can really care about other people. If you are continually judging and criticizing yourself while trying to be kind to others, you are drawing artificial boundaries and distinctions that only lead to feelings of separation and isolation. This is the opposite of oneness, interconnection, and universal love—the ultimate goal of most spiritual paths, no matter which tradition.

I remember talking to my new fiancé, Rupert, who joined me for the weekly Buddhist group meetings, and shaking my head in amazement. "You mean you're actually allowed to be *nice* to yourself, to have compassion for yourself when you mess up or are going through a really hard time? I don't know . . . If I'm too self-compassionate, won't I just be lazy and selfish?" It took me a while to get my head around it. But I slowly came to realize that self-criticism—despite being socially sanctioned—was not at all helpful, and in fact only made things worse. I wasn't making myself a better person by beating myself up all the time. Instead, I was causing myself to feel inadequate and insecure, then taking out my frustration on the people closest to me. More than that, I wasn't owning up to many things because I was so afraid of the self-hate that would follow if I admitted the truth.

What Rupert and I both came to learn was that instead of relying on our relationship to meet all our needs for love, acceptance, and security, we could actually provide some of these feelings for *ourselves*. And this would mean that we had even more in our hearts to give to each other. We were both so moved by the concept of self-compassion that in our marriage ceremony later that year, each of us ended our vows by saying "Most of all, I promise to help you have compassion for yourself, so that you can thrive and be happy."

After getting my Ph.D., I did two years of postdoctoral training with a leading self-esteem researcher. I wanted to know more about how people determine their sense of self-worth. I quickly learned that the field of psychology was falling out of love with self-esteem as the ultimate marker of positive mental health. Although thousands of articles had been written on the importance of self-esteem, researchers were now starting to point out all the traps that people can fall into when they try to get and keep a sense of high self-esteem: narcissism, self-absorption, self-righteous anger, prejudice, discrimination, and so on. I realized that self-compassion was the perfect alternative to the relentless pursuit of self-esteem. Why? Because it offers the same protection against harsh self-criticism as self-esteem, but without the need to see ourselves as perfect or as better than others. *In other words, self-compassion provides the same benefits as high self-esteem without its drawbacks.*

When I got a job as an assistant professor at the University of Texas at Austin, I decided that as soon as I got settled I would conduct research on self-compassion. Although no one had yet defined self-compassion from an academic perspective—let alone done any research on it—I knew that this would be my life's work.

So what is self-compassion? What does it mean exactly? I usually find that the best way to describe self-compassion is to start with a more familiar experience—compassion for others. After all, compassion is the same whether we direct it to ourselves or to other people.

## Compassion for Others

Imagine you're stuck in traffic on the way to work, and a homeless man tries to get you to pay him a buck for washing your car windows. *He's so pushy!* you think to yourself. *He'll make me miss the light and be late. He probably just wants the money for booze or drugs anyway. Maybe if I ignore him, he'll just leave me alone.* But he doesn't ignore you, and you sit there hating him while he washes your window, feeling guilty if you don't toss him some money, resentful if you do.

Then one day, you're struck as if by lightning. There you are in the same commuter traffic, at the same light, at the same time, and there's the homeless man, with his bucket and squeegee as usual. Yet for some unknown reason, today you see him differently. You see him as a *person* rather than just a mere annoyance. You notice his suffering. *How does he survive? Most people just shoo him away. He's out here in the traffic and fumes all day and certainly isn't earning much. At least he's trying to offer something in return for the cash. It must be really tough to have people be so irritated with you all the time. I wonder what his story is? How he ended up on the streets?* The moment you see the man as an actual human being who is suffering, your heart connects with him. Instead of ignoring him, you find—to your amazement—that you're taking a moment to think about how difficult his life is. You are moved by his pain and feel the urge to help him in some way. Importantly, if what you feel is true compassion rather than mere pity, you say to yourself, *There but for the grace of God go I. If I'd been born in different circumstances, or maybe had just been unlucky, I might also be struggling to survive like that. We're all vulnerable.*

Of course, that might be the moment when you harden your heart completely—your own fear of ending up on the street causing you to dehumanize this horrid heap of rags and beard. Many people do. But it doesn't make them happy; it doesn't help them deal with the stresses of their work, their spouse, or their child when they get home. It doesn't help them face their own fears. If anything, this hardening of the heart, which involves feeling *better* than the homeless man, just makes the whole thing that little bit worse.

But let's say you don't close up. Let's say you really do experience compassion for the homeless man's misfortune. How does it feel? Actually, it feels pretty good. It's wonderful when your heart opens—you immediately feel more connected, alive, present.

Now, let's say the man wasn't trying to wash windows in return for some cash. Maybe he *was* just begging for money to buy alcohol or drugs—should you still feel compassion for him? Yes. You don't have to invite him home. You don't even have to give him a buck. You may decide to give him a kind smile or a sandwich rather than money if you feel that's the more responsible thing to do. But yes, he is still worthy of compassion—all of us are. Compassion is not only relevant to those who are blameless victims, but also to those whose suffering stems from failures, personal weakness, or bad decisions. You know, the kind you and I make every day.

Compassion, then, involves the recognition and clear seeing of suffering. It also involves feelings of kindness for people who are suffering, so that the desire to help—*to ameliorate suffering*—emerges. Finally, compassion involves recognizing our shared human condition, flawed and fragile as it is.

## Compassion for Ourselves

Self-compassion, by definition, involves the same qualities. First, it requires that we stop to recognize our own suffering. We can't be moved by our own pain if we don't even acknowledge that it exists in the first place. Of course, sometimes the fact that we're in pain is blindingly obvious and we can think of nothing else. More often than you might think, however, we *don't* recognize when we are suffering. Much of

Western culture has a strong "stiff-upper-lip" tradition. We are taught that we shouldn't complain, that we should just *carry on* (to be read in a clipped British accent while giving a smart salute). If we're in a difficult or stressful situation, we rarely take the time to step back and recognize how hard it is for us in the moment.

And when our pain comes from self-judgment—if you're angry at yourself for mistreating someone, or for making some stupid remark at a party—it's even harder to see these as moments of suffering. Like the time I asked a friend I hadn't seen in a while, eyeing the bump of her belly, "Are we expecting?" "Er, no," she answered, "I've just put on some weight lately." "Oh . . ." I said as my face turned beet red. We typically don't recognize such moments as a type of pain that is worthy of a compassionate response. After all, I messed up, doesn't that mean I should be punished? Well, do you punish your friends or your family when they mess up? Okay, maybe sometimes a little, but do you feel good about it?

Everybody makes mistakes at one time or another, it's a fact of life. And if you think about it, why should you expect anything different? Where is that written contract you signed before birth promising that you'd be perfect, that you'd never fail, and that your life would go absolutely the way you want it to? *Uh, excuse me. There must be some error. I signed up for the "everything will go swimmingly until the day I die" plan. Can I speak to the management, please?* It's absurd, and yet most of us act as if something has gone terribly awry when we fall down or life takes an unwanted or unexpected turn.

One of the downsides of living in a culture that stresses the ethic of independence and individual achievement is that if we don't continually reach our ideal goals, we feel that we only have ourselves to blame. And if we're at fault, that means we don't deserve compassion, right? The truth is, *everyone* is worthy of compassion. The very fact that we are conscious human beings experiencing life on the planet means that we are intrinsically valuable and deserving of care. According to the Dalai

Lama, "Human beings by nature want happiness and do not want suffering. With that feeling everyone tries to achieve happiness and tries to get rid of suffering, and everyone has the basic right to do this. . . . Basically, from the viewpoint of real human value we are all the same." This is the same sentiment, of course, that inspired the Declaration of Independence: "We hold these Truths to be self-evident, that all Men are created equal, that they are endowed by their Creator with certain unalienable Rights, that among these are Life, Liberty and the pursuit of Happiness." We don't have to earn the right to compassion; it is our birthright. We are human, and our ability to think and feel, combined with our desire to be happy rather than to suffer, warrants compassion for its own sake.

Many people are resistant to the idea of self-compassion, however. Isn't it really just a form of self-pity? Or a dressed-up word for self-indulgence? I will show throughout this book that these assumptions are false and run directly counter to the actual meaning of self-compassion. As you'll come to see, self-compassion involves wanting health and well-being for oneself and leads to proactive behavior to better one's situation, rather than passivity. And self-compassion doesn't mean that I think my problems are more important than yours, it just means I think that my problems are *also* important and worthy of being attended to.

Rather than condemning yourself for your mistakes and failures, therefore, you can use the experience of suffering to soften your heart. You can let go of those unrealistic expectations of perfection that make you so dissatisfied, and open the door to real and lasting satisfaction. All by giving yourself the compassion you need in the moment.

The research that my colleagues and I have conducted over the past decade shows that self-compassion is a powerful way to achieve emotional well-being and contentment in our lives. By giving ourselves unconditional kindness and comfort while embracing the human experience, difficult as it is, we avoid destructive patterns of fear, negativity, and isolation. At the same time, self-compassion fosters positive mind-states such as happiness and optimism. The nurturing quality of self-compassion allows us to flourish, to appreciate the beauty and richness of life, even in hard times. When we soothe our agitated minds with self-compassion, we're better able to notice what's right as well as what's wrong, so that we can orient ourselves toward that which gives us joy.

Self-compassion provides an island of calm, a refuge from the stormy seas of endless positive and negative self-judgment, so that we can finally stop asking, "Am I as good as they are? Am I good enough?" Right here at our fingertips we have the means to provide ourselves with the warm, supportive care we deeply yearn for. By tapping into our inner well-springs of kindness, acknowledging the shared nature of our imperfect human condition, we can start to feel more secure, accepted, and alive.

In many ways self-compassion is like magic, because it has the power to transform suffering into joy. In her book *Emotional Alchemy: How the Mind Can Heal the Heart,* Tara Bennett-Goleman uses the metaphor of alchemy to symbolize the spiritual and emotional transformation that's possible when we embrace our pain with caring concern. When we give ourselves compassion, the tight knot of negative self-judgment starts to dissolve, replaced by a feeling of peaceful, connected acceptance—a sparkling diamond that emerges from the coal.

## Exercise One

### *How Do You React to Yourself and Your Life?*

#### HOW DO YOU TYPICALLY REACT TO YOURSELF?

- What types of things do you typically judge and criticize yourself for—appearance, career, relationships, parenting, and so on?
- What type of language do you use with yourself when you notice some flaw or make a mistake—do you insult

yourself, or do you take a more kind and understanding tone?

- If you are highly self-critical, how does this make you feel inside?
- What are the consequences of being so hard on yourself? Does it make you more motivated, or does it tend to make you discouraged and depressed?
- How do you think you would feel if you could truly accept yourself exactly as you are? Does this possibility scare you, give you hope, or both?

## How Do You Typically React to Life Difficulties?

- How do you treat yourself when you run into challenges in your life? Do you tend to ignore the fact that you're suffering and focus exclusively on fixing the problem, or do you stop to give yourself care and comfort?
- Do you tend to get carried away by the drama of difficult situations, so that you make a bigger deal out of them than you need to, or do you tend to keep things in balanced perspective?
- Do you tend to feel cut off from others when things go wrong, with the irrational feeling that everyone else is having a better time of it than you are, or do you try to remember that all people experience hardship in their lives?

If you feel that you lack sufficient self-compassion, check in with yourself—are you criticizing yourself for this, too? If so, stop right there. Try to feel compassion for how difficult it is to be an imperfect human being in this extremely competitive society of ours. Our culture does not emphasize self-compassion, quite the opposite. We're told that no matter how hard we try, our best just isn't good enough. It's time for something different. We can all benefit by learning to be more self-compassionate, and now is the perfect time to start.

So how is all this relevant to you, the reader? This and every chapter contain exercises that will help you understand how your continual self-judgment is harming you. There are also exercises to help you develop greater self-compassion so that it becomes a habit in daily life, allowing you to establish a healthier way of relating to yourself. You can determine your precise level of self-compassion using the self-compassion scale I developed for my research. Go to my website—www.self-compassion.org—and click on the "How Self-Compassionate Are You?" link. After filling out a series of questions, your level of self-compassion will be calculated for you. You may want to record your score and take the test again after reading the book, to determine if you've increased your level of self-compassion with practice.

You can't always have high self-esteem and your life will continue to be flawed and imperfect—but self-compassion will always be there, waiting for you, a safe haven. In good times and bad, whether you're on top of the world or at the bottom of the heap, self-compassion will keep you going, helping you move to a better place. It does take work to break the self-criticizing habits of a lifetime, but at the end of the day, you are only being asked to relax, allow life to be as it is, and open your heart to yourself. It's easier than you might think, and it could change your life.

## Exercise Two

### *Exploring Self-Compassion Through Letter Writing*

#### PART ONE

Everybody has something about themselves that they don't like; something that causes them to feel shame, to feel insecure or not "good enough." It is the human condition to be imperfect, and feelings of failure and inadequacy are part of the experience of living. Try thinking about an issue that tends to make you feel inadequate or bad about yourself (physical appearance, work or relationship issues, etc.). How does this aspect of yourself make you feel inside—scared, sad, depressed, insecure, angry? What emotions come up for you when you think about this aspect of yourself? Please try to be as emotionally honest as possible and to avoid repressing any feelings, while at the same time not being melodramatic. Try to just feel your emotions exactly as they are—no more, no less.

#### PART TWO

Now think about an imaginary friend who is unconditionally loving, accepting, kind, and compassionate. Imagine that this friend can see all your strengths and all your weaknesses, including the aspect of yourself you have just been thinking about. Reflect upon what this friend feels toward you, and how you are loved and accepted exactly as you are, with all your very human imperfections. This friend recognizes the limits of human nature and is kind and forgiving toward you. In his/her great wisdom this friend understands your life history and the millions of things that have happened in your life to create you as you are in this moment. Your particular inadequacy is connected to so many things you didn't necessarily choose: your genes, your family history, life circumstances—things that were outside of your control.

Write a letter to yourself from the perspective of this imaginary friend—focusing on the perceived inadequacy you tend to judge yourself for. What would this friend say to you about your "flaw" from the perspective of unlimited compassion? How would this friend convey the deep compassion he/she feels for you, especially for the discomfort you feel when you judge yourself so harshly? What would this friend write in order to remind you that you are only human, that all people have both strengths and weaknesses? And if you think this friend would suggest possible changes you should make, how would these suggestions embody feelings of unconditional understanding and compassion? As you write to yourself from the perspective of this imaginary friend, try to infuse your letter with a strong sense of the person's acceptance, kindness, caring, and desire for your health and happiness.

After writing the letter, put it down for a little while. Then come back and read it again, really letting the words sink in. Feel the compassion as it pours into you, soothing and comforting you like a cool breeze on a hot day. Love, connection, and acceptance are your birthright. To claim them you need only look within yourself.

*Chapter Two*

# ENDING THE MADNESS

*What is this self inside us, this silent observer,*
*Severe and speechless critic, who can terrorize us*
*And urge us on to futile activity*
*And in the end, judge us still more severely*
*For the errors into which his own reproaches drove us?*
—T. S. Eliot, *The Elder Statesman*

BEFORE EXAMINING SELF-COMPASSION IN MORE DETAIL, IT'S WORTH considering what our more habitual, unhealthy states of mind look like. As we begin to see the workings of our psyches more clearly, we start to recognize how much we skew our perceptions of the world in order to feel better about ourselves. It's as if we're continually airbrushing our self-image to try to make it more to our liking, even if it radically distorts reality. At the same time, we mercilessly criticize ourselves when we fall short of our ideals, reacting so harshly that reality is equally distorted in the opposite direction. The result can look like a Salvador Dalí picture (extra warped). As we first start to learn about self-compassion as a viable alternative to this madness, it's easy for us to end up judging our ego dysfunctions themselves. "I'm so full of myself, I should be more humble!" Or else, "I get so down on myself, I should be more kind and self-accepting!" It's very important to stop condemning yourself for these patterns, fruitless as they may be. The only way to truly have compassion for yourself is to realize that these neurotic ego cycles are not of your own choosing, they are natural and universal. Put simply, we come by our dysfunctions honestly—they are part of our human inheritance.

So why do we vacillate between self-serving distortions and ruthless self-criticism? Because we want to be safe. Our development, both as a species and as individuals, is predicated on basic survival instincts. Because human beings tend to live in hierarchical social groups, those who are dominant within their group are less likely to be rejected and have more access to valued resources. In the same way, those who accept their subordinate status also have a secure place in the social order. We can't take the risk of being outcast by the people who keep us out of harm's way. Not if we want to stay alive. Surely this behavior need not be judged—how could the desire to be safe and secure be anything other than normal and natural for any living organism?

## The Need to Feel Better Than Others

Garrison Keillor famously describes the fictional town of Lake Wobegon as a place where "all the women are strong, all the men are good-looking, and all the children are above average." For this reason, psychologists sometimes use the phrase "Lake Wobegon effect" to describe the common tendency to think of oneself as superior to others on a long list of desirable personality traits. Research has shown that fully 85 percent of students think that they're above average in terms of getting along with others, for instance. Ninety-four percent of college faculty members think they're better teachers than their colleagues, and 90 percent of drivers think they're more skilled than their road mates. Even people who've recently caused a car accident think they're superior drivers! Research shows that people tend to think they're funnier, more logical, more popular, better looking, nicer, more trustworthy, wiser, and more intelligent than others. Ironically, most people also think they're above average in the ability to view themselves objectively. Logically speaking, of course, if our self-perceptions were accurate, only half of all people would say they're above average on any particular trait, the other half admitting they were below average. But this almost never happens. It's unacceptable to be average in our society, so pretty much everyone wears a pair of rose-colored glasses, at least when they're looking in the mirror. How else can we explain all those *American Idol* contestants with marginal talent who seem so genuinely shocked when they're booted off the show?

One might assume that the tendency to see oneself as better than and superior to other people is primarily found in individualistic cultures such as the United States, where self-promotion is a way of life. Where else could Muhammad Ali have gotten away with the line, "I'm not the greatest; I'm the *double* greatest"? In more collectivistic Asian cultures, where conceit is frowned upon, aren't people more modest? The answer is yes, most Asians think they're more modest than others. Research suggests that all people self-enhance, but only on those traits valued by their culture. Whereas Americans tend to think they're more independent, self-reliant, original, and leader-like than the average American, Asians tend to think they're more cooperative, self-sacrificing, respectful, and humble than their peers. *I'm more modest than you are!* It's the same almost everywhere.

And we don't just see ourselves as "better," we also see others as "worse." Psychologists use the term "downward social comparison" to describe our tendency to see others in a negative light so that we can feel superior by contrast. If I'm trying to gild my own ego, you can be damn sure I'll try to tarnish yours. "Sure you're rich, but look at that bald spot!" This tendency was brilliantly illustrated in the film *Mean Girls*. The movie was actually based on the nonfiction book *Queen Bees and Wannabes* by Rosalind Wiseman, which describes how female cliques in high school maintain their social status. *Mean Girls* tells the story of three beautiful, rich, and well-dressed girls who seem to have it all. Certainly they think so. As one says, "I'm sorry that people are so jealous of me . . . I can't help it that I'm so popular." The girls, however, are hated despite their popularity. The clique keeps something called the "Burn Book"—a top secret notebook filled with rumors, secrets, and gossip about the other girls in school. "See," says one, "we cut out girls' pictures from the yearbook, and then we wrote comments. 'Trang Pak is a grotsky little byotch.' Still true. 'Dawn Schweitzer is a fat virgin.' Still half true." When the existence of the book is revealed to the school body at large, it ends up causing a riot. The film was a blockbuster hit in the United States and struck a huge chord with audiences. While exaggerated for comedic effect, the mean girl (or boy) phenomenon is something we're all too familiar with.

Although most of us don't go to the lengths of keeping a "Burn Book," it's very common to look for flaws and shortcomings in others as a way to feel better about ourselves. Why else do we love pictures of stars spilling out of their swimsuits, making fashion flubs, or having a bad hair day? This approach, while ego gratifying for a few moments, has some serious drawbacks. When we are always seeing the worst in others, our perception becomes obscured by a dark cloud of negativity. Our thoughts become malevolent, and this is the mental world we then inhabit. Downward social comparisons actually harm rather than help us. By putting others down to puff ourselves up, we are cutting off our nose to spite our face, creating and maintaining the state of disconnection and isolation we actually want to avoid.

# Exercise One

## *Seeing Yourself as You Are*

Many people think they're above average on personal traits that society values—like being friendlier, smarter, more attractive than average. This tendency helps us to feel good about ourselves, but it also can lead us to feel more separate and cut off from others. This exercise is designed to help us see ourselves clearly and accept ourselves exactly as we are. All people have culturally valued traits that might be considered "better" than average, some traits that are just average, and some that are "below" average. Can we accept this reality with kindness and equanimity?

A.  List five culturally valued traits for which you're *above average:*

1. _____
2. _____
3. _____
4. _____
5. _____

B.  List five culturally valued traits for which you're *just average:*

1. _____
2. _____
3. _____
4. _____
5. _____

C.  List five culturally valued traits for which you're *below average:*

1. _____
2. _____
3. _____
4. _____
5. _____

D.  Consider the full range of traits listed above. Can you accept all these facets of yourself? Being human does not mean being better than others. Being human means you encompass the full range of human experience, the positive, the negative, and the neutral. Being human means you *are* average in many ways. Can you celebrate the experience of being alive on this planet in all your complexity and wonder?

## Why Is It So Hard to Stop Beating Ourselves Up?

Perhaps more perplexing than the desire to think well of ourselves is our equally strong tendency toward self-criticism. As British novelist Anthony Powell noted, "Self-love seems so often unrequited." When we don't succeed in reinterpreting reality so that we feel better than others, when we're forced to finally face up to the fact that our self-image is more blemished than we would like it to be, what happens? All too often, Cruella De Vil or Mr. Hyde emerges from the shadows, attacking our imperfect selves with a surprising viciousness. And the language of self-criticism cuts like a knife.

Most of our self-critical thoughts take the form of an inner dialogue, a constant commentary and evaluation of what we are experiencing. Because there is no social censure when our inner dialogue is harsh or callous, we often talk to ourselves in an especially brutal way. "You're so fat and disgusting!" "That was a totally stupid thing to say." "You're such a loser. No wonder nobody wants you." Ouch! Yet such self-abuse is incredibly common. *Floccinaucinihilipilification,* defined as the habit of estimating something as worthless, is one of the longest words in the English language. The mystery of why we do it is as baffling as how to pronounce it.

Perhaps our behavior becomes more understandable, however, when we remember that just like self-aggrandizement, self-criticism is a type of safety behavior designed to ensure acceptance within the larger social group. Even though the alpha dog gets to eat first, the dog that shows his belly when snarled at still gets his share. He's given a safe place in the pack even if it's at the bottom of the pecking order. Self-criticism serves as a submissive behavior because it allows us to abase ourselves before imaginary others who pronounce judgment over us—then reward our submission with a few crumbs from the table. When we are forced to admit our failings, we can appease our mental judges by acquiescing to their negative opinions of us.

Consider, for example, how people often criticize themselves in front of others: "I look like a cow in this dress," "I'm hopelessly inept with computers," "I have the worst sense of direction of anyone I know!" (I'm prone to spouting this last line, especially when I'm driving friends somewhere and have gotten lost for the umpteenth time.) It's as if we're saying, "I'm going to beat you to the punch and criticize myself before you can. I recognize how flawed and imperfect I am so you don't have to cut me down and tell me what I already know. Hopefully you will then have sympathy for me instead of judging me and assure me that I'm not as bad as I think I am." This defensive posture stems from the natural desire not to be rejected and abandoned and makes sense in terms of our most basic survival instincts.

## The Role of Parents

The social group that is most important for survival, of course, is the immediate family. Children rely on their parents to provide food, comfort, warmth, and shelter. They instinctively trust parents to interpret the meaning of things, to help deal with scary new challenges, to keep them safe from harm's way. Children have no choice but to rely on parents in order to get by in the world. Sadly, however, many parents don't provide comfort and support, but rather try to control their children through constant criticism. Many of you have grown up this way.

When mothers or fathers use harsh criticism as a means to keep their kids out of trouble ("don't be so stupid or you'll get run over by a car"), or to improve their behavior ("you'll never get into college if you keep getting such pathetic grades"), children assume that criticism is a useful and necessary motivational tool. As comedian Phyllis Diller notes, "We spend the first twelve months of our children's lives teaching them to walk and talk and the next twelve telling them to sit down and shut up." Unsurprisingly, research shows that individuals who grow up with highly critical parents in childhood are much more likely to be critical toward themselves as adults.

People deeply internalize their parents' criticisms, meaning that the disparaging running commentary they hear inside their own head is often a reflection of parental voices—sometimes passed down and replicated throughout generations. As one man told me, "I just can't shut the voice up. My mom used to pick on me no matter what I did—for eating my dinner like a pig, wearing the wrong clothes to church, watching too much TV, whatever. 'You're never going to amount to anything,' she'd say over and over again. I hated her and promised myself I'd never raise my children that way. The irony is that even though I'm a loving, supportive dad to my kids, I'm a complete bastard to myself. I tear myself to shreds all the time, even worse than my mother did." People with critical parents learn the message early on that they are so bad and flawed that they have no right to be accepted for who they are.

Critical parents tend to play the role of both good and bad cop with their kids in the hope that they will be able to mold their children into who they want them to be. Bad cop punishes undesirable behavior, and good cop rewards desirable behavior. This leads to fear and distrust among children, who soon come to believe that only by being perfect will they be worthy of love. Given that perfection is impossible, children come to expect that rejection is inevitable.

While most research into the origins of self-criticism focuses on parents, the truth is that constant criticism by *any* significant figure in a child's life—a grandparent, a sibling, a teacher, a coach—can lead that child to experience inner demons later on in life. I have an English friend named Kenneth who is extremely hard on himself. No matter how much success he achieves, he is continually plagued by feelings of inadequacy and insecurity—which makes sense once he talks about his childhood: "Almost everyone in my life told me how crap I was. My sister was the worst. She'd scream 'you're disgusting!' just because she thought I was breathing too loudly, and hide under her bed until I left the room. My mother didn't defend me, but instead often made me apologize to my sister as a way to calm her and keep the peace."

The natural response of children who are being verbally pummeled is to protect themselves, and sometimes the surest means of defense is to have nothing to attack. In other words, children start to believe that self-criticism will prevent them from making future mistakes, thereby circumventing others' criticism. At the very least, they can blunt the force of others' criticism by making it redundant. A verbal assault doesn't have quite the same power when it merely repeats what you've already said to yourself.

## The Role of Culture

The tendency to criticize ourselves and feel worthless as a result can be traced in part to larger cultural messages. In fact, there is a well-known story about a group of Western scholars who were meeting with the Dalai Lama, who asked him how to help people suffering from low self-esteem. His Holiness was confused, and the concept of self-esteem had to be explained to him. He looked around this room of educated, successful people and asked, "Who here feels low self-esteem?" Everyone looked at one another and replied, "We all do." One of the downsides of living in a culture that stresses the ethic of independence and individual achievement is that if we don't reach our ideal goals, we feel that we only have ourselves to blame.

It is not only Westerners who are harshly judgmental toward themselves, of course. We recently conducted a study in the United States, Thailand, and Taiwan and found that in Taiwan—where there is a strong Confucian ethic—there is also strong belief in self-criticism as a motivating force. The Confucian ideal is that you should criticize yourself in order to keep yourself in line—focusing on meeting the needs of others instead of yourself. In countries where Buddhism plays a stronger role in daily life, such as Thailand, people are much more self-compassionate. In fact, in our cross-cultural study we found that people had the highest levels of self-compassion in Thailand and the lowest in Taiwan, with the United States falling in between. In all three countries, however, we found that self-criticism was strongly related to depression and dissatisfaction with life. It appears that the negative impact of self-criticism may be universal, even though different cultures encourage it to a greater or lesser degree.

## A Means to an End

If we look more deeply, we see that harsh self-criticism is often used as a cover for something else: the desire for control. Given that the parents of self-critics are usually overly controlling, the message is received early on that self-control is possible. When parents blame their children for making mistakes, children learn that they are personally responsible for all their failures. The implication is that failure is an option box that need not be checked. That falling short of perfection is something that can and *should* be avoided. Surely if I just try hard enough I should always be able to succeed, shouldn't I?

Wouldn't that be nice! If only we could wriggle our nose like Samantha from the TV show *Bewitched* and never fall off our diet, drop the ball on an important work assignment, say something in anger that we would later regret. But life doesn't work that way. Things are too complicated for us to be able to fully control either our external circumstances or our internal responses to them. To expect otherwise is like expecting the sky to be green instead of blue.

Ironically, there is also a way in which our desire to be superior is *fed* by the process of self-criticism. Our self-concept is multifaceted, and we can identify with different parts of ourselves at any one time. When we judge and attack ourselves, we are taking the role of both the criticizer and the criticized. By taking the perspective of the one holding the whip as well as the one quivering on the ground, we are able to indulge in feelings of righteous indignation toward our own inadequacies. And righteous indignation feels pretty good. "At least I'm smart enough to see how stupid that comment I just made was." "Yes, I did treat that person in an unforgivably bad way, but I'm so just and fair that I will now punish myself without mercy." Anger often gives us a feeling of strength and power, and so when we angrily cut ourselves down for our failings, we have a chance to feel superior to those aspects of ourselves that we judge and thus buttress our sense of authority (in the words of

Thomas Hobbes, "The privilege of absurdity, to which no living creature is subject but man only").

Similarly, by setting unrealistically high standards for ourselves and getting so upset when we fail to meet them, we can subtly reinforce feelings of supremacy associated with having such high standards in the first place. When complaining miserably about "ballooning" up to those size 6 jeans, for instance, or receiving that one minor negative comment from our boss on an otherwise glowing yearly review, we are sending the message that normally we are very much above average in our success, and that "good" just isn't good enough for someone so used to excellence.

When served up with a slice of humor, of course, cutting ourselves down can be a way of endearing ourselves to others. "Better to have them laugh *with* you than laugh *at* you," as the saying goes. A great example of this can be found in the opening scene of Al Gore's *An Inconvenient Truth*. The former presidential candidate takes the stage in front of an enormous audience, with an even more enormous screen behind him, and the first words out of his mouth are, "Hello, my name is Al Gore, and I used to be the next president of the United States." By highlighting his failure in a lighthearted way, Gore had the audience eating out of his hand. There is a difference, however, between healthy self-deprecating humor and unhealthy self-disparagement. The first indicates that someone is self-confident enough to poke fun at him- or herself. The second reveals deep-seated insecurities about personal worth and value.

## A Self-Fulfilling Prophecy

Because self-critics often come from unsupportive family backgrounds, they tend not to trust others and assume that those they care about will eventually try to hurt them. This creates a steady state of fear that causes problems in interpersonal interactions. For instance, research shows that highly self-critical people tend to be dissatisfied in their romantic relationships because they assume their partners are judging them as harshly as they judge themselves. The misperception of even fairly neutral statements as disparaging often leads to oversensitive reactions and unnecessary conflicts. This means that self-critics often undermine the closeness and supportiveness in relationships that they so desperately seek.

My friend Emily was like this. She was awkward, gangly, and painfully shy as a child. Her mother was embarrassed by Emily and told her so constantly. "Why do you always cower in the corner? Stand up straight. Learn your manners. Why can't you be more like your big sister?" Emily grew up to become a professional dancer, in part to appease her mother's criticisms. A beautiful, graceful woman, you'd think it would have been easy for her to find a good relationship, to find the love and acceptance she craved. Not so. Emily certainly had no problems attracting men and starting relationships, but she did have a hard time getting them to last. She was so certain she was being judged as inadequate that she would overreact to the tiniest perceived slight by her partner. Innocent behaviors like forgetting to call the first night he was away on a business trip would be seen as proof that he didn't really care about her. Not complimenting her new dress would be interpreted to mean that he thought she looked ugly. These overreactions would eventually cause her partners to get fed up and leave. In this way, Emily's fear of rejection was transformed into reality over and over again.

To make things even worse, people who harshly judge themselves are often their own worst enemy when it comes to choosing relationship partners in the first place. Social psychologist Bill Swann argues that people want to be known by others according to their firmly held beliefs and feelings about themselves—a model known as "self-verification theory." That is, they want their self-views to be validated because it helps to provide a sense of stability in their lives. His research shows that even people who make strong negative evaluations of themselves follow this pattern. They seek to interact with others who dislike them, so that their experiences will be more familiar and coherent.

So now you know why you—or your wonderful, successful friend— keep picking the wrong guy or gal. Self-critics are often attracted to judgmental romantic partners who confirm their feelings of worthlessness. The certainty of rejection feels safer than not knowing what to expect next. It's the devil they know. Unfortunately, I'm all too familiar with this unhealthy pattern.

## My Story: Abandoned and Unlovable

I was never an exceptionally ferocious self-critic; at least, I wasn't out of the ordinary. Luckily my mother was a loving rather than critical presence while growing up. But I was still pretty bad. Self-criticism is incredibly common in our society, especially among women. And I was hamstrung by the same troubles that afflict many women: daddy issues.

My mother and father met at a college in Southern California. She was a homecoming queen, a beauty whose belt, shoes, and purse always matched. He was a "big man on campus." Smart, athletic, ambitious, handsome. After he graduated they got married, rented a house in the suburbs, and had two lovely children—a boy and a girl. Soon my father was a rising young executive in a large corporation while my mother dropped her studies and stayed home to watch the kids. The American dream. Except that the fifties were over and it was now the sixties—an era of unprecedented social revolution.

My father tuned in to the changes happening around him and recognized the coffin of conventionality that his life had become. But he didn't handle it in a mature way. He left my mother, brother, and me when I was only three, dropped out to become a hippie, and moved into a commune on Maui, Hawaii. Given how far away he lived from our home in Los Angeles, I saw him only every two or three years while growing up, mainly during summer vacations. Although he was affectionate and loving during our visits, he was trapped in Hippieville to the point that he couldn't see very clearly, couldn't even admit to himself that he had abandoned us. "It's all just our karma" he was fond of saying.

One day when I was about eight, after using the word *Dad* in the course of asking him some question, he turned to me and my brother in all seriousness and asked that we please not call him Dad anymore. He wanted us to use his new name, "Brother Dionysus," because "we are all just brothers and sisters at the end of the day—children of God." I had been clinging to the flimsy, occasional father-daughter relationship that we had, but now his rejection of the father role seemed complete. My dad had truly left me, emotionally as well as physically. The bottom dropped out of my stomach, but I couldn't cry. I couldn't express any reaction whatsoever. I didn't want to risk harming any small thread of connection that might still be there. So for more than twenty years I found myself in the awkward situation of not knowing how—on those rare occasions when he *was* around—to address him. I couldn't bring myself to use his ridiculous hippie name, so ended up using no name at all. "Um, hey, uh, excuse me, could you pass the salt, please?" Needless to say, this rejection caused some deep scars in my psyche.

You should have seen the boys I chose as boyfriends in high school. Although I was a straight A student in all honors classes, attractive and friendly, I basically only liked guys who didn't like me. I was drawn to the boys who had a lot less going for them than I did, but who still acted equivocally toward me. I had no idea of my own worth and value, and at some level I was trying to recapture my relationship with my father— unconsciously hoping that I could magically transform the experience of rejection into one of acceptance. Almost every single one of my boyfriends ended up dumping me eventually, which surprised me at the time but makes sense given what I know now. I was simply re-creating situations that validated my sense of self as an unlovable girl who would always be abandoned.

## How Bad Can It Get?

Even though my feelings of insecurity caused me to make some bad decisions, not to mention making me unhappy, it was not *that* extreme. Sadly, the damage caused by self-judgment can get much, much worse. Feelings of inadequacy and inferiority are associated with acts of self-harm—like drug and alcohol abuse, reckless driving on purpose, and cutting—which are really attempts to externalize and release emotional pain. In extreme cases, when self-criticism goes unchecked for years, when ruthless self-pummeling becomes a way of life, some choose to escape the pain by escaping life itself. A number of large-scale studies have found that extreme self-critics are much more likely to attempt suicide than others. Feelings of shame and insignificance can lead to a devaluing of oneself to the extent that it even overpowers our most basic and fundamental instinct—the will to stay alive. The thought patterns linking self-criticism to suicide are apparent in this blog posting taken from a depression website:

> *All my life I've been depressed. I've always felt like there was something wrong with me and that I was stupid and ugly and gross. I want to have more friends but I can't figure out how to do it. I've been able to have one or two friends at a time, but they really never last. Some of them betray me and hurt me and I can never figure out what I did that made them hate me so much. I don't say things out in public much because I might say something stupid and someone will laugh at me and humiliate me. So even if someone is nice and wants to be with me, I end up*

*driving them away. I'm so lonely sometimes that it seems like I'd*
*be better off dead. I think about dying because I'm just so worth-*
*less and no one loves me. I don't love me. Being all the way dead*
*has to be better than feeling dead inside.*

This tragic train of thought is much more common than might be assumed. Worldwide, there are an estimated ten to twenty million attempted suicides each year. Sadly, this shocking act of violence is often just an outward manifestation of the inner violence more familiar to us: harsh self-criticism.

## The Way Out

Although it's important for us to see our psychological patterns clearly, it's equally important that we do not judge ourselves for them. If you are a habitual self-critic, remember that your behavior actually represents a convoluted form of self-care, an attempt to keep yourself safe and on track. *You don't want to beat yourself up for beating yourself up in the vain hope that it will somehow make you stop beating yourself up.* Just as hate can't conquer hate—but only strengthens and reinforces it—self-judgment can't stop self-judgment.

The best way to counteract self-criticism, therefore, is to understand it, have compassion for it, and then replace it with a kinder response. By letting ourselves be moved by the suffering we have experienced at the hands of our own self-criticism, we strengthen our desire to heal. Eventually, after banging our heads against the wall long enough, we'll decide that enough is enough and demand an end to our self-inflicted pain.

Fortunately, we can actually provide ourselves with the security and nurturance we want. We can recognize that weakness and imperfection are part of the shared human experience. We can feel more connected to our fellow life travelers who are just as flawed and vulnerable as we are.

At the same time, we can let go of the need to feel better than others. We can see through the self-serving distortions that inflate our own egos at others' expense.

And who wants to be stuck in a box labeled "good" anyway? Isn't it more interesting to revel in the full range of human experience? Instead of trying to control ourselves and our lives to obtain a perfectionistic ideal, why not embrace life as it is—both the light and the shadow? What adventures might follow if we free ourselves in this way? Happiness is found when we go with the flow of life, not when we rail against it, and self-compassion can help us navigate these turbulent rapids with a wise, accepting heart.

## Exercise Two

### *The Criticizer, the Criticized, and the Compassionate Observer*

This exercise is modeled on the two-chair dialogue studied by Gestalt therapist Leslie Greenberg. In this exercise, clients sit in different chairs to help get in touch with different, often conflicting parts of their selves, experiencing how each aspect feels in the present moment.

To begin, put out three empty chairs, preferably in a triangular arrangement. Next, think about an issue that often troubles you, and that often elicits harsh self-criticism. Designate one chair as the voice of your inner self-critic, one chair as the voice of the part of you that feels judged and criticized, and one chair as the voice of a wise, compassionate observer. You are going to be role-playing all three parts of yourself— you, you, and you. It may feel a bit silly at first, but you may be surprised at what comes out once you really start letting your feelings flow.

1. Think about your "issue," and then sit in the chair of the self-critic. As you take your seat, express out loud what the self-critical part of you is thinking and feeling. For example, "I hate the fact that you're such a wimp and aren't self-assertive enough." Notice the words and tone of voice the self-critical part of you uses, and also how it is feeling. Worried, angry, self-righteous, exasperated? Note what your body posture is like. Strong, rigid, upright?

2. Now take the chair of the criticized aspect of yourself. Try to get in touch with how you feel being criticized in this manner. Talk about how you feel, responding directly to your inner critic. For example, "I feel so hurt by you" or "I feel so unsupported." Just speak whatever comes into your mind. Again, notice the tone of your voice. Is it sad, discouraged, childlike, scared, helpless? What is your body posture like? Are you slumped, downward facing, frowning?

3. Conduct a dialogue between these two parts of yourself for a while, switching back and forth between the chair of the criticizer and the criticized. Really try to experience each aspect of yourself so each knows how the other feels. Allow each to fully express its views and be heard.

4. Now occupy the chair of the compassionate observer. Call upon your deepest wisdom, the wells of your caring concern, and address both the critic and the criticized. What does your compassionate self say to the critic, what insight does it have? For example, "You sound very much like your mother" or, "I see that you're really scared, and you're trying to help me so I don't screw up." What does your compassionate self say to the criticized part of yourself? For example, "It must be incredibly difficult to hear such harsh judgment day after day. I see you're really hurting" or "All you want is to be accepted for who you are." Try to relax, letting your heart soften and

open. What words of compassion naturally spring forth? How is your tone of voice? Tender, gentle, warm? What is your body posture like—balanced, centered, relaxed?

5. After the dialogue finishes—stop whenever it feels right—reflect upon what just happened. Do you have any new insights about where your patterns come from, new ways of thinking about your situation that are more productive? As you contemplate what you have learned, set your intention to relate to yourself in a kinder, healthier way in the future. A truce can be called in your inner war. Peace is possible. Your old habits of self-criticism don't need to rule you forever. What you need to do is listen to the voice that's already there, even if a bit hidden—your wise, compassionate self.

*Part Two*

# THE CORE COMPONENTS OF SELF-COMPASSION

*Chapter Three*

# BEING KIND TO OURSELVES

*When you begin to touch your heart or let your heart be touched,
you begin to discover that it's bottomless, that it doesn't have any
resolution, that this heart is huge, vast, and limitless. You begin
to discover how much warmth and gentleness is there, as well as
how much space.*
—Pema Chödrön, *Start Where You Are*

As I've defined it, self-compassion entails three core components. First, it requires *self-kindness,* that we be gentle and understanding with ourselves rather than harshly critical and judgmental.
Second, it requires recognition of our *common humanity,* feeling connected with others in the experience of life rather than feeling isolated
and alienated by our suffering. Third, it requires *mindfulness*—that we
hold our experience in balanced awareness, rather than ignoring our
pain or exaggerating it. We must achieve and combine these three essential elements in order to be truly self-compassionate. This chapter and
the next two focus on each component separately, as they are all equally

important. We'll start with what is perhaps the most obvious ingredient of self-compassion: self-kindness.

## The Path of Self-Kindness

Western culture places great emphasis on being kind to our friends, family, and neighbors who are struggling. Not so when it comes to ourselves. When we make a mistake or fail in some way, we're more likely to hit ourselves over the head with a club than put a supportive arm around our own shoulder. Most likely, even the thought of comforting ourselves in this way seems absurd. And even when our problems stem from forces beyond our control, self-kindness is not a culturally valued response. Somewhere along the line we get the message that strong individuals should be stoic and silent toward their own suffering—like John Wayne in a western. Unfortunately, these attitudes rob us of one of our most powerful coping mechanisms when dealing with the difficulties of life.

Self-kindness, by definition, means that we stop the constant self-judgment and disparaging internal commentary that most of us have come to see as normal. It requires us to *understand* our foibles and failures instead of condemning them. It entails clearly seeing the extent to which we harm ourselves through relentless self-criticism, and ending our internal war.

But self-kindness involves more than merely stopping self-judgment. It involves *actively* comforting ourselves, responding just as we would to a dear friend in need. It means we allow ourselves to be emotionally moved by our own pain, stopping to say, "This is really difficult right now. How can I care for and comfort myself in this moment?" With self-kindness, we soothe and calm our troubled minds. We make a peace offering of warmth, gentleness, and sympathy *from* ourselves *to* ourselves, so that true healing can occur.

And if our pain is caused by a misstep we have made—this is *precisely* the time to give ourselves compassion. I remember once during high school I went on a first date with a boy I had a huge crush on. I had a slight cold but didn't think much about it. At one point while I was talking and laughing, trying to impress him with how clever and funny I was, he looked at me sideways and raised his eyebrows. I paused, wondering what was the matter. "Nice snot bubble," he said.

The shame and humiliation floored me for weeks. I felt totally lame and told myself so over and over again. I wish I knew then what I know now.

Rather than relentlessly cutting ourselves down when we fall, even if our fall is a spectacular one, we do have another option. We can recognize that everyone has times when they blow it, and treat ourselves kindly. Maybe we weren't able to put our best foot forward, but we tried, and falling flat on one's face is an inevitable part of life. An honorable part, in fact.

Sadly, however, many people believe that they *shouldn't* be kind to themselves, especially if they received that message in childhood. And even among those who *want* to be kinder to themselves, who would happily do away with their inner tyrant if they could, there is often the belief that change is not possible. Because they've developed such a strong habit of self-criticism, they don't think they are actually *capable* of self-kindness. Luckily, however, being kind to yourself is easier than you think.

## The Attachment and Caregiving System

Our brains and bodies have the innate capacity to both give and receive care. It's part of our genetic inheritance. Not only does survival depend on the fight-or-flight instinct, it also depends on the "tend and befriend" instinct. In times of threat or stress, animals that are protective of their offspring are more likely to pass their genes successfully on to the next generation, meaning that caregiving behavior has a strong adaptive function.

For this reason, all mammals are born with an "attachment system"— a set of behaviors that allow for strong emotional bonds between caregivers and their young. Unlike reptiles, who could care less about their offspring once they've slithered out of their eggs—often eating them, in fact—mammals spend considerable time and energy nurturing their young, making sure they are adequately fed, warm, and safe. Mammals are born in an immature state. They can't take care of themselves as newborns, and they rely on parents to be their lifeline until they are ready to leave home. Evolution ensured that mammals could both give and receive nurturance, so that parents wouldn't abandon their children after birth and children wouldn't wander off alone into the dangerous wild. The emotion of care comes naturally to us, because without it our species would not be able to survive. This means that the capacity to feel affection and interconnection is part of our biological nature. *Our brains are actually designed to care.*

The well-known psychologist Harry Harlow was one of the first to examine the development of the mammalian attachment system back in the 1950s. In a series of clever (if ethically questionable) experiments, Harlow studied the behavior of newborn rhesus monkeys who were separated from their mothers and reared alone in a cage. The question was whether the baby monkeys would spend more time with a soft, terrycloth pretend mother—who at least offered some degree of warmth and comfort—or a stark, wire-mesh figure that held a milk-dispensing bottle but provided little comfort. The answer was clear. The baby monkeys clung to their cloth mommies as if their life depended on it, only moving to the stark wire-mesh figures long enough to take a quick drink. What's striking about this finding is that the emotional comfort offered by a snuggly cloth appeared to create a stronger drive in the monkeys than food itself. Care was as powerful a survival need as nutrition. As the Bible says, "Man cannot live by bread alone." Harlow interpreted his experiments as providing evidence for the biological underpinnings of the attachment system.

John Bowlby, another influential psychologist working in the same period, took the study of attachment a step further—to humans. He proposed that infants develop a secure attachment bond to parents when their needs are consistently met. If children are consoled and supported by parents when they're upset or frightened, they learn to trust them. Every time a mom picks up and rocks her crying baby, the baby starts to feel that the world is a safe place, that he or she can turn to mommy for support when needed. This then allows children to use their parents as a "secure base," meaning they can safely explore the world around them because they know help is always at hand. If parents provide inconsistent support, however, or are cold and rejecting, children develop what's called an insecure attachment bond. This insecurity means that children can't trust their parents to soothe their distress—to kiss the boo-boo and make it go away. They learn that the world is really *not* safe, that their parents can't be relied upon. This tends to impair children's confidence in exploring the world—an impairment that often extends to adulthood.

Bowlby argued that early attachment bonds with parents affect the formation of our "internal working model" of self in relation to others. This is an unconscious, deep-seated mental portrait of who we are and what we can expect from other people. If children are securely attached to parents, they feel they are worthy of love. They typically grow up to be healthy and happy adults, secure in the belief they can count on others to provide comfort and support. But if children are insecurely attached, they tend to feel they are unworthy and unlovable, and that other people cannot be trusted. This creates a pervasive feeling of insecurity that can cause long-term emotional distress and affect the ability to form close, stable relationships later on in life.

It probably comes as no surprise then that our research shows people who are insecurely attached have less self-compassion than those who are securely attached. In other words, our internal working models of self have a significant impact on how we treat ourselves—with compassion or contempt. And if our internal working models tell us that we can't rely on others to be there for us in times of need, we will not allow ourselves to depend on them. Just like Emily, the professional dancer whose story was told in the last chapter, we may find it easier to assume the worst and act accordingly rather than make ourselves vulnerable by allowing others into our heart. But in doing so we cut ourselves off from human happiness.

The good news is that our internal working models are not etched in stone—they can be changed. Because the ability to give and receive care is inborn, our attachment buttons can be reset. A person who is insecurely attached as a child but somehow manages to find a loving, supportive romantic partner as an adult can eventually learn to become securely attached. Healthy romantic relationships allow us to realize that actually, we *are* valuable and worthy of care, that others *can* be trusted to meet our needs. Skilled therapists can also help change insecure attachment bonds by providing unconditional support to their clients. The safe space and deep listening provided by a therapist allows access to the deep-rooted patterns formed in our childhood, bringing them to the surface so they can be *re*-formed.

Of course, there are problems with depending solely on other people to change how we feel about ourselves. Romantic relationships may end, therapists may move away or become unaffordable. And those we rely upon often have their own dragons to slay—sickness, depression, job stress—that prevent them from being there for us when we need them. Fortunately, we don't have to solely rely on others to change our self views. When we consistently give *ourselves* nurturance and understanding, we also come to feel worthy of care and acceptance. When we give ourselves empathy and support, we learn to trust that help is always at hand. When we wrap ourselves in the warm embrace of self-kindness, we feel safe and secure.

Luckily, Emily was finally able to learn this. She came to realize that unless she had compassion for the feelings of insecurity woven deep within the fabric of her personality, she would keep driving men away with her defensive reactions. So Emily started to practice being kinder and more accepting of herself. Every time a wave of insecurity came over her she would silently say, "I love and accept myself exactly as I am." Every time she started to criticize herself, or to interpret someone else's actions as a deliberate rejection, she would repeat, "I love and accept myself exactly as I am." Eventually, deep wells of grief arose as she let herself experience the full extent of the pain caused by her mother's rejection and disapproval. But as long as she repeated her phrase, she found she could feel her emotions without being overwhelmed by them.

Finally, as her pain started to subside, she began to trust others once more. She started to realize how much she had to offer others, and that her past no longer had anything to do with her present. The last time I heard from her, Emily was engaged to a wonderful man who deeply loved and appreciated her, and whose love and appreciation she could finally allow herself to receive.

## The Chemicals of Care

The power of self-kindness is not just an idea—some feel-good but in-substantial notion that doesn't really change anything. It's very real. When we soothe our own pain, we are tapping into the mammalian caregiving system. And one important way the caregiving system works is by triggering the release of oxytocin. Researchers have dubbed oxyto-cin the "hormone of love and bonding" because of the important role it plays in social relationships. For instance, one study found that levels of oxytocin measured in pregnant mothers during their first trimester predicted the strength of mother-child bonding after birth. Research has also shown that increased levels of oxytocin strongly increase feelings of trust, calm, safety, generosity, and connectedness and also facilitate the ability to feel warmth and compassion for ourselves. Oxytocin reduces fear and anxiety and can counteract the increased blood pressure and cortisol associated with stress. Interestingly, the party drug MDMA (otherwise known as Ecstasy) mimics the actions of oxytocin, which is why people report feeling more relaxed, loving, and accepting toward themselves and others when taking the drug.

Oxytocin is released in a variety of social situations, including when a mother breast-feeds her child, when parents interact with their young children, or when someone gives or receives a soft, tender caress. Because thoughts and emotions have the same effect on our bodies whether they're directed to ourselves or to others, this research suggests that self-compassion may be a powerful trigger for the release of oxytocin.

Self-criticism appears to have a very different effect on our body. The amygdala is the oldest part of the brain and is designed to quickly detect threats in the environment. When we experience a threatening situation, the fight-or-flight response is triggered: the amygdala sends signals that increase blood pressure, adrenaline, and the hormone cortisol, mobilizing the strength and energy needed to confront or avoid a threat. Although this system was designed by evolution to deal with physical attacks, it is activated just as readily by emotional attacks—from ourselves or others. Over time increased cortisol levels lead to depression by depleting various neurotransmitters involved in the ability to experience pleasure.

There is also neurological evidence showing that self-kindness and self-criticism operate quite differently in terms of brain function. A recent study examined reactions to personal failure using fMRI (functional magnetic resonance imaging) technology. While in a brain scanner, participants were presented with hypothetical situations such as "A third job rejection letter in a row arrives in the post." They were then told to imagine reacting to the situation in either a kind or a self-critical way. Self-criticism was associated with activity in the lateral prefrontal cortex and dorsal anterior cingulate—areas of the brain associated with error processing and problem solving. Being kind and reassuring toward oneself was associated with left temporal pole and insula activation—areas of the brain associated with positive emotions and compassion. Instead of seeing ourselves as a problem to be fixed, therefore, self-kindness allows us to see ourselves as valuable human beings who are worthy of care.

When we experience warm and tender feelings toward ourselves, we are altering our bodies as well as our minds. Rather than feeling worried and anxious, we feel calm, content, trusting, and secure. Self-kindness allows us to feel safe as we respond to painful experiences, so that we are no longer operating from a place of fear—and once we let go of insecurity we can pursue our dreams with the confidence needed to actually achieve them.

## Exercise One

### *Hugging Practice*

One easy way to soothe and comfort yourself when you're feeling badly is to give yourself a gentle hug. It seems a bit silly at first, but your body doesn't know that. It just responds to the physical gesture of warmth and care, just as a baby responds to being held in its mother's arms. Our skin is an incredibly sensitive organ. Research indicates that physical touch releases oxytocin, provides a sense of security, soothes distressing emotions, and calms cardiovascular stress. So why not try it?

If you notice that you're feeling tense, upset, sad, or self-critical, try giving yourself a warm hug, tenderly stroking your arm or face, or gently rocking your body. What's important is that you make a clear gesture that conveys feelings of love, care, and tenderness. If other people are around, you can often fold your arms in a nonobvious way, gently squeezing yourself in a comforting manner. You can also simply *imagine* hugging yourself if you can't make the actual physical gesture.

Notice how your body feels after receiving the hug. Does it feel warmer, softer, calmer? It's amazing how easy it is to tap into the oxytocin system and change your biochemical experience.

Try giving yourself a hug in times of suffering several times a day for a period of at least a week. Hopefully you'll start to develop the habit of physically comforting yourself when needed, taking full advantage of this surprisingly simple and straightforward way to be kind to ourselves.

## The Power of a Gentle Caress

The warm embrace of self-kindness makes our suffering bearable, providing a soothing balm that softens the hard edges of our pain. When we treat ourselves as a kind friend would, we are no longer totally absorbed by playing the role of the one who is suffering. *Yes, I hurt. But I also feel care and concern. I am both the comforter and the one in need of comfort. There is more to me than the pain I am feeling right now, I am also the heartfelt response to that pain.* When we are moved by how difficult life is in the moment, somehow that moment isn't as difficult as it was just a second ago. We add a new ingredient to our experience, providing relief like a cool spring bubbling up in a hot, dry desert.

I remember once I was feeling really down after hearing something mean someone had said about me—someone who didn't know me at all, but who nonetheless was making negative assumptions about my honesty and integrity. I felt like I had been hit by a car. This is so unfair! The nerve! Who does she think she is? I created all sorts of "payback" scenarios in my mind—of showing this person up, publicly proving her wrong, making her feel so horrible about herself that she would cringe in shame. These mental movies were only making me feel worse, however, causing me to relive the pain over and over again. Then I remembered. *What I need to do is give myself compassion for how difficult the situation is.* I gently stroked my arms and spoke to myself in kind, sympathetic tones. *Poor darling. This is really hard right now.* I comforted myself for the pain of being treated so unfairly.

This is what I *actually* needed in the moment. Rather than merely venting my anger, I needed to feel loved and understood, to be seen for who I really was. This was the only remedy that could heal my pain. The moment I changed my approach, I felt my mood start to lift. I stopped obsessing about payback scenarios and instead realized that this person's negativity had nothing to do with me; it was her own issue. Relatively quickly I was able to let go and move on, my equilibrium restored and the impact of her words greatly lessened.

Choosing to relate to ourselves with kindness rather than contempt is highly pragmatic. We don't have a lot of control over our personal characteristics—our inborn personality, our body type, our health, the good or bad fortune of our circumstances. But what we *can* do is start being kind to ourselves when confronting our limitations, and we can suffer less because of them.

One of the most important ways we can be kind to ourselves involves changing our critical self-talk. Marshall Rosenberg, author of the bestselling book *Nonviolent Communication,* stresses the importance of using sympathetic rather than judgmental language when we talk to ourselves. He argues that to be at peace with ourselves, we should reframe our inner dialogues so that they express empathy for our basic human needs. Rosenberg's suggested method for doing so involves asking four simple questions:

- What am I observing?
- What am I feeling?
- What am I needing right now?
- Do I have a request of myself or someone else?

These four questions allow us to listen deeply to what we need most in the moment.

For example, let's say you're working from home and take a break to make yourself some tea. When you come into the kitchen, you see that there are dirty dishes piled up a mile high. The first step involves noticing if your self-talk is critical or judgmental. Are you saying things like "I'm such a hopeless slob"? The next step involves tuning into the feelings underlying your harsh words. Are you feeling frustrated, overwhelmed, irritated with yourself or the situation? The third step entails examining the unmet needs driving your reaction. Perhaps you're frustrated because you know you need a sense of order to deal with the pressing demands of your work, and that the chaos in the kitchen is hindering you. Finally, you consider whether there is anything you want to request of yourself or someone else that may help to meet your needs. Perhaps you can ask your best friend to lend a hand until your work deadline passes. Or maybe you can ask yourself to put off working on your project for a half hour while you clean up, so that you can have the sense of harmony you need to concentrate. The main point is that you validate and listen to what you really need in the moment, and you express empathy toward yourself rather than condemnation.

## Exercise Two

### *Changing Your Critical Self-Talk*

This exercise should be done over several weeks and will eventually form the blueprint for changing how you relate to yourself long term. Some people find it useful to work on their inner critic by writing in a journal. Others are more comfortable doing it via internal dialogues. If you are someone who likes to write things down and revisit them later, journaling can be an excellent tool for transformation. If you are someone (like me) who never manages to be consistent with a journal, then do whatever works for you. You can speak aloud to yourself, or think silently.

1. The first step toward changing the way you treat yourself is to notice when you are being self-critical. It may be that—like many of us—your self-critical voice comes up so frequently that you don't even notice when it is present. Whenever you're feeling bad about something, think about what you've just said to yourself. Try to be as accurate as possible, noting your inner speech verbatim. What words do you actually use when you're self-critical? Are there key phrases that come up over and over again? What is the tone of your voice—harsh, cold, angry? Does the voice remind you of anyone in your past who was critical of you? You want to be able to get to know the inner self-critic very well, and to become aware of when your inner judge is active. For instance, if you've just eaten half a box of Oreos, does your inner voice say something like "you're so disgusting," "you make me sick," and so on? Really try to get a clear sense of how you talk to yourself.

2. Make an active effort to soften the self-critical voice,

but do so with compassion rather than self-judgment (i.e., don't say "you're such a bitch" to your inner critic!). Say something like "I know you're trying to keep me safe, and to point out ways that I need to improve, but your harsh criticism and judgment is not helping at all. Please stop being so critical, you are causing me unnecessary pain."

3. Reframe the observations made by your inner critic in a kind, friendly, positive way. If you're having trouble thinking of what words to use, you might want to imagine what a very compassionate friend would say to you in this situation. It might help to use a term of endearment that strengthens expressed feelings of warmth and care, but only if it feels natural rather than schmaltzy. For instance, you can say something like "Darling, I know you ate that bag of cookies because you're feeling really sad right now and you thought it would cheer you up. But you feel even worse and are not feeling good in your body. I want you to be happy, so why don't you take a long walk so you feel better?" While engaging in this supportive self-talk, try gently stroking your arm, or holding your face tenderly in your hands (as long as no one's looking). Even if you're having trouble calling up emotions of kindness at first, physical gestures of warmth can tap into the caregiving system, releasing oxytocin that will help change your biochemistry. The important thing is that you start acting kindly, and feelings of true warmth and caring will eventually follow.

The healing power of self-kindness was demonstrated in a recent study of chronic acne sufferers. People who have chronic acne are often depressed and experience intense shame and self-judgment. For this reason, researchers held a two-week intervention in which participants were taught how to soothe the negative emotions and self-criticism associated with their acne. For instance, they were told, "There is an inner critic inside of each of us that can say mean and negative things about ourselves in a hostile way . . . We also have an 'inner soother' (a compassionate part within us) that has the ability to soothe ourselves by saying accepting things in a warm and compassionate way." Participants were then given a series of exercises designed to help them self-soothe. They were instructed to write five compassionate phrases on cue cards, such as "I feel upset about my acne and it is okay to feel this way" or "I would be accepting of a friend in my position. I want to be this way to myself too." They were also taught how to challenge and confront their inner critic. They were asked to write five additional phrases on cue cards, such as "It's not true that people will reject me just because I have acne" and "I have the inner strength to fight my distress and my role in creating it."

Participants were then instructed to read the cue cards three times a day over the course of the next two weeks, as well as doing other exercises like writing a compassionate letter to themselves (see exercise one, chapter 1). It was found that the intervention significantly lessened people's feelings of depression and shame due to their acne. Interestingly, it also lessened the degree to which their acne bothered them physically, reducing sensations of burning and stinging.

When faced with our human imperfection, we can either respond with kindness and care, or with judgment and criticism. An important question to ask is, what qualities of heart and mind do we want to encourage in ourselves? We can't stop our judgmental thoughts, but we don't have to encourage or believe in them either. If we hold our self-judgments with gentleness and understanding, the force of self-contempt will eventually fade and wither, deprived of the sustenance needed to survive. We have the power to live with joy and contentment by responding to our suffering with kindness. Although this habit is not taught by the larger culture, change is possible. I know this from personal experience.

## My Story: To Err Is Human

As mentioned at the start of this book, I first learned about self-compassion in the Buddhist meditation group I joined during my last year of graduate school. The main reason I joined was because I was drowning in feelings of shame, guilt, and unworthiness; and I was desperately looking to find some inner peace. It was just months before Rupert and I were set to marry, and I was still reeling from the mess I had made of my personal life some years previous.

You see, I had been married before, to a man called John (not his real name) whom I had met while a junior in college. After the string of losers I had dated as a teenager, I thought I had finally met a keeper. John was handsome, intelligent, and cultured. He was also extremely judgmental. When he tried to break up with me due to my perceived shortcomings, a standard theme in my relationships up to that point, I resisted. *This one is too good to lose,* I thought. And of course, his rejection just hooked me even more. I pulled out every resource of charm I had, and we ended up staying together. A few years later we got married.

John was basically a good man, but his judgmental nature meant that he was extremely skeptical about any sort of spirituality. He certainly did not approve of the spiritual beliefs I had been raised with—he thought they were complete hogwash and did not shy away from telling me so. Because I wanted so desperately to be loved and accepted, I began to change myself into the person he thought I should be. I started becoming a skeptic myself, giving up the one thing that had probably been most important in my life up to that point—my relationship with God, or Universal Consciousness as I often thought of it. To be fair, however, some part of me was already starting to question the concepts of reincarnation, karma, and enlightenment I had put so much faith in during my New Age childhood. Who could say whether these ideas were real or merely wishful thinking—a type of feel-good science fiction? John's skeptical nature was the perfect springboard for my crisis of faith, and I dove right in.

Shortly after starting our relationship, I dropped all spiritual pursuits and enrolled in graduate school at Berkeley to become a research psychologist. Rationality became my new God. This period lasted about seven years. What I didn't realize, of course, was how firmly my heart shut down when I closed off the door to spirituality. My rational mind alone was not enough to make me happy, but I didn't know it. I wasn't happy in my marriage, either, but because it was stable and there were no obvious problems, my dissatisfaction remained largely unconscious. I had never experienced what it felt like to be really seen, cherished, and loved by a man for who I was. So I assumed that having someone who didn't leave me was as good as it got.

Until I met someone who did actually understand and appreciate the real me, that is—an older man (let's call him Peter) who was wiser and more experienced than I. After a friendship that grew increasingly close over about a year, Peter and I started having an affair. I could tell things to Peter that I had never felt safe telling to anyone before, and it made him love me even more. In one way I was happier with Peter than I ever had been in my life. My heart broke wide open and I felt a joy, an aliveness, a self-acceptance more intense than I had ever thought possible. My spiritual side was reawakened. I felt whole and complete for the first time in a long while. The fact that Peter was so much older than me also played into it, no doubt. His desire for me was probably some sort of substitute for feeling unwanted by my father.

Because I felt so terrible about being unfaithful to John, however, I couldn't really acknowledge what was happening, even to myself. My self-judgment made it impossible to own up to what I was doing—such a damning self-portrait was just too painful. It was as if I had developed a split personality, with each side of my life completely disconnected and out of touch with the other. There was an awful period of lying and self-deception that lasted about three months, and I was actually relieved when we were finally found out.

To make a long story short, I left John for Peter, believing that surely we must be soul mates destined to be together forever. How else could I justify the horrible pain I had caused my husband if it wasn't for something pure and noble? Peter, however, did not leave his wife for me.

I sank to one of the lowest points in my life. I hated myself for hurting John so deeply, but I also hated Peter for not making an honest— or at least partially honest—woman out of me. Thank goodness I had already arranged to spend a year studying in India to conduct my dissertation research. (It was on reasoning about rights and responsibilities within Indian marriages, and no, the irony was not lost on me.) The time abroad afforded me the opportunity to get away for a while and lick my wounds. It was in India that I met Rupert, a British travel writer working on a guidebook to the region. Even though I told him I was an emotional mess and that he shouldn't touch me with a ten-foot pole— which for him was like waving a red flag at a bull—it somehow worked out between us.

But when I eventually returned to Berkeley to finish my dissertation, I still had to face up to the chaos I had left behind. Apologizing to John didn't help. He was still furious and not about to forgive me. He still hasn't to this day. But blaming things on Peter didn't help either. And I couldn't remain angry once I learned that he had developed cancer shortly after our breakup and only had a few months left to live.

It was precisely at this point that I started learning about self-compassion in my weekly Buddhist forays, and you can imagine what a lifesaver it was for me. I started to judge myself a little less, to have compassion for my early childhood wounds, and to accept the limitations that led to my unfaithfulness. I wish I had been mature enough to realize that my marriage wasn't working and been able to choose a more honorable way of making a change. I wish I had been wise enough to see that the source of the aliveness and passion I had discovered wasn't in my lover, but in myself. But I wasn't able to do so at the time. I failed to live up to my ideals, and that was a very human thing to do.

It was hard for me to let go of my self-criticism though. Looking back, I see that I was trying to salvage my self-esteem in a convoluted way. At least the part of me that was constantly judging and criticizing myself was good, even if the rest of me was bad.

Another stumbling block was the belief that if I forgave myself it would just amount to letting myself off the hook. But to my surprise I found that when I started to accept myself with more kindness and compassion, I could actually be more honest about the ways in which I had harmed others. Not only John, but also Peter and his wife. Peter, being more worldly and experienced than I was, had realized that my first flush of passion for a much older man was unlikely to last. I have to admit he was probably right. In some ways I was just using Peter as an escape route from an unhappy marriage. Though I didn't realize it at the time, I probably would have left him once that goal was accomplished. It was the right choice for him to stay with his wife, who was rock solid and his main source of strength during his months of chemotherapy.

What amazed me about my newfound practice of self-compassion was the incredible ability it gave me to see myself clearly, and to learn from the mistakes I had made. Once I stopped cringing and found the bravery to look closely, I could see more precisely where I had gone wrong. With the blessing of my fiancé—Rupert—I took several long, peaceful mountain walks with Peter and we came to a place of mutual understanding, the urgency of our discussions being intensified by Peter's impending death. I could understand why I had made the choices I did, and why Peter had made the choices he did. It wasn't pretty, but it was how life had unfolded.

After Peter passed away, I could finally let go of my shame and self-judgment. I saw that relentlessly attacking myself for my weakness and immaturity was a complete waste of time and wasn't helping myself or anybody else. I realized that by giving myself kindness and understanding, I could start to heal. This new place of inner warmth, peace, and emotional stability not only brought me great happiness, it also allowed me to give more in my relationship with Rupert.

## A Precious Gift

Self-compassion is a gift available to anyone willing to open up to themselves. When we develop the habit of self-kindness, suffering becomes an opportunity to experience love and tenderness from within. No matter how difficult things get, we can always wrap our torn and tattered selves in our own soft embrace. We can soothe and comfort our own pain, just as a child is soothed and comforted by her mother's arms. We don't have to wait until we are perfect, until life goes exactly as we want it to. We don't need others to respond with care and compassion in order to feel worthy of love. We don't need to look outside ourselves for the acceptance and security we crave. This is not to say that we don't need other people. Of course we do. But who is in the best position to know how you really feel underneath that cheerful façade? Who is most likely to know the full extent of the pain and fear you face, to know what you need most? Who is the only person in your life who is available 24/7 to provide you with care and kindness? You.

*Chapter Four*

# WE'RE ALL IN THIS TOGETHER

*A human being is part of the whole, called by us "Universe," a part limited in time and space. He experiences himself, his thoughts and feelings, as something separate from the rest—a kind of optical delusion of consciousness. This delusion is a kind of prison for us, restricting us to our personal desires and to affection for a few persons nearest to us. Our task must be to free ourselves from this prison by widening our circle of compassion to embrace all living creatures and the whole of nature in its beauty.*
—EINSTEIN, *The Einstein Papers*

THE SECOND FUNDAMENTAL ELEMENT OF SELF-COMPASSION IS RECOGnition of the common human experience. Acknowledgment of the interconnected nature of our lives—indeed of life itself—helps to distinguish self-compassion from mere self-acceptance or self-love. Although self-acceptance and self-love are important, they are incomplete by themselves. They leave out an essential factor—other people. Compassion is, by definition, relational. Compassion literally means "to suffer *with*," which implies a basic mutuality in the experience of suffering. The emotion of compassion springs from the recognition that the human experience is imperfect. Why else would we say "it's only human" to comfort someone who has made a mistake? Self-compassion honors the fact that all human beings are fallible, that wrong choices and feelings of regret are inevitable, no matter how high and mighty one is. (As the saying goes, a clear conscience is usually the sign of a bad memory.)

When we're in touch with our common humanity, we remember that feelings of inadequacy and disappointment are shared by all. This is what distinguishes self-compassion from self-pity. Whereas self-pity says "poor me," self-compassion remembers that everyone suffers, and it offers comfort because everyone is human. The pain I feel in difficult times is the same pain that you feel in difficult times. The triggers are different, the circumstances are different, the degree of pain is different, but the process is the same. *You can't always get what you want.* This is true for everyone, even the Rolling Stones.

We often become scared and angry when we focus on undesired aspects of ourselves or our lives. We feel helpless and frustrated by our inability to control things—to get what we want, to be who we want to be. We rail against things as they are, and we cling to our narrow vision of how things *should* be. Every single human is in the same boat. The beauty of recognizing this basic fact of life—the silver lining so to speak—is that it provides deep insight into the shared human condition.

## Isolated and Alone

Sadly, however, most people don't focus on what they have in common with others, especially when they feel ashamed or inadequate. Rather than framing their imperfection in light of the shared human experience, they're more likely to feel isolated and disconnected from the world around them when they fail.

When we focus on our shortcomings without taking the bigger human picture into account, our perspective tends to narrow. We become absorbed by our own feelings of insufficiency and insecurity. When we're in the confined space of self-loathing, it's as if the rest of humanity doesn't even exist. This isn't a logical thought process, but a type of emotional tunnel vision. Somehow it feels like *I* am the only one who is being dumped, proven wrong, or made a fool of. As Tara Brach (author of *Radical Acceptance)* writes: "Feeling unworthy goes hand in hand with feeling separate from others, separate from life. If we are defective, how can we possibly belong? It seems like a vicious cycle: the more deficient we feel, the more separate and vulnerable we feel."

And even when we're having a painful experience that is not our fault—perhaps we've been laid off our job because of an economic down-turn, for instance—we often irrationally feel that the rest of the world is happily employed while it's only me sitting at home watching reruns all day. Or when we become ill, it feels like sickness is an unusual, ab-normal state (like the dying eighty-four-year-old man whose final words were "why me?"). Once we fall into the trap of believing that things are "supposed" to go well, we tend to think something has gone terribly amiss when they suddenly don't. Again, this isn't a conscious thought process but a hidden assumption that colors our emotional reactions. If we were to take a completely logical approach to the issue, we'd consider the fact that thousands of things can go wrong in life at any one time, so it's highly likely—in fact inevitable—that we'll experience hardships on a regular basis. But we don't tend to be rational about these matters. Instead, we suffer, and we feel all alone in our suffering.

## The Need to Belong

Abraham Maslow was a well-known American psychologist working in the mid-twentieth century who led the humanistic psychology movement. He argued that needs for individual growth and happiness can't be met without first satisfying the more basic need for human connection. Without bonds of love and affection with others, he argued, we cannot go on to achieve our full potential as human beings. Similarly, psychoanalyst Heinz Kohut, who developed a model called "self psychology " in the early 1970s, proposed that belongingness was one of the core needs of the self. He defined belongingness as the feeling of being "human among humans," a feeling that allows us to feel connected to other people. One of the major causes of mental health problems, he felt, was a lack of belongingness, the perception that we are cut off from our fellows.

Loneliness stems from the feeling that we don't belong, whether or not we're in the presence of others. If you attend a large party where you don't quite fit in, you're still likely to feel alone. Loneliness comes from feeling disconnected from others, even if they're only inches away. Public speaking anxiety, the number one phobia experienced in our culture, is also caused by fear of rejection and isolation. Why does the instruction to imagine your audience in their underwear work? Because it reminds you that the audience is vulnerable and imperfect too, and the image boosts your sense of shared humanity.

Even the fear of death itself stems largely from apprehension about losing companionship, closeness, and relationships to others. And feelings of isolation can actually help make that fear a reality. Research indicates that social isolation increases the risk of coronary heart disease by two or three times. In contrast, involvement in a support group lessens the anxiety and depression experienced by cancer victims, while increasing their long-term chances of survival. One of the key reasons support groups are so effective is because members feel less isolated throughout their ordeal. The need to belong, therefore, is fundamental to both physical and emotional health.

Feelings of connectedness, like feelings of kindness, activate the brain's attachment system. The "befriend" part of the "tend and befriend" instinct has to do with the human tendency to affiliate, to come together in groups in order to feel secure. For this reason, people who feel connected to others are not as frightened by difficult life circumstances and are more readily able to roll with the punches.

Of course, it's wonderful when we can get our need to belong met by loved ones such as friends or family. But if you're someone who has trouble sustaining good relationships, this type of social support may be missing in your life. And even in the best of circumstances, other people aren't always able to make us feel that we belong and are accepted. In the cavernous halls of our own minds, we may feel isolated in any moment, even if this isn't the way things actually are. Our fears and self-judgments are like blinders that often prevent us from seeing the hands that are being held out to help us. We may also be ashamed to admit our feelings of inadequacy to those we love, for fear that they wouldn't love us anymore if they knew the way we really were. Hiding our true selves from others then makes us feel even more alone.

That's why it's so important to transform our relationship with ourselves by recognizing our *inherent* interconnectedness. If we can compassionately remind ourselves in moments of falling down that failure is part of the shared human experience, then that moment becomes one of togetherness rather than isolation. When our troubled, painful experiences are framed by the recognition that countless others have undergone similar hardships, the blow is softened. The pain still hurts, but it doesn't become compounded by feelings of separation. Sadly, however, our culture tells us to notice how we are *unique* from others, not how we are the same.

## The Comparison Game

Because our culture demands that we perceive ourselves as "special and above average," we routinely engage in an egoistic process of social comparison with others. When we're deeply invested in seeing ourselves positively, we tend to feel threatened if others do better than we do.

Liz, for instance, felt great after getting her first annual review at her new job. The report praised her hard work and effort and also promised a 5 percent raise starting the next fiscal year. Elated, she rang her boyfriend with the news. "Fantastic!" he said. "I'll have the champagne ready when you get home." Later in the parking lot, however, Liz overheard a colleague talking excitedly on her cell phone. "The report said I was the most promising new employee of the year! And get this, they're giving me a 10 percent raise! That's twice the 5 percent everyone else gets. Isn't that amazing?" In half a second Liz went from feeling fabulous to feeling like a complete failure. Instead of celebrating her good fortune with her boyfriend when she got home, she ended up crying on his shoulder.

One of the saddest consequences of social comparison is how we distance ourselves from people whose success makes us feel bad about ourselves. Interestingly, one study found this to be true both literally and figuratively. Researchers told study participants they were assessing student interest in and knowledge of various topics for an upcoming College Bowl competition. Students thought they were being tested in pairs, but the other student was really part of the research team. A mock competition was held, and students fielded a series of questions about topics such as rock music or football. The experimenters told students either that they had outperformed their partner, or else that their partner had outperformed them. Next, experimenters assessed how close participants felt to their study partner by asking how much they thought they had in common and how much they wanted to work with their partner in the future. They even looked at how physically close they sat to their partner when both were moved to another room. Students felt more distant from partners, and also sat farther away from them, when they were told that they had been outperformed.

The sad irony is that the very reason we want to succeed in the first place is because we want to feel accepted and worthy, to be close to others, to feel that we belong. It's a classic catch-22. The very act of competing with others for success sets up an unwinnable situation in which the feelings of connectedness we crave are forever out of reach.

## Us Against Them

And we don't just compare ourselves to other individuals. We also compare the groups we belong to—Americans, Russians, Republicans, Democrats, Christians, Muslims, and so on—to other groups. That's why we tend to wear the mantle of our group affiliations on our sleeves (or our car bumpers). Our sense of self is imbued with social labels that define us and make us feel safe and accepted within clearly defined group boundaries. Although a sense of belongingness can be found within these group identities, it is still limited. As long as we're identifying with subsets of people rather than the entire human race, we're creating divisions that separate us from our fellows.

Sadly, these divisions often lead to prejudice and hatred. Just as we like to feel we are superior and above average in terms of personal traits, we also like to feel that our groups are superior to others. According to Henri Tajfel's social identity theory, when we incorporate a group into our identity, we derive our sense of self-worth from being a member of that group. We therefore become heavily invested in seeing "us" positively and "them" negatively. It's our investment in social identities that underlies group discrimination and racism. The reason I want to see your gender-ethnic-racial-political-national group as inferior is because it validates the preeminence of my own group, thereby giving me a sense of pride and righteous superiority. When the Ku Klux Klan member dons his white hood and robe, or the would-be terrorist attends a hate rally, his sense of self-worth gets a hit more powerful—and more dangerous—than any drug.

Tajfel's research showed that the process of group prejudice occurs even when the groups we belong to are based on arbitrary criteria. For instance, putting people into different groups based on their preference for the abstract artists Klee or Kandinsky, or even based on the flip of a coin, leads people to like their own group members better, to provide them with more resources, and to distrust members of the other group.

Group identity lies at the root of most violent conflicts—whether it's a scuffle between two local high school football teams or a full-scale international war. Tajfel understood the ramifications of this type of group bias firsthand. A Polish Jew who studied at the Sorbonne in Paris during the outbreak of World War II, he was drafted into the French army and captured by the Nazis. He was put in a prisoner of war camp but survived only because no one discovered he was Jewish. Most of his friends and family back in Poland were killed, however. The Holocaust was one of the worst—but sadly not the last—examples of the degree to which people can mistreat each other by classifying the self and others into distinct groups.

Fortunately, psychologists have discovered that when our sense of belonging extends to the whole human community rather than stopping at the boundaries of our own social groups, conflict is dramatically lessened. As long as we recognize that we are interconnected rather than distinct entities, understanding and forgiveness can be extended to oneself and others with fewer barriers in between. One study illustrates this point quite well. Jewish college students were asked about their willingness to forgive modern-day Germans for what happened in the Holocaust. The study had two conditions—either the Holocaust was described as an event in which Germans behaved aggressively toward Jews, or as an event in which humans behaved aggressively toward other humans. The Jewish participants were more willing to forgive modern-day Germans when the event was described as occurring between humans rather than distinct social groups, and they also saw Germans as more similar to themselves in this condition. By simply shifting our frame of reference from distinctiveness to similarity with others, we can dramatically alter our perceptions and emotional reactions.

There's a wonderful program called Challenge Day that provides a powerful experience of common humanity for adolescents. The program puts a group of high school students through a daylong series of activities designed to promote feelings of connectedness with their peers. In an exercise called "Lines that divide us," for example, teens are asked to line up on one side of the school gym. Then, a team leader calls out a series of painful experiences and asks people to cross over to the other side of the gym if they've ever had that experience. Each event is called out slowly, providing ample time for everyone to see who among them has suffered as they have. "Please cross the line if you've ever felt hurt or judged because of the color of your skin. . . . Been humiliated in a classroom by a teacher or a student. . . . Been bullied or teased or hurt for wearing glasses, braces, a hearing aid . . . for the way that you talked, for the clothes that you wore, or for the shape, size, or appearance of your body." At some point, almost every single person in the room crosses the line, making it vividly clear that all teens suffer from judgmental cruelty at one point or another. Typically, even the toughest kids will tear up after participating in the exercise, as compassion flows for themselves and others. The experience shatters the imaginary walls that make teens feel all alone, allowing them to realize that their sense of isolation has been an illusion, and lessening the chance of conflicts between them.

This is why the recognition of common humanity embedded in self-compassion is such a powerful healing force. When our sense of self-worth and belonging is grounded in simply being human, we can't be rejected or cast out by others. Our humanity can never be taken away from us, no matter how far we fall. The very fact that we are imperfect affirms that we are card-carrying members of the human race and are therefore always, automatically, connected to the whole.

## The Illusion of Perfection

All too often, however, our minds fool us into thinking that we can, and in fact *should,* be other than we are. Nobody likes to feel they're flawed. But for some, imperfection is especially hard to bear. Perfectionism is defined as the compulsive need to achieve and accomplish one's goals, with no allowance for falling short of one's ideals. Perfectionists experience enormous stress and anxiety about getting things exactly right, and they feel devastated when they don't. The unrealistically high expectations of perfectionists mean that they will inevitably be disappointed. By seeing things in black-and-white terms—either I'm perfect or I'm worthless—perfectionists are continually dissatisfied with themselves.

Tom, for example, was a writer who made a decent living writing historical fiction novels, but he had never had a major success. While able to pay his living expenses from his royalties (no mean feat for a writer), Tom felt he wouldn't be satisfied until he had written a national best seller. Then, finally, he got his big break. His latest novel got a glowing review from the *New York Times,* and shortly thereafter he was invited for interviews on various TV and radio stations. Sales of his book started to take off. It didn't take long before he started to envision the words "Number one best-selling novel" written on the cover of the paperback edition. Although he did see a peak in sales, and the book did in fact make the best-seller list (number 23), Tom still wasn't happy. He could only focus on the fact that his sales weren't higher. He wasn't number one, he wasn't even in the top ten. Ironically, Tom felt more depressed *after* his sales went up than before, the possibility of being "the best" now having been firmly entrenched in his mind. Good just wasn't good enough, so he ended up feeling like a failure even though in fact he was a bona fide success. Tom's story highlights the insidious nature of perfectionism, and the suffering it so often causes.

So does perfectionism have an upside? The positive aspect of perfectionism has to do with the determination to do your best. Striving to achieve and setting high standards for yourself can be a productive and healthy trait. But when your *entire* sense of self-worth is based on being productive and successful, when failure is simply not allowed, then the striving to achieve becomes tyrannical. And counterproductive. Research indicates that perfectionists are at much greater risk for eating disorders, anxiety, depression, and a whole host of other psychological problems.

If we were perfect, we wouldn't be human; we'd be Barbie and Ken—plastic figurines that look good but are also dead as doorknobs. Warm, breathing, human life is a constantly unfolding wonder, not a static state of flawless sameness. Being alive involves struggle and despair as well as joy and glory. To demand perfection is to turn our backs on real life, the full range of human experience. And perfection is boring! The popular YouTube character Kelly (an adolescent girl played by comedian Liam Kyle Sullivan) captures this sentiment perfectly when she says in a typically bored teen-girl voice: "I've already been to heaven. After five minutes I was like, let's go!" Isn't it so true? Would you really want to inhabit a world where everything and everyone was absolutely perfect? It's precisely *because* of the unwanted and unexpected that our lives have such intrigue and interest.

Imperfection also makes growth and learning possible. Like it or not, the main way we learn is by falling flat on our face, just as we did when we first learned to walk. Our parents may tell us a million times not to touch that hot stove, but it's only after we actually burn ourselves that we really understand why it's not such a great idea. The learning opportunities provided by failure can actually help us to achieve our dreams. In the words of restaurateur Wolfgang Puck, "I learned more from the one restaurant that didn't work than from all the ones that were successes." Yes, failure is frustrating. But it's also temporary and eventually yields wisdom. We can think of failure as part of life's apprenticeship. If we were perfect and had all the answers, we'd never get to ask questions, and we wouldn't be able to discover anything new.

## Interconnectedness

When we judge ourselves for our inadequacies, we typically assume that there is in fact a separate, clearly bounded entity called "me" that can be blamed for failing. But is this really true? Who we are, how we think, and what we do is inextricably interwoven with other people and events, which makes the assignment of blame quite ambiguous. Let's say you have an anger issue that you habitually criticize yourself for. What are the causes and conditions that led you to be so angry? Perhaps inborn genetics plays a role. But did you choose your genes before entering this world? Of course not, your genetic makeup stems from factors completely beyond your control. Or maybe you grew up in a conflict-filled household in which shouting and anger were the only ways to get heard. But did you choose for your family to be this way?

If we closely examine our "personal" failings, it soon becomes clear that they are not there by choice. Typically, outside circumstances conspired to form our particular patterns without our input. If you had control over your maladaptive thoughts, emotions, and behaviors, you wouldn't still have them. You would have already jettisoned your dark, anxious, neurotic persona and become a calm, confident ray of sunshine. Clearly you don't have complete control over your actions, or else you'd only act in ways that you approved of. So why are you judging yourself so harshly for the way you are?

We are the expression of millions of prior circumstances that have all come together to shape us in the present moment. Our economic and social background, our past associations and conversations, our culture, our family history, our genetics—they've all had a profound role in creating the person we are today. Zen master Thich Nhat Hahn calls this "interbeing."

> *If you are a poet, you will see clearly that there is a cloud floating in this sheet of paper. Without a cloud there will be no water;*

*without water, the trees cannot grow; and without trees, you cannot make paper. So the cloud is in here. The existence of this page is dependent upon the existence of a cloud. Paper and cloud are so close.*

Many people are scared to acknowledge their essential interconnectedness, because it means they must admit they don't have complete control over how they think and act. This makes them feel powerless. However, the illusion of being in control is just that—an illusion. And a harmful one at that, because it encourages self-judgment and self-blame. In reality, it doesn't make any more sense to harshly blame ourselves than it does to blame a hurricane. Despite the fact that we give hurricanes names like Katrina and Rita, a hurricane isn't a self-contained unit. A hurricane is an impermanent, ever-changing phenomenon arising out of a particular set of interacting conditions—air pressure, ground temperature, humidity, wind, and so on. The same applies to us: we aren't self-contained units either. Like weather patterns, we are also an impermanent, ever-changing phenomenon arising out of a particular set of interacting conditions. Without food, water, air, and shelter, we'd be dead. Without our genes, family, friends, social history, and culture, we wouldn't act or feel as we do.

When we recognize that we are the product of countless factors that we don't normally identify with, we don't need to take our "personal failings" so personally. When we acknowledge the intricate web of causes and conditions in which we are all imbedded, we can be less judgmental of ourselves and others. A deep understanding of interbeing allows us to have compassion for the fact that we're doing the best we can given the hand life has dealt us.

"But" is often the interjection at this point. What's wrong with judgment? Don't we need judgment to figure out right from wrong? To take personal responsibility for our mistakes?

It's useful here to draw a distinction between judgment and discriminating wisdom. Discriminating wisdom recognizes when things are harmful or unjust, but also recognizes the causes and conditions that lead to situations of harm or injustice in the first place. When wrongdoers are treated with compassion rather than harsh condemnation, cycles of conflict and suffering can be broken.

Imagine hearing a story about a young man who robs a bank and shoots a teller in the arm as she tries to call for help. At first you might make a ruthless judgment of the man—he's a monster and should be locked in jail for eternity. End of story. But then, you learn more about the criminal's background and history. His parents were drug addicts. By eleven he was out on the streets in a neighborhood where he had to fight and steal to survive. He tried to get a job and go straight but kept getting fired because he didn't know how to read or write properly, and eventually he turned to crime again. Your hard-line attitude toward the offender might begin to soften. You might even come to have compassion for him. This compassion wouldn't mean that you absolve the man of responsibility for his crimes, or think that what he did was okay. You might still decide that he needs to be put away in prison to ensure the safety of society. But you would have a deeper understanding of the conditions that led him to act as he did, and you would retain respect for his humanity in the process. And who knows, it's even possible that with the right help and encouragement—in other words, a new set of conditions—he could change.

This is discriminating wisdom rather than judgment. Judgment defines people as bad versus good and tries to capture their essential nature with simplistic labels. Discriminating wisdom recognizes complexity and ambiguity. It acknowledges that life has unfolded in such a way as to cause something to happen, but also allows for the possibility that with a new set of circumstances things might well go differently.

Jesus famously said, "Let him who is without sin cast the first stone." And later, as he hung dying on the cross, he said, "Father, forgive them, for they know not what they do." The message was clear: we need to have understanding and compassion for even the worst wrongdoers, ourselves included.

## Exercise One

*Letting Go of Our Self-Definitions by*
*Identifying Our Interconnectedness*

Think about a trait that you often judge yourself for, and that is an important part of your self-definition. For example, you may think of yourself as a shy person, lazy, angry, and so on. Then ask yourself the following questions:

1. How often do you display this trait—most of the time, sometimes, only occasionally? Who are you when you don't display the trait? Are you still you?

2. Are there particular circumstances that seem to draw out the trait, and others in which the trait is not apparent? Does this trait really define you if particular circumstances must be present in order for the trait to emerge?

3. What are the various causes and conditions that led to having the trait in the first place (early family experiences, genetics, life pressures, etc.)? If these "outside" forces were partly responsible for you having this trait, is it accurate to think of the trait as reflecting the inner you?

4. Did you choose to have this trait, and do you have much choice about whether or not you display this trait? If not, why are you judging yourself for this trait?

5. What happens when you reframe your self-description so that you are not defining yourself in terms of the trait? For example, instead of saying "I am an angry person," what happens when you say "Sometimes, in certain circumstances, I

get angry." By not identifying so strongly with this trait, does anything change? Can you sense any more space, freedom, peace of mind?

We are all subject to human limitations. Every single one of us is in the same predicament. The British novelist Jerome K. Jerome once wrote, "It is in our faults and failings, not in our virtues, that we touch each other, and find sympathy. It is in our follies that we are one." In recognizing the shared nature of our imperfection, self-compassion provides the sense of connectedness needed to truly thrive and reach our full potential. Instead of looking outside ourselves for a sense of acceptance and belonging, we can directly satisfy these needs by looking within.

## My Story: What's Normal, Anyway?

The practice of self-compassion, and especially of remembering our shared humanity, helped me deal with the greatest challenge in my life so far. A couple of years after getting a job at the University of Texas at Austin, I gave birth to a beautiful little boy named Rowan. At eighteen months, we knew there was something wrong with him. He wasn't pointing, something most babies do by their first birthday. He didn't turn his head when we called his name, didn't call me Mama, didn't call me anything at all. He only had about five words—all starting with the letter B—and a few names, mostly of Thomas the Tank engine trains. He would spend hours obsessively lining up his toy animals. He would tantrum violently at the drop of a hat. I'd known parenthood would be hard, but not this hard. Why couldn't I stop his disruptive behaviors? Was it because I was a bad mother? Was I not being firm enough?

I did wonder whether Rowan might have some sort of developmental disorder. Could it be hearing problems, speech delay, central auditory processing disorder? I took him to all sorts of specialists. Ordered any book I thought might help. Did anything and everything *except* seriously investigate if Rowan was showing signs of autism. Looking back, I must have unconsciously suspected he was autistic, but my conscious mind wouldn't allow me to admit it. Whatever's wrong with Rowan, I thought, there's no way that this adorable, charming, funny child could be autistic. After all, he was so loving and affectionate, and he made direct eye contact. Autistic children aren't supposed to do that, are they? I remember once after Rowan gave me one of his beautiful, heartwarming smiles, I even half-jokingly said to my husband, Rupert—"At least we know he's not autistic!"

Then one day, as I was packing for a silent meditation retreat that was to start later that afternoon, I couldn't ignore the nagging worry any longer. I took a few deep breaths, turned toward the computer, and typed in the words "Autism, early signs of." The web page said that if your child showed at least three out of a list of ten signs, he or she had a good chance of being autistic and should be taken in for professional evaluation as soon as possible. Rowan had nine out of ten. Lack of eye contact was the only sign he *didn't* have.

At that moment, I knew Rowan was autistic. I called Rupert and told him. He was as stunned as I was. "I'll cancel my retreat," I said. "No, you should go," he said. "You need it. And I'll need you to be strong and centered so you can help *me* when you get back." I cried during the entire two-hour drive to the retreat center, and for the next four days I quite literally sat with the pain of knowing my son was autistic. "How can this be happening?" "Is Rowan slipping away from us?" "How are we going to cope?" I allowed myself to fully feel my fear and grief. I gave myself as much loving-kindness and compassion as I could. If a guilty thought would creep in—"How can I be grieving for Rowan, when I love him so much?"—I wouldn't allow myself to run away with self-judgment. My feelings of grief were only natural, something all parents in such situations go through.

When I got back from the retreat, Rupert and I had to deal with the fact that this was now our life. All our dreams of having the perfect son—we assumed that he would go on to get a Ph.D. like me, of course, or maybe become a successful writer like his father—flew out the window. We had an autistic child.

I freely admit that at times, the experience pushed me into self-pity. When at the park with Rowan, for instance, watching other moms with their "normal" kids, I would start to feel very sorry for myself. Why can't I have a normal child? Why can't Rowan even respond when another child asks him his name? Why are the other kids making faces at how weird he's being? I would start to feel isolated, alone, cut off from the world of "normal" families. I found myself internally screaming, *"HAVING CHILDREN IS NOT SUPPOSED TO BE THIS WAY! THIS IS NOT THE PLAN I SIGNED UP FOR! WHY ME?"* But luckily self-compassion saved me from going too far down this path. While watching the other kids playing on the swings or swooshing down the slide, I would remind myself that most families had difficulties raising their kids. Maybe the challenge wasn't autism, but it could be any number of other issues—depression, eating disorders, drug addiction, being bullied at school, serious illness. I would look at the other families at the park and remember that they surely had their woes and sorrows too, if not now then sometime in the future. Instead of feeling "poor me," I would try to open my heart to all parents everywhere who were trying to do their best in challenging circumstances. What about the millions of parents in developing countries whose children didn't even have enough to eat? I certainly wasn't the only one having a hard time.

Two things would happen as a result of this line of thinking. First, I would begin to feel deeply in touch with the unpredictability of being human. My heart would swell up with tenderness for all the challenges and sorrows involved in being a parent, but also for all the joy, love, and wonder that children bring us. Second, my situation was put into much clearer perspective. Rather than falling into the trap of believing that other parents were having an easier time than I was, I remembered that it could be worse—much worse. In the overall scheme of things, autism wasn't so bad, and there were things we could do to help Rowan tremendously. The real gift of self-compassion, in fact, was that it gave me the equanimity needed to take actions that *did* ultimately help him.

Perhaps more important, focusing on common humanity helped me to love Rowan for who he was. Once I remembered that having problems and challenges *was* normal, I could more easily get over the disappointment of not having a "normal" child.

And what is "normal" anyway? Maybe Rowan had difficulty expressing himself with language, or engaging in appropriate social interactions, but he was a loving, happy kid. Being human is not about being any one particular way; it is about being as life creates you—with your own particular strengths and weaknesses, gifts and challenges, quirks and oddities. By accepting and embracing the human condition, I could better accept and embrace Rowan and also my role as the mother of an autistic child.

*Chapter Five*

# BEING MINDFUL OF WHAT IS

*You can't stop the waves, but you can learn to surf.*
—JON KABAT-ZINN, *Wherever You Go, There You Are*

THE THIRD KEY INGREDIENT OF SELF-COMPASSION IS MINDFULNESS. Mindfulness refers to the clear seeing and nonjudgmental acceptance of what's occurring in the present moment. Facing up to reality, in other words. The idea is that we need to see things as they are, no more, no less, in order to respond to our current situation in the most compassionate—and therefore effective—manner.

## Stopping to Notice Moments of Suffering

To give ourselves compassion, we first have to recognize that we are suffering. We can't heal what we can't feel. As mentioned earlier, we often fail to recognize feelings of guilt, defectiveness, sadness, loneliness, and so on, as moments of suffering that can be responded to with compassion. When you look in the mirror and decide you're too short, or that your nose is too big, do you immediately tell yourself that these feelings of inadequacy are painful and deserving of a kind, caring response? When your boss calls you into his office and tells you that your job performance is below par, is your first instinct to comfort yourself for going through such a difficult experience? Probably not.

We certainly feel the sting of falling short of our ideals, but our mind tends to focus on the failure itself, rather than the pain caused by failure. This is a crucial difference. The moment we see something about ourselves we don't like, our attention tends to become completely absorbed by our perceived flaws. In that moment, we don't have the perspective needed to recognize the suffering caused by our feelings of imperfection, let alone to respond to them with compassion.

And it's not just the pain of personal inadequacy that we tend to ignore. We are surprisingly brusque toward ourselves when the more general circumstances of our life go wrong through no fault of our own. Let's say your mother becomes seriously ill, or you get rear-ended on the freeway. Most people, even if they don't blame themselves for their current circumstances, tend to immediately go into problem-solving mode in such situations. We are likely to spend enormous amounts of time and energy dealing with the crisis, making doctors appointments, calling insurance companies, and so on. Although all this is certainly necessary, it's also very important to recognize that these experiences take a lot out of us emotionally. We need to stop for a breath or two and acknowledge that we're having a hard time, and that our pain is deserving of a kind, caring response. Otherwise, our suffering will go unattended, and feelings of stress and worry will only mount. We risk getting burned out, exhausted, and overwhelmed, because we're spending all our energy trying to fix external problems without remembering to refresh ourselves internally.

It's not surprising that we often ignore our own pain, given that we're physiologically programmed to avoid it. Pain signals that something is wrong, triggering our fight-or-flight response. It screams PROBLEM, GET AWAY, DANGER!!! Imagine if pain couldn't signal something as basic as "finger caught in car door, open door and remove finger immediately!" Because of our innate tendency to move away from pain, it can be extremely difficult to turn toward our pain, to hold it, to be with it as it is. This is why so many people shut themselves off from their emotions. It's a very natural thing to do.

Jacob was one of these people. He avoided conflict and was quick to appease anyone who showed any signs of getting upset. He just didn't want to deal with any sort of emotional intensity. Jacob was a good man, but he was unwilling to face up to the pain of his past. His mother had been a well-known television actress who was seriously devoted to her acting career. She often left Jacob in the hands of nannies while she worked on various production sets. On an unconscious level, Jacob deeply resented all the time his mother spent away from him, feeling that she prioritized her career over him. If he were to allow his feelings of anger in, however, he was afraid he'd start hating his mother, destroying the feelings of love and connection he felt with her. So basically, he just suppressed his rage.

Several years ago, Jacob became depressed and entered therapy. The therapist helped him to realize that his depression stemmed in part from the deep wells of anger he was harboring toward his mother, and the effort it was taking to repress his rage. What he needed was to get in touch with his true feelings. When Jacob did finally turn toward his anger, however, rather than simply holding it in mindful awareness, it took him over, and he ended up wielding his anger like an assault rifle. He dove into his rage with full force, getting more and more riled up as he thought about the "horrible" way his mother had treated him. He started seeing her as a narcissistic monster—Norma Desmond in *Sunset Boulevard*. In short, he became hysterical rather than mindful. Unfortunately, this type of extreme pendulum swing is common when people first start working with difficult emotions.

# Running Away with Painful Feelings

Like Jacob, suppressing and then exploding with our emotions is something most of us have experienced. I like to term this process "overidentification." Our sense of self becomes so wrapped up in our emotional reactions that our entire reality is consumed by them. There's no mental space left over to say, "Gosh, I'm getting a bit worked up here. Maybe there's another way to look at this." Rather than stepping back and objectively observing what's occurring, we're lost in the thick of it. What we think and feel seems like a direct perception of reality, and we forget that we are putting a personal spin on things.

I remember once my mother and mother-in-law were both visiting from out of town and they borrowed my car for an outing with my son, Rowan. I have a silver Toyota hybrid with keyless technology, meaning that you just have to hold the key near the car door and it will open. There is no button to push or key to insert. This novel technology made them a bit nervous—they just didn't trust it. After going on the outing and coming back to the parking lot, they tried holding the magical key thingy next to the car door and, of course, it didn't work. My mother tried the key over and over again, and nothing happened. "See! You can't rely on these newfangled gimmicks!" They both got very upset—here they were, almost an hour from home, stranded with a confused child, all because of some goddamned modern technology. What were they to do?

They called the local Toyota dealership, who told them to call a locksmith. Once the locksmith had been arranged and was on his way, they saw a parking lot security person. Maybe he could help in the meantime. "Sir, we're locked out of our Toyota hybrid that has this weird key thing; have you ever used one of these before?" The man looked at the key, then looked at the car. "Uh, ladies, you said it was a Toyota hybrid? This car isn't a hybrid. It isn't even a Toyota." My car was actually three spaces down. They had become so lost in their reactions that neither of them thought to take a very sensible next step: checking to see whether they were trying to get into the right car! In the immortal words of Charlie Chaplin, "Life is a tragedy when seen in a close-up, but a comedy when seen in a long-shot."

There's another reason I call this process overidentification. Extreme reactions—or perhaps more accurately, overreactions—are especially common when the sense of self is involved. If I am afraid of other people judging me—let's say I have to give a public speech and am nervous about it—then the feelings that come up when thinking about the speech will tend to wildly distort reality. Rather than simply noticing that I am nervous, I might create elaborate scenarios in my mind of rejection, people laughing at me, throwing rotten vegetables, and so on.

What often drives this type of emotional overreaction is the attempt to avoid seeing ourselves as flawed or "bad." When our self-concept is threatened, things ramp up very quickly. I can think of a recent example (very recent, I must admit), of my own "overidentified" reaction. I thought I'd lost an important tax certificate sent to me by the IRS, which I had applied for months earlier and had just received in the mail. The deadline for filing the certificate was fast approaching. I was about to send it to my accountant but couldn't find it anywhere. I looked and looked but to no avail. Panic ensued. I was racked with anxiety. What a catastrophe! I'm in deep jeopardy! I became angry, distraught—losing it, in other words. Underlying my reaction was the fear that I was just a screwup, that my lack of organization skills (mail tends to pile up on my kitchen table like leaves in autumn) had finally come back to haunt me. Luckily, I eventually recognized what was happening and was able to be mindful of my reactions. Yes, I was feeling anxious about losing the certificate, but was it really all that bad? I could always ask the IRS for another copy, which, though a hassle, wouldn't be the end of the world. I even managed to remember to have compassion for the anxiety I felt, and to recognize that my life was very busy and I was actually pretty organized considering everything. I stopped to comfort myself in this painful situation, remembering that these things happen.

A few hours later, my husband, Rupert, came home with a sheepish look on his face. He told me that he had accidentally used the back of the IRS envelope for a shopping list, so it wasn't really lost after all. Rather than lambasting him, which I probably would have done if I was still wrestling with the self-judgment that I was incompetent, I was able to laugh at the whole situation. How often do we make mountains out of molehills? How often do we create the illusion that things are worse than they really are? If we can be mindful of our fears and anxieties rather than overidentifying with them, we can save ourselves from a lot of unwarranted pain. As the seventeenth-century French philosopher Montaigne once said, "My life has been filled with terrible misfortune, most of which never happened."

Mindfulness brings us back to the present moment and provides the type of balanced awareness that forms the foundation of self-compassion. Like a clear, still pool without ripples, mindfulness perfectly mirrors what's occurring without distortion. Rather than becoming lost in our own personal soap opera, mindfulness allows us to view our situation with greater perspective and helps to ensure that we don't suffer unnecessarily.

## Awareness of Awareness

When we notice our pain without exaggerating it, this is a moment of mindfulness. Mindfulness entails observing what is going on in our field of awareness just as it is—right here, right now. I remember quite clearly the first time I experienced mindfulness. I was about twelve years old, home alone after school. My mother had a copy of Ram Dass's book *Be Here Now* lying on the coffee table. Although the book had been there for several months, one day, for whatever reason, I actually thought about what the words meant. BE HERE NOW. Hmmm. I *am* here, and it *is* now. I walked across the living room. Still here, still now. Then I walked into the kitchen. Still here, still now. Where else could I be but here? When else could it be but now? Then it dawned on me—there is *only* here and *only* now. No matter where we go or what we do, we are here, now. I felt a giddy excitement and ran around the house laughing with amazement. HERE! NOW! HERE! NOW! HERE! NOW! I had gained insight into one of the most fundamental truths of life—*that conscious awareness only exists in the here and now.*

Why is this important? Because this insight allows us to see that thoughts about the past and the future are just that: thoughts. The past doesn't exist except in our memories, and the future doesn't exist except in our imagination. Rather than being lost in our train of thought, therefore, we can take a step back and say—ahh, this is what I'm thinking, feeling, and experiencing *right now.* We can awaken to the reality of the present moment.

Mindfulness is sometimes seen as a form of "meta-awareness," which means awareness of awareness. Instead of simply feeling anger, I am aware that I am now feeling anger. Rather than just feeling the blister on my heel, I am aware that I now feel the blister on my heel. Not only am I thinking about what I'm going to say at the meeting tomorrow, I am aware that I'm now thinking about what I'm going to say tomorrow. This may seem like a vague, insubstantial distinction, but it makes all the difference in the world in terms of our ability to respond effectively to difficult situations. When we can see our situation with clarity and objectivity, we open the door to wisdom. When our awareness narrows and gets lost in our thoughts and emotions, we can't reflect on our reactions and question whether they are out of line. This limits our ability to act wisely.

A commonly used analogy among those who write about mindfulness is that of a movie theater. When you're lost in the story line of a movie—perhaps a thriller—sometimes you suddenly remember that you're watching a movie. A moment earlier, when you thought the heroine might be pushed out of the window by the villain, you were gripping your armrests in fear. Then the man next to you sneezes and you realize that there isn't really any danger—*it's just a movie.* Rather than being totally consumed by the plot, your awareness broadens and you recognize what is actually happening in the present moment. You are simply watching pixels of light dancing across a scene. So you loosen your grip on the armrest, your heartbeat returns to normal, and you allow yourself to become lost in the story once again.

Mindfulness operates in a very similar manner. When you focus on the fact that you are having certain thoughts and feelings, you are no longer lost in their story line. You can wake up and look around you, taking an outsider's perspective on your experience. You can turn your awareness in on itself, as if you were gazing in a reflective pool and see an image of yourself gazing in a reflective pool. Try it right now. You've been reading the words on this page without realizing that you were reading, but now you can read this sentence with the *awareness* that you are reading. If you're sitting, you probably haven't noticed the sensations in your feet as they touch the floor. Now focus on the fact that your feet feel a certain way. Not only do your feet tingle (or are warm, cold, cramped, etc.), you are now *aware* that your feet feel this way. This is mindfulness.

Fortunately, Jacob finally learned how to become mindful of the anger spurred by his mother's acting career instead of just "letting it all hang out." His therapist taught him how to fully feel and experience the hurt and resentment he had been harboring toward his mother all those years, without necessarily believing that the story line he was telling himself was *real and true.* The anger was true, but the gentle, nonjudgmental awareness that held his anger helped him realize that his mother's deep love for him was also true. Yes, she loved her career and was devoted to it—perhaps to a fault—but this was partly because it gave her the financial resources needed to provide the advantages in life she so wanted for him. Before confronting his mother with angry accusations, therefore, Jacob was able to calm and center himself with mindfulness. He then had a frank but kind conversation with his mother about the difficulties of his childhood that actually ended up bringing them closer together. If he had not chosen the path of mindfulness, he might have caused a destructive rift in their relationship that would have taken years to heal.

## Shining the Light of Consciousness

One key to understanding mindfulness lies in distinguishing awareness itself from the contents of awareness. All sorts of different things arise within the frame of our awareness—physical sensations, visual perceptions, sounds, smells, tastes, emotions, thoughts. These are all contents—things that come and go. And the contents of awareness are always changing. Even when staying perfectly still, our breath rises and falls, our heart beats, our eyes blink, sounds arise and pass away. If the contents of awareness didn't change, we'd be dead. Life, by definition, entails transformation and change.

What about the awareness that holds all these phenomena, however? The light of consciousness that illuminates the sights, sounds, sensations, and thoughts? Awareness does not change. It is the only thing in our waking experience that remains still and constant, the calm foundation on which our ever-changing experience rests. Experiences continually vary, but the conscious awareness that illuminates those experiences does not.

Imagine a red cardinal bird flying across a clear blue sky. The bird represents a particular thought or emotion we're experiencing, and the sky represents mindfulness, which holds the thought or emotion. The bird might start doing crazy loops, take a nose dive, land on a tree branch, whatever, but the sky is still there, unperturbed. When we identify with the sky rather than with the bird, or in other words, when our attention rests in awareness itself, rather than the particular thought or emotion arising within that awareness, we can stay calm and centered.

This is important, because when we are mindful, we find our resting place—our seat, as it's sometimes called. Rather than having our sense of self caught up in and carried away by the contents of awareness, our sense of self remains centered in awareness itself. We can notice what is happening—an angry thought, a fear, a throbbing sensation in our temple—without falling into the trap of thinking that we are *defined* by this anger, fear, or pain. We can't be defined by *what* we are thinking and feeling when our consciousness is *aware* that we are thinking and feeling: otherwise, who is it that is being aware of our thoughts and feelings?

## Exercise One

### *Noting Practice*

(Also available as a guided meditation in MP3 format at www.self-compassion.org)

An important tool used to develop mindfulness is the practice of noting. The idea is to make a soft mental note whenever a particular thought, emotion, or sensation arises. This helps us to become more consciously aware of what we're experiencing. If I note that I feel angry, for instance, I become consciously aware that I'm angry. If I note that my back is uncomfortable as I'm sitting at my desk, I become consciously aware of my discomfort. This then provides me with the opportunity to respond wisely to my current circumstances. Perhaps I should take a few deep breaths to calm down or stretch to relieve my back pain. The noting practice can be used in any situation and helps engender mindfulness in daily life.

For this exercise, find a relaxed position and sit down for about ten to twenty minutes. Get comfortable, close your eyes, and simply note whatever thoughts, emotions, smells, sounds, or other physical sensations arise in your awareness. For example: "breathing in," "sound of children playing," "itch in left foot," "wondering what to wear for the party," "insecurity," "excitement," "plane flying overhead," and so on. Every time you become aware of a new experience, acknowledge the experience with a quiet mental note. Then allow your attention to settle on the next experience it is drawn to.

Sometimes you'll find yourself lost in thought and realize that for the last five minutes you've been thinking about your lunch and have forgotten entirely about your noting practice. Not to worry. As soon as you notice that you've been lost in thought, simply note "lost in thought" and turn your attention back to your noting practice.

We can train our brains to pay better attention and become more aware of what's happening to us moment to moment. This skill offers a big payoff in terms of allowing us to be more fully engaged in the present, and it also provides us with the mental perspective needed to deal with challenging situations effectively.

## Responding Rather Than Reacting

Mindfulness provides incredible freedom, because it means we don't have to believe every passing thought or emotion as *real and true*. Rather, we can see that different thoughts and emotions arise and pass away, and we can decide which are worth paying attention to and which are not. We can question the accuracy of our perceptions and ask if our thoughts and emotions need to be taken quite so seriously. The real treasure offered by mindfulness—its most amazing gift—is that mindfulness provides us with the opportunity to *respond* rather than simply *react*.

When I am lost in the story of a powerful emotion—let's say I feel insulted by something my friend just said and I'm feeling hurt and indignant—I am likely to react in a way I'll later regret. For instance, I was once talking with a friend on the phone and we got into an argument. I was trying to convince her that a choice I was making was in fact a good one. At first it was just a discussion—I was presenting my reasons for making this choice and my friend was presenting her concerns about whether or not it was actually right for me. At some point, however, my friend voiced her fear that I was being "naive." It's funny how quickly the tenor of the discussion changed. I felt insulted, then angry. I started raising my voice and was soon shouting. I was defending my point of view as if my life depended on it, exaggerating my claims to know what was right for me and portraying my friend as the one who was ignorant and confused. Before I knew it, I had hung up on her.

Luckily we're old friends and I called her back a few minutes later to apologize. Once we started talking calmly, I realized she didn't mean to be insulting by voicing her fear that I was being naive about this particular issue. She was really concerned I was making a decision without having the experience or knowledge needed to make a good one. Sure, it wasn't the most politic choice of words on her part, but her intentions were good and I certainly overreacted. The fact that I had had a stressful day at work that day probably hadn't helped things either.

If I had been able to be mindful during our conversation, I would have been able to say to myself: *I am aware that I am feeling hurt, insulted, and angry right now. I'm going to take a deep breath and pause before I start shouting accusations. What are her motives—is she really trying to hurt me?* In other words, when we're able to recognize what we're feeling in the moment, we don't have to let those feelings immediately propel us into action. We can stop to question whether we really want to say what's on the tip of our tongue and choose to say something more productive instead.

To have any choice in how we respond, however, we need the mental space to consider our options. We need to be able to ask ourselves— what is really happening right here, right now? Is the danger real, or am I only having *thoughts* of danger, like pixels of light dancing on a screen? What is the *actual* situation that needs to be responded to? This is how we gain the freedom needed to make wise choices.

And even when we aren't able to be mindful in the moment—which is admittedly very difficult to do when our emotions are running high— mindfulness allows us to recover from our overreactions more quickly. No, I wasn't able to stop myself before hanging up on my friend. But I didn't have to spend the next few hours, days, or weeks justifying my behavior either. I was quickly able to recognize what had just happened, to be mindful of the reality that I regretted my behavior, to make amends, and move on.

There is remarkable power in mindfulness—it gives us the breathing room needed to respond in a way that helps rather than harms us. And of course, one of the ways we harm ourselves most is through the reactive habit of self-criticism. Whether due to our parents, our culture, or our personality type, many of us have built up lifelong patterns of beating ourselves up when we fail or make some mistake. Our automatic reaction when we see something about ourselves we don't like is to put ourselves down. Or when faced with adversity, our first reaction might be to immediately go into problem-solving mode without first stopping to tend to our emotional needs. But if we can be mindful, even for just a moment, of the pain associated with failure or the stress and hardship entailed by difficult circumstances, we can take a step back and respond to our pain with kindness. We can soothe and comfort ourselves with compassionate understanding. We can reframe our situation in light of our shared humanity, so that we don't feel so isolated by adversity. Not only am I suffering, *I am aware that I am suffering,* and therefore I can try to do something about it.

After some practice you can actually make a habit of this, so that as soon as you notice you're suffering you automatically embrace yourself with compassion. Think of it as pushing the reset button on your computer when it gets locked up. Rather than staying stuck in painful feelings of self-judgment or merciless stoicism, you can reboot your heart and mind so that they start flowing freely again. Then, whatever actions are needed to help your situation can be carried out with more calm, stability, and grace—not to mention effectiveness.

## Suffering = Pain x Resistance

Suffering stems from a single source—comparing our reality to our ideals. When reality matches our wants and desires, we're happy and satisfied. When reality doesn't match our wants and desires, we suffer. Of course, we have about a snowball's chance in hell of our reality completely matching our ideals 100 percent of the time. That's why suffering is so ubiquitous.

I once went on a meditation retreat with a wonderful teacher named Shinzen Young, who gave me words of wisdom that I'll never forget. He said that the key to happiness was understanding that suffering is caused by *resisting* pain. We can't avoid pain in life, he said, but we don't necessarily have to suffer because of that pain. Because Shinzen was a bit of a Buddhist "nerd" (he even wore horn-rimmed glasses), he chose to express these words of wisdom with an equation: "Suffering = Pain x Resistance." He then added, "Actually, it's an exponential rather than a multiplicative relationship." His point was that we can distinguish between the normal pain of life—difficult emotions, physical discomfort, and so on—and actual *suffering,* which is the mental anguish caused by fighting against the fact that life is sometimes painful.

Let's say you get caught in a nasty traffic jam. This situation may be mildly stressful and annoying. You'll probably be a few minutes late for work and somewhat bored while sitting there. No big deal. If, however, you resist the fact that you are caught in a traffic jam, mentally screaming "THIS SHOULD NOT BE HAPPENING!!!!" you are likely to suffer a great deal. You'll become much more upset, agitated, and angry than you would be otherwise. Road rage incidents are due to precisely this type of overreaction. There are about three hundred serious injuries or deaths caused by road rage in the United States alone each year.

Our emotional suffering is caused by our desire for things to be other than they are. The more we resist the fact of what is happening right now, the more we suffer. Pain is like a gaseous substance. If you allow it to just *be* there, freely, it will eventually dissipate on its own. If you fight and resist the pain, however, walling it into a confined space, the pressure will grow and grow until there is an explosion.

Resisting pain truly is banging your head against the wall of reality. When you fight against the fact that pain is arising in your conscious experience, you are piling on feelings of anger, frustration, and stress on top of the pain. This only exacerbates your suffering. Once something has occurred in reality, there is nothing you can do to change that reality in the present moment. *This is how things are.* You can choose to accept this fact or not, but reality will remain the same either way.

Mindfulness allows us to stop resisting reality because it holds all experience in nonjudgmental awareness. It allows us to accept the fact that something unpleasant is occurring, even if we don't like it. By mindfully relating to our difficult emotions, they have the chance to take their natural course, arising and eventually passing away. If we can wait out the storm with relative equanimity, we won't make things any worse than they already are. Pain is unavoidable; suffering is optional.

## Exercise Two

### *Mindfully Working with Pain*

Conduct this small experiment to observe how mindfulness and self-compassion can help us suffer less when we're in pain.

1. Hold an ice cube in your hand for several seconds (this will be mildly uncomfortable). Just react as you normally would, and put the ice cube down when the discomfort becomes overwhelming. Notice how intense your discomfort was, and how long you could hold the ice cube before needing to put it down.

2. Hold an ice cube in your other hand for several seconds. This time, as you feel the discomfort, try not to resist it. Relax around the sensation and allow it just to be. Mindfully note the qualities of the sensation—cold, burning, tingling, and so on. As you do so, give yourself compassion for any discomfort you feel. (For example, you might say "Ouch, this really hurts. It's difficult to feel this sensation. But it's okay, I'll get through it.") Put the ice cube down when the discomfort becomes overwhelming. Once again, notice how intense your discomfort was, and how long you could hold the ice cube.

After you're done, compare the two experiences. Did anything change when you didn't resist the pain? Were you able to hold the ice cube for a longer time? Was your discomfort less intense? Were you able to provide empirical support for the proposition that "Suffering = Pain × Resistance"? The less you resist, the less you suffer.

# Relating to That Which Is Beyond Our Control

Sometimes—not always, but sometimes—there is the possibility of making changes to your current situation so that your future circumstances will improve. If you relate to the present moment mindfully, you'll be in a better place to wisely consider what you want to do in the next moment. If you judge and resist the present moment, however, not only will you cause yourself extra frustration and anger, you will also cloud your ability to choose your next steps wisely. Mindfulness, then, allows us to consider what proactive steps might be taken to improve our situation, but also to recognize when things cannot be changed and must be accepted.

The serenity prayer—made famous by Alcoholics Anonymous and other twelve-step programs—captures this idea beautifully:

> *God grant me the serenity to accept the things I cannot change,*
> *the courage to change the things I can, and the wisdom to know*
> *the difference.*

Mindfulness allows us to distinguish between those aspects of our experience we can change and those we can't. If a heavy object falls on my foot, I can take the object off—that's something I can change. But the throbbing I feel in my foot can't be changed, at least in the moment. If I accept that the event has happened—maybe even throwing in a dash of humor—I will still feel the pain but remain relatively peaceful as it fades away. I won't add to my predicament by getting frustrated and agitated, or kicking the offending object in anger (you laugh but you know we've all done it!). My calm state will also help me to make a wise decision, like wrapping my foot in an ice pack before it swells up.

Although it may be counterintuitive, one thing that we have little power to change is what goes on inside our own heads. What arises within our field of conscious awareness is a mystery. Thoughts and emotions arise unbidden and often overstay their welcome. We may wish we had an internal filter for our thoughts and emotions—similar to the lint filter on a dryer—that would prevent any negative thoughts and emotions from entering our awareness. Then all we'd have to do is peel off the accumulated bundle of painful, critical, and self-sabotaging thoughts and throw them in the trash. That's not how our minds work, however.

Thoughts and feelings arise based on our history, our past experiences and associations, our hardwiring, our hormonal cycle, our physical comfort level, our cultural conditioning, our previous thoughts and feelings, and numerous other factors. As discussed in the last chapter, there are untold prior causes and conditions that have come together to produce our current mental and emotional experience—conditions beyond our conscious choosing. We can't control which thoughts and emotions pass through the gates of awareness and which do not. If our particular thoughts and feelings aren't healthy, we can't make these mental experiences go away. However, *we can change the way we relate to them.*

When we judge ourselves for our mental experience, we are only making things worse. "What a horrible person I am for having that thought!" "A nicer person would feel sympathy rather than annoyance in this situation!" Did you choose to have that particular thought or emotion, however? If not, should you be judging yourself so? We can release ourselves from the tangled knot of self-judgment by accepting the fact of our experience in the here and now. "These are the thoughts and emotions that are arising in my conscious awareness in the present moment." A simple statement of fact, with no blame attached. We don't need to lambast ourselves for thinking those nasty thoughts or feeling those destructive emotions. We can simply let them go. As long as we don't get lost in a story line that justifies and reinforces them, they will tend to dissipate on their own. A weed that is not given water will eventually wither and fade away. At the same time, when a wholesome thought or feeling arises, we can hold it in loving awareness and allow it to fully blossom.

A Native American wisdom story tells of an old Cherokee who is teaching his grandson about life. "A fight is going on inside me," he said to the boy. "It is a terrible fight and it is between two wolves. One is evil—he is anger, envy, sorrow, regret, greed, arrogance, self-pity, guilt, resentment, inferiority, lies, false pride, superiority, and ego. The other is good—he is joy, peace, love, hope, serenity, humility, kindness, benevolence, empathy, generosity, truth, compassion, and faith. The same fight is going on inside you—and inside every other person, too." The grandson thought about it for a minute and then asked his grandfather, "Which wolf will win?" The old Cherokee simply replied, "The one you feed."

The gift of mindfulness, then, is that by accepting the present moment you are better able to shape your future moments with wisdom and clarity. Not only do you reduce your own suffering, you are also able to make good choices about how to act next. It makes perfect sense, if you think about it, but it's not a habit that many of us were taught as children. In the West we are raised to be knowledgeable, to work hard, and to be productive members of society, but no one teaches us how to deal productively with our own emotions, especially the difficult ones.

## Learning to Be Mindful

Fortunately, this is starting to change. Western scientists are starting to document the health benefits of mindfulness, bringing attention to an idea that originated in Eastern meditation traditions thousands of years ago. Many hundreds of studies have now shown that people who are able to pay attention to their present moment experience in a mindful way have greater emotional balance. For instance, brain scans using fMRI technology have shown that people who are more mindful are less reactive to scary or threatening images, as measured by amygdala activation (the reptilian part of our brain responsible for the fight-or-flight response). In short, they are less easily "freaked out" and therefore less at the mercy of circumstance. For this reason, mindfulness skills are commonly taught by therapists and other health professionals to help people deal with stress, addiction, physical pain, and other forms of suffering.

Jon Kabat-Zinn's Mindfulness-Based Stress Reduction (MBSR) program is one of the most ubiquitous and successful stress-reduction programs in the country. MBSR courses are offered by hundreds of hospitals, clinics, and medical centers around the United States and elsewhere in the world. The eight-week intensive program guides people through a series of exercises to help them learn to be more mindful. Research has shown that learning to be more mindful by taking an MBSR course helps people cope with life challenges with less stress and greater ease. MBSR also helps people cope with chronic pain. One of Kabat-Zinn's early studies, for instance, found that people experiencing debilitating back pain reported substantial decreases in pain (around 50% less) after taking an MBSR course.

One of the key practices taught in MBSR courses is mindfulness meditation. This type of meditation typically involves reducing sensory input by sitting quietly and closing one's eyes, so that it is easier to pay attention to what's arising in one's present moment experience without getting overwhelmed by too many outside sensations. People often start their meditation by focusing on their breath for a period to quiet their minds and sharpen their attention. Then, once the mind is fairly quiet, the attention moves freely to any thought, sound, or sensation that arises in one's field of awareness. The idea is to observe whatever arises without judgment, without trying to push any particular experience away or else hold on to it. One simply allows thoughts and feelings to come and go, like a bird flying across a wide-open sky. Tracking the arising and passing away of mental phenomena builds skills that increase one's ability to be mindful during the course of everyday life.

It's important to note, however, that although meditation is a powerful way to strengthen one's mindfulness muscle, there are other ways to quiet the mind and break the reverie of thought—like silent prayer, or even taking a solitary walk in the woods. Another tried and true method is to take a few slow, deep breaths, carefully paying attention to all the sensations generated during the in-breath and the out-breath. Mindfulness is not some special esoteric practice we have to pull out of a magician's hat: we're all innately gifted with the ability to be aware of our own field of awareness. This means that it is fully within our power to be mindful. Mostly, the key is *intentionally choosing* to focus on the thoughts, emotions, and sensations that are arising in the present moment in a friendly, nonjudgmental way.

## Exercise Three

### *Mindfulness in Daily Life*

Pick one activity a day in which you'll be mindful. It may be while you brush your teeth, while you walk from the parking garage to work, when you eat your breakfast, or whenever your cell phone rings. You might want to choose an activity that occurs early in the day, to help you remember to be mindful before you get overwhelmed with the daily tasks of life. As you're engaging in your mindful activity—let's say you choose the walk from the parking lot to your office—bring your focused awareness to your actual experience in the present moment.

Try not to immediately start thinking of what you need

to do once you get to your office. Simply notice how it feels to be walking. How do your feet feel as they touch the ground? Can you notice the change in sensations as each foot rises and falls? How do your legs feel as they move, as the weight shifts from the right to left? What is the air temperature like as you walk? Warm? Cold? Try to bring your awareness to as many aspects of the experience of walking as possible. It's helpful to focus on one distinct sensation at a time, so that you don't become overwhelmed. If you become lost in thoughts or emotions, simply note this and bring your awareness back to the experience of walking.

What you're doing is sharpening your skills of attention, building your mindfulness muscle. This will eventually help you when challenging situations arise, so that you can be aware of difficult emotions without running away with them. We are all capable of being mindful, but in the midst of our hectic lives, we must choose to slow down and notice—if even just for a moment—what's happening to us right here, right now.

Because mindfulness is one of the core components of self-compassion, when we improve our mindfulness skills, we automatically increase our ability to be self-compassionate. Several studies have demonstrated that participation in an eight-week MBSR course increases self-compassion levels. Similarly, studies have demonstrated that experienced mindfulness meditators have more self-compassion than those who are less experienced.

While increasing our mindfulness skills is an important way to foster self-compassion, the two other components of self-compassion—self-kindness and common humanity—also enhance our ability to be mindful, creating a positive and self-reinforcing cycle. One of the enemies of mindfulness is the process of overidentification—becoming so carried away by our personal drama that we can't clearly see what is occurring in the present moment. If you're upset because you're lost in self-judgment or are feeling isolated from others, it will be much harder for you to be mindful of your painful emotions. If you are able to calm and soothe your feelings by giving yourself kindness or by putting things into the larger human perspective, however, you can give yourself the space needed to break out of your melodrama, and therefore your suffering. Realizing that you're overreacting isn't so difficult when you feel cared for and connected.

## Three Doorways In

The beauty of using self-compassion as a tool for dealing with difficult emotions is that it has three distinct doorways in. Whenever you notice you are in pain, you have three potential courses of action.

- You can give yourself kindness and care.
- You can remind yourself that encountering pain is part of the shared human experience.
- You can hold your thoughts and emotions in mindful awareness.

Engaging any one of the three components of self-compassion when confronting difficult feelings will then make it easier to engage the others. Sometimes you'll find it easier to enter in through one doorway than another depending on your mood and the current situation, but once you're in, you're in. You'll have tapped into the power of self-compassion, allowing you to transform your relationship with the pain of life in a revolutionary, creative way. From the stable platform of self-compassion, you'll be able to wisely guide your next steps in a manner that leads to greater health, happiness, and well-being. Instead of letting your difficult emotions carry you away, you can carry your difficult emotions to a better place. You can hold them, accept them, and be compassionate toward yourself when you feel them. And the amazing thing is that you don't have to rely on anyone or anything else to give yourself this gift. Nor do you have to wait until circumstances are exactly right. It's precisely *when* you've fallen on hard times and things are looking their worst that self-compassion is most available.

## Exercise Four

### *Self-Compassion Journal*

Try keeping a daily self-compassion journal for one week (or as long as you like). Journaling is an effective way to express emotions and has been found to enhance both mental and physical well-being. At some point during the evening when you have a few quiet moments, review the day's events. In your journal, write down anything that you felt bad about, anything you judged yourself for, or any difficult experience that caused you pain. (For instance, maybe you got angry at a waitress at lunch because she took forever to bring the check. You made a rude comment and stormed off without leaving a tip. Afterward, you felt ashamed and embarrassed.) For each event, use mindfulness, a sense of common humanity, and kindness to process the event in a self-compassionate way.

#### MINDFULNESS

This will mainly involve bringing awareness to the painful emotions that arose due to your self-judgment or difficult circumstances. Write about how you felt: sad, ashamed, frightened, stressed, and so on. As you write, try to be accepting and nonjudgmental of your experience, not belittling it nor making it overly dramatic. (For example, "I was frustrated because she was being so slow. I got angry, overreacted, and felt foolish afterward.")

## COMMON HUMANITY

Write down the ways in which your experience was connected to the larger human experience. This might include acknowledging that being human means being imperfect, and that all people have these sorts of painful experiences. ("Everyone overreacts sometimes; it's only human.") You might also want to think about the various causes and conditions underlying the painful event. ("My frustration was exacerbated by the fact that I was late for my doctor's appointment across town and there was a lot of traffic that day. If the circumstances had been different, my reaction probably would have been different.")

## SELF-KINDNESS

Write yourself some kind, understanding words of comfort. Let yourself know that you care about yourself, adopting a gentle, reassuring tone. *(It's okay. You messed up but it isn't the end of the world. I understand how frustrated you were and you just lost it. I know how much you value being kind to other people and how badly you feel right now. Maybe you can try being extra patient and generous to any waitstaff this week . . .)*

Practicing the three components of self-compassion with this writing exercise will help organize your thoughts and emotions, while helping to encode them in your memory. If you're the type who likes to keep a journal regularly, your self-compassion practice will become even stronger and translate more easily into daily life.

## My Story: Getting Through the Dark Times

I can tell you from firsthand experience what a lifesaver self-compassion can be. It pulled me back from the precipice of despair over and over again as I struggled to deal with Rowan's autism. When my mind would start to walk down the dark alley of fear—*What's going to happen to him? Will he ever live independently? Will he ever have a job, a family?*—I would try to stay in the present moment. *I am right here, right now. Rowan is safe and happy. I have no idea what's going to happen to him, or what his future holds. It's a mystery, but running away with my fear is not going to help. Let me focus on calming and comforting myself. Poor darling, I know how incredibly difficult it is for you right now . . .* When I soothed my troubled mind with this kind of caring concern, I was able to stay centered without being overwhelmed, realizing that whatever Rowan's future held, I loved him exactly as he was.

At times when I thought I couldn't cope a moment longer, self-compassion got me through. When Rowan would launch into an ear-splitting tantrum because he momentarily mislaid his toy zebra, or because of some other seemingly insignificant trigger, I would try to mindfully watch my breath, sending myself compassion for the pain rather than fighting and resisting it. Autistic children's tantrums are neurological in origin and are often due to an overloaded sensory system. They literally can't stop their reaction or be consoled. The only thing parents can do is try to keep their children from hurting themselves, and wait till the storm passes.

When people gave me disapproving looks in the grocery store because they assumed Rowan was a spoiled brat and that I was a bad mother for not being able to control his behavior (one autism mother told me a stranger actually slapped her child because she thought he needed some "real discipline"), I would send myself compassion. I would hold my feelings of pain in mindful, spacious awareness so that they didn't overwhelm me.

Rowan's autism forced me to surrender any pretense of control, and mindfulness taught me that maybe this wasn't such a bad thing. No matter how much I wanted to be off that airplane, trapped twenty thousand feet in the air as Rowan screamed away, every other passenger looking at us like they wished we were dead, having to run to the bathroom (which was occupied, of course) to change Rowan's poop-filled underpants, I had no other choice but to deal with it. NO OTHER CHOICE. All I could do was try to get through the situation with as much grace as I could muster. Once I surrendered, a sense of deep calm descended. I felt a quiet joy, knowing that my peace of mind didn't depend on external circumstances. If I could get through this moment, I could get through anything.

Self-compassion helped me steer clear of anger and self-pity, allowing me to remain patient and loving toward Rowan despite the feelings of despair and frustration that would inevitably arise. I'm not saying that I didn't have times when I lost it. I had many. But in those times I still had my practice of self-compassion to fall back on. I could forgive myself for reacting badly, for making mistakes, for being human. If I hadn't been aware of the power of self-compassion at that time, I don't know how I would have gotten through those especially difficult early years. And for that reason, I'll always be eternally grateful, knowing that the angel of self-compassion sits on my shoulder, available whenever I need it.

#### Part Three

# THE BENEFITS OF
# SELF-COMPASSION

*Chapter Six*

# EMOTIONAL RESILIENCE

*You know quite well, deep within you, that there is only
a single magic, a single power, a single salvation . . . and
that is called loving. Well, then, love your suffering. Do not
resist it, do not flee from it. It is your aversion that hurts,
nothing else.*
—HERMAN HESSE, *Wer lieben kann ist glücklich.*
*Über die Liebe.*

SELF-COMPASSION IS AN INCREDIBLY POWERFUL TOOL FOR DEALING
with difficult emotions. It can free us from the destructive cycle
of emotional reactivity that so often rules our lives. This chapter looks
more closely at the ways that self-compassion provides emotional resilience and enhances well-being. By changing the way we relate to ourselves and our lives, we can find the emotional stability needed to be
truly happy.

## Self-Compassion and Negative Emotions

One of the most robust and consistent findings in the research literature is that people who are more self-compassionate tend be less anxious and depressed. The relationship is a strong one, with self-compassion explaining one-third to one-half of the variation found in how anxious or depressed people are. This means that self-compassion is a major protective factor for anxiety and depression. As discussed earlier, self-criticism and feelings of inadequacy are implicated in the experience of depression and anxiety. When we feel fatally flawed, incapable of handling the challenges life throws our way, we tend to shut down emotionally in response to fear and shame. All we see is doom and gloom, and things go down from there, as our negative mind-set colors all our experiences. I like to call this mental state "black goo" mind.

Though sticky and unpleasant, this process is actually quite natural. Research has demonstrated that our brains have a negativity bias, meaning we're more sensitive to negative than to positive information. When evaluating others or ourselves, for instance, negative facts are given more weight than positive ones. Think about it. If you glance in a mirror before heading out for a party and see that you have a pimple on your chin, you're not going to notice the fact that your hair looks great or that your outfit is fabulous. All you'll see is that pimple, flashing at you like the red emergency light on top of an ambulance. Your sense of how you look for your big evening out will be skewed accordingly. There's a reason for this.

In the natural environment, negative information usually signals a threat. If we don't notice that crocodile lurking in the banks of the river immediately, we'll soon become his lunch. Our brains evolved to be highly sensitive to negative information so that the fight-or-flight response could be triggered quickly and easily in the brain's amygdala, meaning that our chances of taking action to ensure our survival would be maximized. Positive information isn't as crucial to immediate survival as it is to long-term survival. Noticing that the river has fresh, clean water is important, especially if you're thirsty or deciding on a place to camp, but there's not the same urgency to act on these data. Thus, our brains give less time and attention to positive than to negative information. As Rick Hanson, author of *The Buddha's Brain,* says, "our brain is like Velcro for negative experiences but Teflon for positive ones." We tend to take the positive for granted while focusing on the negative as if our life depended on it.

Once our minds latch on to negative thoughts, they tend to repeat over and over again like a broken record player. This process is called "rumination" (the same word that's used for a cow chewing the cud) and involves a recurrent, intrusive, and uncontrollable style of thinking that can cause both depression and anxiety. Rumination about negative events in the past leads to depression, while rumination about potentially negative events in the future leads to anxiety. This is why depression and anxiety so often go hand in hand; they both stem from the underlying tendency to ruminate.

Research indicates that women are much more likely to ruminate than men, which helps explain why women suffer from depression and anxiety about twice as often as men. Although some of these gender differences may be physiological in origin, culture also plays a role. Because women have historically had less power in society than men, they've had less control over what happens to them and have therefore had to be more vigilant for danger.

If you are someone who tends to ruminate, or who suffers from anxiety and depression, it's important that you *don't judge yourself* for this way of being. Remember that rumination on negative thoughts and emotions stems from the underlying desire to be safe. Even though these brain patterns may be counterproductive, we can still honor them for trying so diligently to keep us out of the jaws of that crocodile. Also remember that although some people tend to ruminate more than others, all people have a negativity bias to some extent. It's hardwired in our brains.

## Breaking Free of the Ties That Bind

So how do we release ourselves from this deep-rooted tendency to wallow in black goo? By giving ourselves compassion. Research shows that self-compassionate people tend to experience fewer negative emotions—such as fear, irritability, hostility, or distress—than those who lack self-compassion. These emotions still come up, but they aren't as frequent, long lasting, or persistent. This is partly because self-compassionate people have been found to ruminate much less than those who lack self-compassion. Rumination is often fueled by feelings of fear, shame, and inadequacy. Because self-compassion directly counters these insecurities, it can help unravel the knot of negative rumination as surely as detangling spray.

When we hold negative thoughts and feelings in nonjudgmental awareness, we are able to pay attention to them without getting stuck like Velcro. Mindfulness allows us to see that our negative thoughts and emotions are just that—thoughts and emotions—not necessarily reality. They are therefore given less weight—they are *observed,* but not necessarily *believed.* In this way, negatively biased thoughts and emotions are allowed to arise and pass away without resistance. This allows us to deal with whatever life brings our way with greater equanimity.

A useful method of mindfully relating to our negative emotions is to become aware of them as a physical sensation. This may seem like an unfamiliar concept, but all emotions can be felt in the body. Anger is often experienced as a tight clenching in the jaw or gut, sadness as heaviness around the eyes, fear as a gripping sensation in one's throat. The physical manifestation of emotions will be experienced differently by different people and will shift and change over time, but still they can be tracked in the body if we pay close attention. When we experience our emotions on the physical level, rather than *thinking* about what's making us so unhappy, it's easier to stay present. It's the difference between noticing "tightness in my chest" and thinking *I can't believe she said that to me; who does she think she is?* And so on and so on . . . By staying anchored in our body, we can soothe and comfort ourselves for the pain we're feeling without getting lost in negativity.

For some reason I often wake up at about four A.M. in a negative, anxious mind-state. While I lie there in bed my mind swirls with fear and dissatisfaction, focusing in on everything that's wrong in my life. Because it happens so regularly, I've learned to envision this mood quite literally as a storm passing in the night. Rather than getting caught up in my thoughts, I try to imagine dark clouds passing overhead, complete with violent lightning and thunder. The lightning represents the agitation in my brain, which is somehow triggered by my sleep cycle. Instead of taking the mood too seriously, I try to ground my awareness in my body: the weight of my body on the bed, the feel of the blanket on top of me, the sensations in my hands and feet. I try to remember to be in the here and now, and just watch the storm pass over. And sure enough, I eventually fall back asleep and wake up in a much better mood. This is the power of mindfulness. It allows you to fully experience what's arising in the present moment without being caught by it.

Often, however, mindfulness alone is not enough to avoid getting trapped in depressed and anxious mind-states. Try as we may, sometimes our minds just keep getting stuck in negativity. In this case, we need to actively try to soothe ourselves. By being kind to ourselves when we experience black goo mind, remembering our inherent interconnectedness, we start to feel cared for, accepted, and secure. We balance the dark energy of negative emotions with the bright energy of love and social connection. These feelings of warmth and safety then deactivate the body's threat system and activate the attachment system, calming down the amygdala and ramping up the production of oxytocin. Fortunately, research shows that oxytocin helps dampen our natural negativity bias.

In one study, researchers asked participants to identify the emotions displayed on people's faces in a series of photos. Half were given a nasal spray that contained oxytocin; the other half received a placebo spray (the control group). Volunteers who had received the oxytocin spray were slower to identify fearful facial expression in the photos, and were less likely to mistake positive facial emotions for negative ones, as compared with the control group. This means that oxytocin lessens the tendency of our mind to immediately latch on to negative information.

Relating to our negative thoughts and emotions with compassion, then, is a good way to lessen our negativity bias. Compassion stops rumination in its tracks, engendering a hopeful outlook that asks "How can I calm and comfort myself right now?"

## Exercise One

### Dealing with Difficult Emotions in the Body:
### Soften, Soothe, Allow

(Also available as a guided meditation in MP3 format at www.self-compassion.org)

The next time you experience a difficult emotion and want to work with it directly, try processing the emotion in your body (this exercise will take fifteen to twenty minutes).

To begin, sit in a comfortable position or lie down with your back on the floor. Try to locate the difficult feeling in your body. Where is it centered? In your head, your throat, your heart, your stomach? Describe the emotion using mental noting—tingling, burning, pressure, tightness, sharp stabbing (sorry, but typically sensations like pleasant bubbling don't come up when dealing with emotional pain). Is the sensation hard and solid, or fluid and shifting? Sometimes all you will feel is numbness—you can bring your attention to this sensation as well.

If the feeling is particularly distressing and difficult to experience, go gently. You want to try to soften any resistance you feel toward the sensation, so that you can feel it fully, but you don't want to push yourself beyond your limits. Sometimes it helps to first focus on the outer edge of the sensation, moving inward only if it starts feeling safer and more bearable.

Once you feel in touch with the painful emotion in your body, send it compassion. Tell yourself how difficult it is to feel this right now, and let yourself know you're concerned about your well-being. Try using terms of endearment if it feels comfortable for you, like "I know this is really difficult, darling," or "I'm sorry you're in such pain, dear." Imagine mentally caressing the spot where the painful emotion is lodged, as if you were stroking the head of a child who was crying. Reassure yourself that it's okay, that all will be well, and that you will give yourself the emotional support needed to get through this difficult experience.

When you find yourself carried away by thinking about the situation driving your painful feelings (which you're likely to do), simply bring your awareness back to the physical sensation in your body, and start again.

When doing this exercise, it often helps to silently repeat the phrase "Soften, soothe, allow." This reminds you to accept the feeling as it is, softening any resistance to it, while actively soothing and consoling yourself for any discomfort you feel.

As you give yourself compassion, notice if the physical

sensations you experience change. Is there any lessening or relief from the painful sensations? Do they become easier to bear over time? Does that solid mass of tension feel like it's starting to break up, to move and shift? Whether or not things seem to get better, worse, or stay the same, keep giving yourself compassion for what you're experiencing.

Then, when you feel it's the right time, get up, do a few stretches, and carry on with your day. With some practice you'll find that you can help yourself cope with difficult situations without having to delve deeply into thinking or problem-solving mode, the power of self-compassion working its magic on your body itself.

## Feeling It All

Self-compassion helps lessen the hold of negative emotions, but it's important to remember that self-compassion does not push negative emotions away in an aversive manner either. This point is often confusing, because conventional wisdom (and the famous Johnny Mercer tune) tells us that we should accentuate the positive and eliminate the negative. The problem, however, is that if you try to eliminate the negative, it's going to backfire. Mental or emotional resistance to pain merely exacerbates suffering (remember, Suffering = Pain × Resistance). Our subconscious registers any attempt at avoidance or suppression, so that what we're trying to avoid ends up being amplified.

Psychologists have conducted a great deal of research on our ability to consciously suppress unwanted thoughts and emotions. Their findings are clear: *we have no such ability.* Paradoxically, any attempt to consciously suppress unwanted thoughts and emotions appears to only make them stronger. In one classic study, participants were asked to report the thoughts that were going through their heads for a period of five minutes. Before doing so, however, they were instructed *not* to think of a white bear. If they *did* end up thinking of a white bear, they were asked to ring a small bell. Bells pealed forth like it was Christmastime. In the next study, participants were asked to go ahead and think about a white bear for five minutes, actively visualizing it, before they were asked *not* to think about a white bear. Once again, they were instructed to report on their thoughts for a five-minute interval and ring a bell whenever they thought of a white bear. Bells rang out much less often. The attempt to suppress unwanted thoughts causes them to emerge into conscious awareness more strongly and more frequently than if they were given attention in the first place. (Interestingly, a white bear was chosen for the preceding experiment because it is said that Fyodor Dostoyevsky, while attempting to illustrate the persuasive power of the mind, challenged his brother to stand in the corner of a room and not return until he had stopped thinking of a white bear. Needless to say, his brother missed supper that night.)

Research shows that people with higher levels of self-compassion are significantly less likely to suppress unwanted thoughts and emotions than those who lack self-compassion. They're more willing to experience their difficult feelings and to acknowledge that their emotions are valid and important. This is because of the safety provided by self-compassion. It's not as scary to confront emotional pain when you know that you will be supported throughout the process. Just as it feels easier to open up to a close friend whom you can rely on to be caring and understanding, it's easier to open up to yourself when you can trust that your pain will be held in compassionate awareness.

The beauty of self-compassion is that instead of *replacing* negative feelings with positive ones, new positive emotions are generated by *embracing* the negative ones. The positive emotions of care and connectedness are felt alongside our painful feelings. When we have compassion for ourselves, sunshine and shadow are both experienced simultaneously. This is important—ensuring that the fuel of resistance isn't added to the fire of negativity. It also allows us to celebrate the entire range of human experience, so that we can become whole. As Marcel Proust said, "We are healed from suffering only by experiencing it to the full."

## A Journey to Wholeness

The road to becoming whole takes some time to travel and doesn't happen overnight. Rachel was a good friend of mine back in graduate school, and though she was witty and intelligent, she could also be a bit of a black hole. The T-shirt she was wearing when I first met her pretty much sums it up: LIFE'S A BITCH, 'CAUSE IF IT WAS A SLUT IT'D BE EASY. Rachel was a classic negative thinker, always seeing the glass as half empty rather than half full. Even when everything was going relatively well, with only a few challenges to deal with, Rachel would focus almost exclusively on what was wrong in any given situation. She took everything that was right about her life for granted, because it wasn't a problem and therefore didn't need fixing. This meant she was often anxious, frustrated, and depressed.

I remember one time Rachel made a homemade chocolate cake for my birthday. The cake was delicious, despite the fact that the grocery store had been out of her favorite brand of chocolate and she was forced to use an alternate brand that wasn't as good. No matter how much I told her I loved the cake, she could only focus on its ever-so-slightly-less-sumptuous-than-usual quality. (I think her comment was "tastes like imitation Ding Dongs.") She fell into such a foul mood while obsessing about the cake that she actually ended up leaving my birthday party early.

I could handle Rachel's negativity because she often made me laugh. Like the time I asked her how her blind date went. "A total bore. I asked him how he was and he actually told me." The boyfriend she had during graduate school didn't find her so funny, however, and eventually dumped her for being such a bummer all of the time. She then started to get down on herself for being so negative, which of course just made things worse.

Once she finished her studies, Rachel swore she was going to change her ways. After reading some books on positive thinking, Rachel started saying daily positive affirmations, like "I am a radiant person of positive energy" and "Every day in every way I am getting better and better." She tried to think positively no matter what the circumstances, even if she felt miserable inside. She kept it up for a few months, but it didn't last long. It seemed phony to her and took way too much effort.

Rachel and I kept in touch over the years. When she asked what I was up to, I told her about my research on self-compassion. At first she wasn't impressed. "Isn't that just sugar coating for the fact that life sucks?" But because we were old friends and she valued my opinion, she managed to get through her initial resistance and listened as I explained the concept to her. She didn't say anything for a while, and I assumed she was going to roll her eyes and dismiss everything I had said. Instead, she told me that she wanted to try to be more compassionate with herself and asked for my help. What should she do? So I told her what I did.

I had developed this practice years earlier to help myself remember to be self-compassionate, and I still use it constantly. It's a sort of self-compassion mantra and is highly effective for dealing with negative emotions. Whenever I notice something about myself I don't like, or whenever something goes wrong in my life, I silently repeat the following phrases:

*This is a moment of suffering.*
*Suffering is part of life.*
*May I be kind to myself in this moment.*
*May I give myself the compassion I need.*

I find these phrases particularly useful, not only because they're short and easily memorized, but because they invoke all three aspects of self-compassion simultaneously. The first phrase, "This is a moment of suffering," is important because it brings mindfulness to the fact that you're in pain. If you're upset because you notice you've gained a few pounds, or if you get pulled over for a traffic violation, it's often hard to remember that these are moments of suffering worthy of compassion.

The second phrase, "Suffering is part of life," reminds you that imperfection is part of the shared human condition. You don't need to fight against the fact that things aren't exactly as you want them to be, because this is a normal, natural state of affairs. More than that, it's one that every other person on the planet also experiences, and you're certainly not alone in your predicament.

The third phrase, "May I be kind to myself in this moment," helps bring a sense of caring concern to your present experience. Your heart starts to soften when you soothe and comfort yourself for the pain you're going through.

The final phrase, "May I give myself the compassion I need," firmly sets your intention to be self-compassionate and reminds you that you are worthy of receiving compassionate care.

After a few weeks of practicing this self-compassion mantra, Rachel started to get a small taste of freedom from her constantly negative mind-set. She began to be more aware of her dark, depressive thoughts, so that she didn't become so hopelessly lost in gloominess. She found herself being less self-critical, and she didn't complain as much about what was wrong with her life. Instead, when she experienced negative thoughts and emotions, she said her phrases and tried to focus on the fact that she was hurting and in need of care.

The thing she liked most about self-compassion, she told me, was that "I don't have to fool myself to make it work." Unlike the practice of positive affirmations, in which she tried to convince herself that everything was fine and dandy even when it wasn't, self-compassion enabled

Rachel to accept and acknowledge the fact that sometimes, life *does* suck. But we don't have to make things worse than they already are. The key to self-compassion is not to deny suffering, but to recognize that it's perfectly normal. There isn't anything wrong with the imperfection of life as long as we don't expect it to be other than it is.

"It's weird," she said, "but sometimes my negativity vanishes as soon as I say the phrases. Even though I'm not trying to make them go away, they just go—poof—like a cheesy David Copperfield show."

Rachel didn't become some kind of Pollyanna, however. She is still someone who tends to notice what's wrong about a situation before she sees what's right. But her negativity doesn't cause her to descend into depression anymore. She can laugh at the darkness of her own thoughts, because they no longer fully control her. Once she remembers to be self-compassionate, she can appreciate the half of the glass that's full as well as noticing the half that's empty.

## Exercise Two

### *Developing Your Own Self-Compassion Mantra*

A self-compassion mantra is a set of memorized phrases that are repeated silently whenever you want to give yourself compassion. They are most useful in the heat of the moment, whenever strong feelings of distress arise.

You might find that the phrases I created work for you, but it's worth playing with them to see if you can find phrases that fit you better. What's important is that all three aspects of self-compassion are evoked, not the particular words used.

Other possible wordings for the first phrase, "This is a moment of suffering," are "I'm having a really hard time right now," "It's painful for me to feel this now," and so on.

Other possible wordings for the second phrase, "Suffering is part of life," are "Everyone feels this way sometimes," "This is part of being human," and so on.

Other possible wordings for the third phrase, "May I be kind to myself in this moment," are "May I hold my pain with tenderness," "May I be gentle and understanding with myself," and so on.

Other possible wordings for the final phrase, "May I give myself the compassion I need," are "I am worthy of receiving self-compassion," "I will try to be as compassionate as possible," and so on.

Find the four phrases that seem most comfortable for you and repeat them until you have them memorized. Then, the next time you judge yourself or have a difficult experience, you can use your mantra to help remind yourself to be more self-compassionate. It's a handy tool to help soothe and calm troubled states of mind.

## Self-Compassion and Emotional Intelligence

Self-compassion is a powerful form of emotional intelligence. As defined in Daniel Goleman's influential book of the same name, emotional intelligence involves the ability to monitor your own emotions and to skillfully use this information to guide your thinking and action—in other words, being *aware* of your feelings without being hijacked by them, so that you can make wise choices. If you realize that you're mad at someone who made an insensitive comment, for instance, you might take a walk around the block to cool down before discussing it, rather than spouting the first disparaging remark that springs to mind. Perhaps better *not* to say, "Calling you an idiot would be an insult to all the stupid people," satisfying though it may be at the time.

Research shows that people who are more self-compassionate have more emotional intelligence, meaning they are better able to maintain emotional balance when flustered. For example, one study looked at people's reactions to an awkward and embarrassing task—being videotaped while looking into a camera and making up a children's story that began "Once upon a time there was a little bear . . ." Participants were later asked to watch their taped performances and report on the emotions they experienced while doing so. Those with higher levels of self-compassion were more likely to say they felt happy, relaxed, and peaceful while watching themselves make up the silly story. Those who lacked self-compassion were more likely to feel sad, embarrassed, or nervous.

Another study looked at the way self-compassionate people tend to deal with negative events in their daily lives. Participants were asked to report on problems experienced over a twenty-day period, such as having a fight with a romantic partner or tension at work. Results indicated that people with higher levels of self-compassion had more perspective on their problems and were less likely to feel isolated by them. For example, they felt their struggles were no worse than what lots of other people were going through. Self-compassionate people also experienced less anxiety and self-consciousness when thinking about their problems.

There is also physiological data supporting the claim that self-compassionate people have better emotional coping skills. Researchers measured cortisol levels and heart rate variability among a group of people trained to have more self-compassion. Cortisol is a stress hormone, while heart rate variability is an indicator of the ability to adapt effectively to stress. The more self-compassionate versus self-critical that people were, the lower their cortisol levels and the higher their heart rate variability. This suggests that self-compassionate people are able to deal with the challenges life throws their way with greater emotional equanimity.

Of course, people who experience extreme life challenges—such as almost dying in a car accident or being sexually assaulted—may have an especially hard time coping. In such cases, people may develop posttraumatic stress disorder (PTSD). PTSD is a severe and ongoing emotional reaction to an extreme psychological trauma. It often involves reexperiencing the traumatic event through flashbacks or nightmares, having disturbed sleep patterns, and persistent fear or anger. One of the key symptoms of PTSD is experiential avoidance, which means that trauma victims tend to push away uncomfortable emotions associated with what happened. Unfortunately, such avoidance only makes PTSD symptoms worse, given that suppressed emotions tend to grow stronger as they vie to break through to conscious awareness. The effort needed to keep suppressed emotions at bay can also sap the energy needed to deal with frustration, meaning that PTSD sufferers are often irritable.

There is some evidence that self-compassion helps people get through PTSD. For example, in one study of college students who showed PTSD symptoms after experiencing a traumatic event such as an accident, a fire, or a life-threatening illness, those with more self-compassion showed less severe symptoms than those who lacked self-compassion. In particular, they were less likely to display signs of emotional avoidance and were more comfortable facing the thoughts, feelings, and sensations triggered by what happened. When you're willing to feel painful emotions and hold them with compassion, they're less likely to interfere with everyday life.

Self-compassion gives us the calm courage needed to face our unwanted emotions head-on. Because escape from painful feelings is not actually possible, our best option is to clearly but compassionately experience our difficult emotions just as they are in the present moment. Given that all experiences eventually come to an end, if we can allow ourselves to remain present with our pain, it can go through its natural bell-curve cycle—arising, peaking, and fading away. As it says in the Bible, "This too shall pass." Or as the Buddha said, all emotions are "liable to destruction, to evanescence, to fading away, to cessation."

Painful feelings are, by their very nature, temporary. They will weaken over time as long as we don't prolong or amplify them through resistance or avoidance. The only way to eventually free ourselves from debilitating pain, therefore, is to *be* with it as it is. *The only way out is through.* We need to bravely turn toward our suffering, comforting ourselves in the process, so that time can work its healing magic.

## The Healing Power of Self-Compassion

Penny—a forty-six-year-old divorced sales rep—suffered from near constant anxiety. When her twenty-one-year-old daughter, Erin (who was away at college), didn't call her for a few days, she immediately assumed that something was wrong. She would leave Erin desperate phone messages asking her if she was okay, assuming that no news was bad news. Or when Erin was home, if she overheard her say something like "Oh no!" while talking on her cell, she would interrupt the conversation, frantically asking "What's wrong, what's wrong?" Although Erin loved her mother, she dreaded coming home for visits because her mother was always so tense and nervous. Penny was aware of her daughter's reluctance and harshly judged herself for being such an uptight and uneasy person. It wasn't how she wanted to be.

Erin was pretty convinced her mother's anxiety was caused by unresolved emotional trauma. Penny's father had been declared missing in action in the Vietnam War, when Penny was only six. Penny's mother had a nervous breakdown upon receiving the news, so Penny was raised by her maternal grandmother for two years before her mother was able to take care of her again. Penny's father was never found, and she never really got to properly grieve for him. The result was that Penny irrationally feared losing her daughter, Erin, in the same way she lost her father—anxiety permeating every corner of her life.

Erin had heard a guest lecture on self-compassion at her university and tried to convince her mother that she should have more compassion for herself. "I want you to be happy, Mom," she said, "and I think it would help you. I also think it would help our relationship."

Mainly out of love for her daughter, Penny reluctantly decided to enter therapy, choosing a counselor who explicitly incorporated self-compassion into his therapeutic approach. She wanted to finally get to grips with her anxiety and also to deal with the grief she felt over the loss of her father. Her therapist advised her to go slowly, only feeling as much as was comfortable at any one time.

Penny first tried to focus on having compassion for the anxiety she felt as an adult. She began to realize how much she suffered from having a fist of fear ready to clamp tight over her heart at any time. Her therapist gently reminded her that anxiety was an incredibly common experience, something that millions and millions of other people struggle with on a daily basis. Over time Penny learned to judge herself a little less severely for being anxious, and she instead started trying to comfort herself for having such constant and uncontrollable fear. Once she felt ready, she was then able to turn her attention to the source of her fear: the experience of losing her mother and father at the same time when she was only a small child.

At first Penny mainly focused on the compassion she felt for her mother, which somehow felt more manageable. Her heart started to crack open as she thought about the horror her mother must have experienced when her husband was declared missing, not even knowing for sure if he was dead or alive. Then she tried feeling compassion for herself, for how scared and alone she felt when her father disappeared and her mother had her breakdown. At first she was just numb, unable to feel anything.

The therapist asked her to bring a picture of herself as a young girl to their next session, to see if that would help. The photo was of a six-year-old girl wearing a maroon velvet dress, opening Christmas presents. When Penny looked at the photo, she saw the face of Erin looking back at her. She imagined how Erin would have felt at age six if the same thing had happened to her. This broke through her defenses, and she had a powerful moment of getting in touch with her six-year-old self—the incredible fear, confusion, and sadness she had felt.

For several weeks all Penny could do was sob whenever she thought about her childhood. There was nothing she could do to fix things, to change what had happened. There was nothing she could do to ensure that her daughter would never have any harm befall her. There was only pain, sadness, grief, worry, and fear. But there was also compassion. Whenever she felt that she would be engulfed by her negative emotions, she would think of that picture of herself as a child. She would imagine stroking the child's hair, using a gentle tone of voice and telling her that she was going to be okay. Although the anxiety didn't go away, its edges started to soften. It became more bearable, less overwhelming.

One day Penny came to her therapy appointment extremely excited. "Erin was home yesterday and I heard her say 'That's terrible! Oh my God!' on her cell phone. My instinctive reaction was to immediately demand what was wrong. Instead, I just let myself feel the fear. I managed not to pounce on Erin as soon as she hung up the phone. Instead, I figured that if there was a dire emergency she would tell me. It was hard to wait, but I felt strong enough to handle it. And sure enough, it turns out that her favorite TV character had been killed off in the latest episode. That was all. What a victory!"

Such stories are actually quite common. Especially when helped along by a supportive person such as a therapist, self-compassion has the power to radically transform lives. For this reason, many clinical psychologists are starting to explicitly incorporate self-compassion into their therapeutic approaches.

## Compassionate Mind Training

Paul Gilbert, a clinician at the University of Derby and author of *The Compassionate Mind,* is one of the leading thinkers and researchers on self-compassion as a therapeutic tool. He has developed a group-based therapy model called "Compassionate Mind Training" (CMT), which is designed to help people who suffer from severe shame and self-judgment. His approach focuses on helping clients understand the harm they do themselves through constant self-criticism, while also having compassion for these same tendencies. Gilbert argues that self-criticism is an evolutionarily based survival mechanism designed to help keep oneself safe (see chapter 2) and therefore should not be judged. CMT helps people to understand this mechanism and teaches them how to relate to themselves with compassion rather than self-condemnation. This process can be tricky for some.

Many of Gilbert's patients have a history of being abused by their parents, either physically or emotionally. For this reason, they are often frightened of self-compassion at first, and they feel vulnerable when they are kind to themselves. This is because as children, the same people who gave them care and nurturance—their parents—also betrayed their trust by harming them. Feelings of warmth thus became jumbled together with feelings of fear, making the foray into self-compassion rather complicated. Gilbert cautions that people with a history of parental abuse should proceed slowly down the path of self-compassion, so that they don't become too frightened or overwhelmed. Even among those without histories of physical or mental abuse, Gilbert's research indicates that people are often afraid of being compassionate to themselves. They worry that they will become weak, or that they will be rejected, if they don't use self-criticism as a way of addressing personal shortcomings. This fear of compassion then acts as a roadblock to treating oneself kindly and exacerbates self-judgment and feelings of inadequacy.

CMT relies heavily on the practice of self-compassionate imagery to generate feelings of warmth and safety for clients. Practitioners first instruct patients to generate an image of a safe place to help counter any fears that may arise. They are then instructed to create an ideal image of a caring and compassionate figure. Especially for people who have a hard time having feelings of compassion for themselves, their compassionate image can be used as a proxy source of soothing. Eventually, self-compassion becomes less frightening and can be drawn upon to help deal with feelings of defectiveness and inadequacy.

In a study of the effectiveness of CMT for patients in a treatment program at a mental health hospital—people who were being treated for intense shame and self-criticism—patients were led through weekly two-hour CMT sessions for twelve weeks. The training resulted in significant reductions in depression, self-attacking, feelings of inferiority, and shame. Moreover, almost all of the patients felt ready to be discharged from the hospital at the end of the intervention.

## Exercise Three

### Using Compassionate Imagery

This exercise is adapted from Paul Gilbert, *The Compassionate Mind* (London: Constable, 2009).

1. Sit comfortably in a quiet spot. The first task is to create an image of a safe place. This can be imaginary or real—any place that makes you feel peaceful, calm, and relaxed: a white sandy beach, a forest glade with deer grazing nearby, Grandmother's kitchen, or near a crackling fire. Try to really envisage this place in your mind's eye. What are the colors? How bright is it? What sounds or smells are there? If you ever feel

anxious or insecure during your voyage into self-compassion, you can call up this image of your safe place to help calm and soothe yourself.

2. The next task is to create an image of an ideally caring and compassionate figure, someone who embodies wisdom, strength, warmth, and nonjudgmental acceptance. For some this will be a known religious figure like Christ or the Buddha. For others it will be someone they have known in the past who was very compassionate, like a favorite aunt or teacher. For still others it might be a beloved pet, a completely imaginary being, or even an abstract image like a white light. Try to see this image as vividly as possible, incorporating as many of the senses as possible.

3. If you are suffering in some way right now, think about the type of wise, caring things that this idealized source of compassion would say to comfort you right now. How would his or her voice sound? What feelings would be conveyed in his or her tone? If you're feeling a bit numb or shut down, just let yourself bask in the compassionate presence of your ideal image, simply allowing yourself to be there.

4. Now release your compassionate image, take a few breaths, and sit quietly in your own body, savoring the comfort and ease that you generated in your own mind and body. Know that whenever you want to generate compassion for yourself, you can use this image as a springboard, allowing yourself to receive the gift of kindness.

## Mindful Self-Compassion

Christopher Germer, a clinical psychologist affiliated with Harvard who specializes in the integration of mindfulness and psychotherapy, teaches self-compassion to most of his therapy clients. Chris is also a friend and colleague with whom I teach self-compassion workshops. He wrote the wonderful book *The Mindful Path to Self-Compassion*, which summarizes the knowledge he's gained over the years while helping his clients to relate to themselves more compassionately.

Germer observes that his clients typically go through several distinct stages of self-compassion practice during their therapy. A common experience at the beginning, especially for those who suffer from intense feelings of worthlessness, is "backdraft." When a fire is deprived of oxygen and fresh air is suddenly let in, an explosion often occurs (the process known by firefighters as backdraft). Similarly, people who are used to constant self-criticism often erupt with anger and intense negativity when they first try to take a kinder, more gentle approach with themselves. It's as if their sense of self has been so invested in feeling inadequate that this "worthless self" fights for survival when it's threatened. The way to deal with backdraft, of course, is to mindfully accept the experience and have compassion for how hard it is to experience such intense negativity.

Once the initial resistance softens, clients often feel great enthusiasm for self-compassion practice as they begin to realize what a powerful tool it is. Germer calls this the "infatuation" stage. After battling themselves for so long, people often fall in love with the feeling of peace and freedom they find by relating to themselves in a tender way. Like receiving a kiss from a new lover, they tingle from head to toe. During this stage, people tend to get attached to the good feelings provided by self-compassion, and they want to experience those good feelings constantly.

As time goes on, however, the infatuation typically fades as people realize that self-compassion doesn't magically make all their negative thoughts and feelings go away. Remember that self-compassion doesn't eradicate pain or negative experiences, it just embraces them with kindness and gives them space to transform on their own. When people practice self-compassion as a subtle way of resisting their negative emotions, not only will the bad feelings remain, they will often get worse. Germer says that he sees this phase of the therapy process as a good sign, because it means clients can begin to question their motivations. Are they being compassionate primarily because they want to be emotionally healthy, or because they mainly want to eliminate their pain?

If people can stick with the practice during this tricky middle bit, they eventually discover the wisdom of "true acceptance." During this stage, the motivation for self-compassion shifts from "cure" to "care." The fact that life is painful, and that we are all imperfect, is then fully accepted as an integral part of being alive. It becomes understood that happiness is not dependent on circumstances being exactly as we want them to be, or on ourselves being exactly as we'd like to be. Rather, happiness stems from loving ourselves and our lives exactly as they are, knowing that joy and pain, strength and weakness, glory and failure are all essential to the full human experience.

Chris Germer and I are now working on an exciting new project together; developing an eight-week training program in Mindful Self-Compassion (MSC). The program is similar to Kabat-Zinn's MBSR program, and we hope it will be a useful complement to it. In the first day of the program, we mainly focus on explaining the concept of self-compassion and how it differs from self-esteem (see chapter 7). In the following weeks we focus on how to use self-compassion to deal with difficult emotions using various meditations, homework assignments, and experiential exercises (including those found in this chapter and others). The program appears to be quite powerful in terms of changing people's lives for the better, and hopefully we'll soon have research data that examines the effectiveness of MSC as a therapeutic intervention. We are both convinced that participating in the MSC program will help people maximize their emotional resilience and well-being. (For more information on the program, go to www.self-compassion.org or www.mindfulselfcompassion.org.)

## Exercise Four

### *Compassionate Body Scan*

(Also available as a guided meditation in MP3 format at www.self-compassion.org)

One technique commonly taught in mindfulness courses such as MBSR is "the body scan." The idea is to systematically sweep your attention from the crown of your head to the soles of your feet, bringing mindful awareness to all of the physical sensations in your body. Chris Germer and I also use this technique in our MSC workshops, but with a twist. We add in self-compassion. The idea is that whenever you come into contact with an uncomfortable sensation while scanning your body, you should try to actively soothe the tension, giving yourself compassion for your suffering. By mentally caressing your body in this way, you can help ease your aches and pains to a remarkable extent.

To begin, it's best to lie down on a bed or the floor. Lie flat on your back, and gently rest your arms about six inches away from your sides and hold your legs about shoulder width apart. This is called "the corpse pose" in yoga, and allows you to completely relax all your muscles. Start with the crown of your head. Notice what your scalp feels like. Is it itching, tingling, hot, cold? Then notice if there's any discomfort there. If so, try to relax and soften any tension in this area and extend kind, caring concern to this part of your body. Internal words said in a soothing, comforting voice like "poor darling, there's a lot of tightness there, it's okay, just relax" often help tremendously. Once you've given this body part compassion, or if there was no discomfort in the first place, move on to the next body part.

There are many pathways through the body you can take, but typically I move from the top of my head to my face, to the back of my head, to my neck, my shoulders, my right arm (moving from upper arm to lower arm to hand), my left arm, my chest, my abdomen, my back, my pelvic region, my gluts, my right leg (moving from thigh to knee to calf to foot), then my left leg. Other people start with their feet and move up through their body to the crown of their head. There is no one right way to do it, just what feels right for you.

As you scan each new body part with your awareness, check in to see if there is any tension there, and offer yourself compassion for your pain, consciously trying to soften, relax, and comfort this area. I often try to express gratitude to the body part that aches, appreciating how hard it works for me (like my neck, which has to hold up my big head!). It's an opportunity to be kind to yourself in a very concrete way, and the more slowly and mindfully you do the exercise, the more you'll get out of it.

Once you finish sweeping your awareness from head to toe—this can take anywhere from five minutes to thirty minutes depending on how quickly you do it—bring your attention to your entire body with all its buzzing, pulsating sensations, and send yourself love and compassion. Most people report feeling wonderfully relaxed yet vibrant after this exercise—and it's cheaper than a massage.

## Chapter Seven

# OPTING OUT OF THE SELF-ESTEEM GAME

*Don't take the ego too seriously. When you detect egoic behavior in yourself, smile. At times you may even laugh. How could humanity have been taken in by this for so long?*
—ECKHART TOLLE, *A New Earth:*
*Awakening to Your Life's Purpose*

THE IDEA THAT WE NEED TO HAVE HIGH SELF-ESTEEM TO BE PSYchologically healthy is so widespread in Western culture that people are terrified of doing anything that might endanger it. We're told we must think positively of ourselves at all costs. Teachers are encouraged to give all their students gold stars so that each can feel proud and special. High self-esteem is portrayed as the pot of gold at the end of the rainbow, a precious commodity that must be acquired and protected.

It's true that people with high self-esteem tend to be cheerful, report having lots of friends, and are motivated in life, while people with low self-esteem are lonely, anxious, and depressed. Those with high self-esteem are optimistic, seeing the world as their oyster. Those with low self-esteem often can't even tie their shoes in the morning. The assumption is that self-esteem *causes* these outcomes. The almost religious faith placed in the power of high self-esteem to create mental health has led to a deluge of self-esteem programs in schools, community centers, and mental health facilities. In 1986, the State of California launched a Task Force on Self-Esteem and Personal and Social Responsibility that had an annual budget of a quarter-million dollars a year. The reasoning was that if the self-esteem of California's children were raised, problems such as bullying, crime, teen pregnancy, drug abuse, and academic underachievement would be eased. It was even argued that investing in the self-esteem of children would pay off in tax revenues in the long run, because people with high self-esteem tend to earn more than those with low self-esteem. Dozens of women's magazines have touted the benefits of high self-esteem, and thousands of books have been written on how to get it, raise it, or keep it.

## The Emperor Has No Clothes

This fascination with high self-esteem has largely been fueled by psychologists, who have published more than fifteen thousand journal articles on the topic. More recently, however, psychologists have started questioning whether high self-esteem is truly the panacea it's been made out to be. Reports on the efficacy of California's self-esteem initiative, for instance, suggest that it was a total failure. Hardly any of the program's hoped-for outcomes were achieved. Of course, this didn't stop the Task Force from concluding that "diminished self-esteem stands as a powerful *independent variable* (condition, cause, factor) in the genesis of major social problems. We all know this to be true, and it is really not necessary to create a special California task force on the subject to convince us." In other words, we *know* self-esteem works even though our own data says it doesn't, so we shouldn't have bothered trying to prove what was self-evident in the first place. As humorist Will Rogers once commented, "I don't make jokes. I just watch the government and report the facts."

In one influential review of the self-esteem literature, it was concluded that high self-esteem actually did *not* improve academic achievement or job performance or leadership skills or prevent children from smoking, drinking, taking drugs, and engaging in early sex. If anything, high self-esteem appears to be the *consequence* rather than the cause of healthy behaviors. The report also challenged the assumption that bullies act as they do because they have low self-esteem. In fact, bullies are just as likely to have high self-esteem as others. Picking on other people is one of the key ways they can feel strong and superior. People with high self-esteem tend to be cliquish—they generally like members of the in-groups they belong to better than "outsiders." Accordingly, research shows that people with high self-esteem are just as prejudiced, if not more so, than those who dislike themselves. People with high self-esteem also engage in socially undesirable behavior such as cheating on tests just as often as people with low self-esteem do.

And when people with high self-esteem feel insulted, they frequently lash out at others. In one study, for instance, college students were told they did worse than average on an intelligence test. Those with high self-esteem tended to compensate for the bad news by insulting the other study participants and putting them down. Those with low self-esteem, on the other hand, tended to react by being nicer and complimenting other participants as a way to seem more likable. Who would *you* rather hang out with when yearly performance reviews are being passed out at work?

## What Is Self-Esteem Anyway?

Before going further, it's worth taking a closer look at what actually constitutes self-esteem. At its core, self-esteem is an evaluation of our worthiness, a judgment that we are good, valuable people. William James, one of the founding fathers of Western psychology, argued that self-esteem was a product of "perceived competence in domains of importance." This means that self-esteem is derived from thinking we're good at things that have personal significance to us. I may excel at checkers and be an atrocious chess player, but this will only affect my self-esteem if I value being good at checkers or chess. The dynamic that James identified suggests that we can raise our self-esteem in two main ways.

One approach is to value the things we're good at and devalue the things we're bad at. A teen boy who's good at basketball and bad at math may decide that basketball is really important while math is for the birds. The potential problem with this approach, of course, is that we may undercut the importance of learning valuable skills just because it makes us feel better about ourselves. When a kid focuses all his energy on becoming a pro basketball player and ignores learning math, he's limiting his future employment opportunities—a scenario that happens all too often. In other words, our desire to achieve high self-esteem in the short term may harm our development in the long run.

The other way to raise our self-esteem involves increasing our competence in those areas that are important to us. For instance, a woman who values looking like a model may keep trying to lose that last fifteen pounds in order to reach her desired weight. The problem here is that sometimes striving to improve is counterproductive. The woman who tries to fit into size 2 jeans even though she doesn't have a naturally thin body type will just end up feeling hungry, frustrated, and dejected and would have been better off downplaying the importance of looking model-skinny in the first place. (After all, most men say they prefer curves.)

Charles Horton Cooley, a well-known sociologist writing at the turn of the twentieth century, identified another common source of self-esteem. He proposed that feelings of self-worth stem from the "looking glass self." That is, our perceptions of how we appear in the eyes of others. If we believe that others judge us positively, we'll feel good about ourselves. If we believe that others judge us negatively, we'll feel bad about ourselves. Self-esteem, in other words, stems not only from our own self-judgments, but also the perceived judgments of others. Highlight the word *perceived*.

Research shows that self-esteem is more strongly influenced by the perceived judgments of strangers than close friends and family. Think about it. When your mother tells you how smart or attractive you are, how seriously are you going to take the comment? "*Of course* my mother would say that, she's my mother!" We tend to give more weight to what nameless, faceless "other people" think of us—coworkers, neighbors, other kids at school, and so on, who are supposedly more objective. The big hole in this line of reasoning, of course, is that the thread on which we're hanging our self-esteem is incredibly thin. First, given that people who don't know us very well aren't able to make well-informed judgments of us, why should we be so swayed by their opinions? Second, how well do we know their opinions in the first place?

When I was in college, I used to spend hours getting my Goth hair and makeup just right before going to a popular death-rock nightclub. I wanted to appear cool to the other Goths. I always felt like a "poser," however, and assumed people rolled their eyes at me behind my back. I generally had poor self-esteem when it came to my rocker looks, despite all my white-face-and-big-hair efforts. Years later, some friends told me that other people actually *did* think I looked cool at the time and had even tried to emulate me. In other words, my perceptions of others' perceptions were way off base. And after reviewing the photographic evidence, their perceptions also seem to have been off base. I can definitely say that Goth was *not* a good look for me.

We tend to think it's only young people who fall prey to peer pressure and insecurity of this sort, but how often do we adults feel good or bad about ourselves simply because of some vague and unsubstantiated notion about how "other people" are viewing us? Not only are our perceptions of reality often seriously clouded, our obsession with the impression we're making on others may lead to some serious self-delusion.

## Mirror, Mirror on the Wall

People with high self-esteem describe themselves as being more likable and attractive, and as having better relationships with others, than people with low self-esteem do. Objective observers, however, do not necessarily agree. In one study, researchers examined how college undergraduates rated their interpersonal skills—their ability to start new friendships, talk and open up to others, deal with conflicts, and provide emotional support. Not surprisingly, people with high self-esteem reported that they had these good qualities in spades. According to their roommates, however, their interpersonal skills were merely (God forbid!) average. Similar studies have found that high-self-esteem people are more confident about their popularity, whereas low-self-esteem people assume that others don't like them much. Typically, however, people with high and low self-esteem are equally liked by others. It's just that those with low self-esteem greatly underestimate how much others actually approve of them, while those with high self-esteem greatly overestimate others' approval. In other words, high self-esteem isn't associated with *being* a better person, just with *thinking* you are.

My husband's grandfather Robbie was a wealthy white farmer in Zimbabwe who ran his plantations with an iron fist. Robbie had an extremely high opinion of himself and assumed everyone else did too. On one visit to Zimbabwe, as we were being served tea by Robbie's black manservant (who actually called him "master"), I remember him telling a story about his farmworkers and his relationship with them. At the end of his tale Robbie got a wistful look on his face and said, "You know, I think they rather like me . . ." He had absolutely no idea—or at least he suppressed the idea—that his workers just kissed his butt because they were terrified of losing their jobs. Though friendless (he had alienated most of his family through his tyrannical behaviors), he clung to his delusions of being loved and admired until the day he died. In an interesting postscript, Robbie's death occurred suddenly, just days after Robert Mugabe declared he was taking over all the white farms in Zimbabwe. Perhaps Robbie didn't want to live without his most salient source of self-esteem.

It is true that high self-esteem has at least one tangible, and by no means unimportant, benefit: happiness. When you like yourself, you tend to be cheerful; when you dislike yourself, you tend to be depressed. These mood states then color our feelings about our lives more generally. When we believe *we're* great, life is great; when we don't, life stinks. Happiness is an important feature of living a good life and is definitely worth cultivating. But the price paid for the momentary happiness of high self-esteem can be steep.

## The Pool of Narcissus

Narcissists have extremely high self-esteem and are quite happy most of the time. Of course, they also have inflated, unrealistic conceptions of their own attractiveness, competence, and intelligence and feel entitled to special treatment.

Narcissus, from whose myth *narcissism* was named, was the son of the river god Cephissus and the nymph Liriope. He fell in love with his own image reflected in a pool, being so transfixed that he couldn't pull himself away, eventually wasting away to death. In modern psychology, narcissism is typically measured by examining people's scores on the

Narcissistic Personality Inventory, which includes items such as "I think I am a special person," "I like to look at myself in a mirror," and "If I ruled the world it would be a better place." Research generally finds that people who score high on this scale also report being very satisfied with their lives. Who wouldn't love the show in which they have the starring role?

But narcissists are actually caught in a social trap. Although they hope their personal greatness will be admired by others, winning them friends and devotees, the truth is that over time, narcissists almost always drive people away. People may be impressed by the self-confidence and swagger of narcissists at first but are eventually turned off by these same tendencies. Most report disliking those high in the trait of narcissism, and the relationships of narcissists typically fall apart after a while. It's hard to feel understood or get your needs met when your partner is so self-absorbed.

Many people believe that deep down, narcissists hate themselves, and their inflated self-image is just a cover for insecurity. This idea has penetrated the American popular media. When discussing the troubles of young stars such as Lindsay Lohan or Paris Hilton, for instance, one TV commentator said, "They have everything you'd ever want in life—they've finally achieved their faces on television. Meanwhile that little voice inside is saying, 'You're not good enough. Not good enough.'" The cure for narcissism, it is therefore assumed, must be higher self-esteem. Research has shown this assumption to be false. Scientists have found a way to assess unconscious self-attitudes using something called the Implicit Association Test (IAT). This computer-based test measures how fast people associate the labels "me" and "not me" with positive words like *wonderful* versus negative words like *awful*. People who quickly associate "me" with positive words but are slow to associate "me" with negative words are said to have high implicit self-esteem, while the reverse pattern indicates low implicit self-esteem. It turns out that narcissists think they're wonderful both implicitly and explicitly.

When Paris Hilton claimed "There's nobody in the world like me. I think every decade has an iconic blonde—like Marilyn Monroe or Princess Diana—and right now, I'm that icon," she probably didn't do so because deep down she feels insecure. Trying to help a narcissist by telling her to love herself more is about as effective as throwing oil on a fire.

The metaphor of a fire is an appropriate one. As long as they're receiving the attention and admiration they believe they deserve, narcissists are on top of the world. The problem comes when their position of superiority starts to slip. When confronted with bad reviews, the narcissist typically responds with feelings of rage and defiance.

In one classic study, researchers examined the behavior of narcissists when their ego was threatened. The study required people to write an essay on an important issue, which was supposedly read and evaluated by a research partner in the next room (who the participant never met and who didn't actually exist). The essays were randomly given one of two written comments by the fictitious partner: "This is one of the worst essays I have read!" or "No suggestions, great essay!" In the next part of the study, which was described as a learning task, participants were told that they and their partner would have to press a button as fast as possible after solving a simple problem. They were then told that whoever was slower would receive a blast of noise in order to help them learn. The task was rigged, of course. Participants were told that they had been the fastest and were asked to set the noise level and duration of the blast for their "slow" partner (the same person who they believed had just evaluated their essay). Narcissists who had received derogatory feedback were the most violent, giving long, loud blasts of noise as payback for their partner's earlier insult.

When narcissists receive put-downs from others, their retaliation can be fast and furious, even violent. Narcissistic anger serves an important function for the narcissist: it deflects negative attention away from the self toward others, who can then be blamed for all the dark emotions being experienced. This pattern helps explain why clinician Otto

Kernberg refers to the violence of school shooters as "malignant narcissism." Eric Harris and Dylan Klebold, for instance, the Columbine High School gunmen, committed their atrocious deeds in reaction to relatively minor insults doled out by some school jocks. But in their ego-inflated minds, the jocks were getting their just deserts. Just days before pulling the trigger on their classmates, Eric and Dylan laughingly told each other, "Isn't it fun to get the respect we're going to deserve?"

If you've ever known a narcissist, this pattern will be all too familiar. The narcissist's need and demand for respect is constant. Because narcissists are always trying to hang on to that elusive feeling of high self-esteem, the wrath that descends when their precious ego is jeopardized can be truly something to behold.

My friend Irene once told me a story about a woman who had all the hallmarks of a classic narcissist. She said that at first glance you'd never guess Susan was a narcissist—she was overweight and overworked, and didn't have much of a social life. But she did have one passion in life: helping needy children. She went on volunteer missions to third world countries at least twice a year, and she was a very effective aid worker.

Unfortunately, Irene realized the hard way that Susan was mainly using her charity work as a way to feel superior. Susan was "one of the world's leading experts" on the problem of malnutrition among third world children (at least according to Susan), and she clearly identified with being in the position of helper—a knight in shining armor who rescued those in need. Susan's lifelong dream, as she was fond of telling people, was to open a food bank where she could feed malnourished children year-round. When Irene received an unexpected financial windfall, she was now in a position to make Susan's dream a reality. She decided to found a nonprofit that would build a food bank in rural Bangladesh, employing Susan as the center's manager.

Instead of being grateful for her assistance, however, Susan immediately started to turn on Irene. She started bad-mouthing her behind her back, complaining to anyone who would listen about having to work with such a stupid woman. She was willing to be the manager of the food bank "for the sake of the children" she said, but it would be a penance to do so under the supervision of someone so obviously incompetent. Then she started to spread nasty and false rumors that attacked Irene's personal character and integrity. Luckily, an acquaintance told her what was happening about a week before the food bank was set to open, and Irene managed to pull out of her contract with Susan just in the nick of time.

Irene felt like she'd received a slap in the face. But after a while she began to realize that Susan's behavior had little to do with her. Susan had painted a glowing portrait of herself as world savior, and finding herself in the position of receiving rather than giving assistance was just too much for her ego to bear. Susan had to cast Irene as the devil to maintain her own self-image as an angel. Sadly, narcissism is more common than you might think among people doing good works in the world. But when the force driving philanthropy is the pursuit of high self-esteem, even beautiful acts of charity can be sullied by the needy, greedy ego.

## Indiscriminate Praise

Although problems are associated with the *pursuit* of high self-esteem, high self-esteem is not bad in and of itself. It's clearly much better to feel worthy and valuable than worthless and insignificant. It's just that there are both healthy and unhealthy pathways to high self-esteem. Having a supportive family or working hard to achieve valued goals are healthy sources of high self-esteem. Puffing up your ego and putting other people down is not so great. The majority of research that examines self-esteem, however, does not distinguish healthy self-esteem from its other, less productive forms.

The most commonly used measure of self-esteem, the Rosenberg

Self-Esteem Scale, asks questions that are quite general. For instance, "I feel that I have a number of good qualities," or "I take a positive attitude toward myself." The narcissist who thinks he's the best thing since sliced bread will score quite high on this scale, as will the humble person who likes himself simply because he is a human being intrinsically worthy of respect. Put simply, it's impossible to tell if high self-esteem is healthy or unhealthy until you determine its source.

The problem with many of the school-based programs to increase self-esteem is that they don't distinguish between healthy and unhealthy self-esteem either. They tend to use indiscriminate praise to boost children's self-image, focusing only on the child's level of self-esteem, not on how or why it gets there. As a result, many children come to believe they deserve compliments and admiration no matter what they do.

Jean Twenge writes about this trend in her fascinating book *Generation Me*. She notes that self-esteem programs for schoolkids tend to be ego flattering to the point of nausea. Children are given books to read such as *The Lovables in the Kingdom of Self-Esteem,* where children learn that the gates to self-esteem will open if they repeat "I'm lovable!" three times with pride. Weighty tomes like *Be a Winner: A Self-Esteem Coloring and Activity Book* help children realize how special and important they are. Games such as "The Magic Circle" designate one child a day to wear a badge that says "I'm great" while classmates write up a list of praise for the anointed one. Elementary schools in particular assume that their mission is to raise the self-esteem of their pupils, to prepare children for success and happiness later on in life. For this reason, they discourage teachers from making critical remarks to little ones because of the damage it might do to their self-esteem.

Some schools have even eliminated "F" as a grade category because "F" stands for "fail." Instead, they simply assign the letter "E" for unacceptable work, presumably because it is a nonjudgmental letter that merely follows "D" (and still connotes positive things like "excellent," perhaps?). The desire to raise children's self-esteem has led to some serious grade inflation. One study found that 48 percent of high school students received an A average in 2004, as compared to 18 percent in 1968. Not surprisingly, American students think they're the best and brightest in the world, even though they're beaten by students from other countries on almost every measure of academic success. We might as well change our name to the United States of Lake Wobegon.

Although the emphasis on raising children's self-esteem comes from good motives, and breaks away from the harsh educational practices of the past that often lowered children's self-esteem, indiscriminate praise can hinder children's capacity to see themselves clearly, limiting their ability to reach their full potential.

This emphasis on high self-esteem at all costs has also led to a worrying trend toward increasing narcissism. Twenge and colleagues examined the scores of more than fifteen thousand college students who took the Narcissistic Personality Inventory between 1987 and 2006. During the twenty-year period, scores went through the roof, with 65 percent of modern-day students scoring higher in narcissism than previous generations. Not coincidentally, students' average self-esteem levels rose by an even greater margin over the same period.

Twenge recently coauthored a book called *The Narcissism Epidemic: Living in the Age of Entitlement* with leading narcissism researcher Keith Campbell. The authors examine how the emphasis on raising self-esteem in America has led to a real cultural sickness, writing:

> *Understanding the narcissism epidemic is important because its long-term consequences are destructive to society. American culture's focus on self-admiration has caused a flight from reality to the land of grandiose fantasy. We have phony rich people (with interest-only mortgages and piles of debt), phony beauty (with plastic surgery and cosmetic procedures), phony athletes (with performance-enhancing drugs), phony celebrities (via reality TV and YouTube), phony genius students (with grade inflation), a phony national economy*

*(with $11 trillion of government debt), phony feelings of being special among children (with parenting and education focused on self-esteem), and phony friends (with the social networking explosion). All this fantasy might feel good, but unfortunately, reality always wins. The mortgage meltdown and the resulting financial crisis are just one demonstration of how inflated desires eventually crash to earth.*

Because the praise given by teachers and parents to boost children's self-esteem is so unconditional, some argue that praise should be contingent on hard work and effort, so that kids feel good about themselves *only* if they deserve it. Why bother putting in the effort to do well, the thinking goes, if mediocrity receives the same praise as first-rate work? Subtly embedded in this position is the idea that praise and criticism are effective motivating forces when they're tied to success and failure, and that feeling good about oneself should come in one scenario, not the other. Sadly, however, there is ample evidence that using self-esteem in a conditional way, so that we only feel good about ourselves when we succeed and feel bad about ourselves when we fail, is as problematic as basing our self-esteem on nothing at all.

## Contingent Self-Worth

"Contingent self-worth" is a term psychologists use to refer to a sense of self-esteem that depends on success or failure, on approval or disapproval. Several common areas of contingent self-worth have been identified, such as personal attractiveness, peer approval, competition with others, work/school success, family support, feeling virtuous, and even God's love. People vary in terms of the degree to which their self-esteem is contingent on positive evaluations in these different areas. Some people put all their eggs into one basket, like personal attractiveness, whereas others strive to be good at everything. Research shows that the more your overall sense of self-worth is dependent on success in particular life areas, the more generally miserable you feel when you fail in those areas.

Having contingent self-esteem can feel like Mr. Toad's wild ride—your mood swinging from elation one moment to devastation the next. Let's say you derive your sense of self-worth from doing well at your marketing job. You'll feel like a king when you're named salesperson of the month but a pauper when your monthly sales figures are merely average. Or maybe you tend to base your self-esteem on being liked by others. You'll get an incredible high when you receive a nice compliment but crash in the dust when someone ignores you or—worse—criticizes you.

Once, I actually had the experience of feeling hugely complimented and devastatingly criticized at the exact same moment. I was visiting an equestrian center with Rupert, a lifelong horseman, and the elderly Spanish riding instructor who ran the stable apparently liked my dark Mediterranean looks. In his desire to be gallant he paid me what he clearly thought was the highest compliment: "You are veeerry beautiful. Don't *ever* shave your muuustache."

I didn't know whether to laugh, hit him, hang my head in shame, or say thank you. (I chose the first and last options, but seriously considered the other two!) Rupert was too busy laughing to say anything.

Ironically, people who excel in areas important to their self-esteem are the most vulnerable to letdowns. The straight A student feels crushed if she receives anything less than an A on an exam, whereas the D student might feel on top of the world for merely getting a C. The higher you climb, the farther you have to fall.

And contingent self-esteem has an addictive quality that's hard to shake. Because the initial rush of self-esteem feels so good, we want to keep getting those compliments or winning those competitions. We keep chasing after that initial high, but as with drugs or alcohol, we build up a tolerance so that it progressively takes more and more to get our fix. Psychologists refer to this process as the "hedonic treadmill" (hedonic means pleasure seeking), comparing the pursuit of happiness to a person on a treadmill who has to continually work harder just to stay in the same place.

Trying to continually prove your mettle in areas where your self-esteem is invested can also backfire. If the main reason you want to win that marathon is to feel good about yourself, what happens to your love of running in and of itself? Instead of doing it because you enjoy it, you start doing it to get the reward of high self-esteem. Which means you're more likely to give up if you stop winning races. It's like being a dolphin who jumps through a flaming hoop only because it wants a fish treat. But if the treat isn't given, if you stop getting the self-esteem boost you're so invested in, the dolphin doesn't jump.

Jeanie loved classical piano and learned to play when she was only four. The piano was the biggest source of joy in her life, reliably transporting her to a place of serenity and beauty. As a teen, however, her mother started entering her into piano competitions. Suddenly it wasn't about the music anymore. Because her developing identity was so wrapped up in being a "good" pianist, it mattered hugely (both to Jeanie and her mother) whether she came in first, second, or third in a competition. And if she didn't place at all, she felt utterly worthless. The harder Jeanie tried to play well, the worse she performed, because she would focus more on the competition than the music itself. By the time she entered college, Jeanie dropped piano altogether. It had stopped being fun. Artists and athletes often tell such stories. Once we start basing our self-esteem purely on our performance, our greatest joys in life can start to seem like so much hard work, our pleasure morphing into pain.

## Confusing the Map for the Territory

As human beings with the capacity for self-reflection, with the ability to construct a self-concept, our thoughts and evaluations of ourselves can easily become confused with who we actually are. It's as if we conflate that Cezanne still life of a bowl of fruit with the fruit itself, mistaking the paint and canvas for the actual apples, pears, and oranges that the still life represents, and getting frustrated when we find we can't eat them. Our self-concept is not our *actual* self, of course. It is simply a representation, a sometimes accurate but more often wildly inaccurate portrayal of our habitual thoughts, emotions, and behaviors. And the sad thing is that the broad brush strokes that outline our self-concept don't even begin to do justice to the complexity, subtlety, and wonder of our actual self.

Still, we identify so strongly with our mental self-portrait that painting a positive rather than a negative picture of ourselves can feel like a matter of life and death. If the image I construct of myself is perfect and desirable, the unconscious thought process goes, then *I* am perfect and desirable, and therefore others will accept rather than reject me. If the image I construct is flawed or undesirable, however, then I am worthless and will be cast out and abandoned. Our thinking on these matters tends to be incredibly black and white—either we're all good (phew, breathe a sigh of relief) or we're all bad (might as well throw in the towel now). Any threat to our mental representation of who we are, therefore, feels like an actual, visceral threat, and we respond as powerfully as a soldier defending his very life.

We grasp onto self-esteem as if it were an inflatable raft that will save us—or at least save and prop up the positive sense of self that we so crave—only to find that the raft has a gaping hole and is rapidly running out of air. The truth is this: sometimes we display good qualities and sometimes bad. Sometimes we act in helpful, productive ways and sometimes in harmful, maladaptive ways. But we are not *defined* by these qualities or behaviors. We are a verb not a noun, a process rather than a fixed "thing." Our actions change—mercurial beings that we are—according to time, circumstance, mood, setting. We often forget this, however, and continue to flog ourselves into the relentless pursuit of high self-esteem—the elusive holy grail—trying to find a permanent box labeled good in which to stuff ourselves.

By sacrificing ourselves to the insatiable god of self-esteem, we are trading the ever-unfolding wonder and mystery of our lives for a sterile Polaroid snapshot. Instead of reveling in the richness and complexity of our experience—the joy and the pain, the love and anger, the passion, the triumphs and the tragedies—we try to capture and sum up our lived experience with extremely simplistic evaluations of self-worth. But these judgments, in a very real sense, are just thoughts. And more often than not they aren't even accurate thoughts. The need to see ourselves as superior also makes us emphasize our separation from others rather than our interconnectedness, which in turns leads to feelings of isolation, disconnection, and insecurity. So, one might ask, is it worth it?

## Self-Compassion Versus Self-Esteem

Rather than trying to define our self-worth with judgments and evaluations, what if our positive feelings toward ourselves came from a totally different source? What if they came from our hearts, rather than our minds?

Self-compassion does not try to capture and define the worth or essence of who we are. It is not a thought or a label, a judgment or an evaluation. Instead, self-compassion is a way of *relating* to the mystery of who we are. Rather than managing our self-image so that it is always palatable, self-compassion honors the fact that all human beings have both strengths and weaknesses. Rather than getting lost in thoughts of being good or bad, we become mindful of our present moment experience, realizing that it is ever changing and impermanent. Our successes and failures come and go—they neither define us nor do they determine our worthiness. They are merely part of the process of being alive. Our minds may try to convince us otherwise, but our *hearts* know that our true value lies in the core experience of being a conscious being who feels and perceives.

This means that unlike self-esteem, the good feelings of self-compassion do not depend on being special and above average, or on meeting ideal goals. Instead, they come from caring about ourselves—fragile and imperfect yet magnificent as we are. Rather than pitting ourselves against other people in an endless comparison game, we embrace what we share with others and feel more connected and whole in the process. And the good feelings of self-compassion don't go away when we mess up or things go wrong. In fact, self-compassion steps in *precisely* where self-esteem lets us down—whenever we fail or feel inadequate. When the fickle fancy of self-esteem deserts us, the all-encompassing embrace of self-compassion is there, patiently waiting.

Sure, you skeptics may be saying to yourself, but what does the research show? The bottom line is that according to the science, self-compassion appears to offer the same advantages as high self-esteem, with no discernible downsides. The first thing to know is that self-compassion and self-esteem *do* tend to go together. If you're self-compassionate, you'll tend to have higher self-esteem than if you're endlessly self-critical. And like high self-esteem—self-compassion is associated with significantly less anxiety and depression, as well as more happiness, optimism, and positive emotions. However, self-compassion offers clear advantages over self-esteem when things go wrong, or when our egos are threatened.

In one study my colleagues and I conducted, for instance, undergraduate students were asked to fill out measures of self-compassion and self-esteem. Next came the hard part. They were asked to participate in a mock job interview to "test their interviewing skills." A lot of undergrads are nervous about the interviewing process, especially given that they will soon be applying for jobs in real life. As part of the experiment, students were asked to write an answer to that dreaded but inevitable interview question, "Please describe your greatest weakness." Afterward they were asked to report how anxious they were feeling.

Participants' self-compassion levels, but not their self-esteem levels, predicted how much anxiety they felt. In other words, self-compassionate students reported feeling less self-conscious and nervous than those who lacked self-compassion, presumably because they felt okay admitting and talking about their weak points. Students with high self-esteem, by contrast, were no less anxious than those with low self-esteem, having been thrown off balance by the challenge of discussing their failings. And interestingly, self-compassionate people used fewer first-person singular pronouns such as "I" when writing about their weaknesses, instead using more third-person plural pronouns such as "we." They also made references to friends, family, and other humans more often. This suggests that the sense of interconnectedness inherent to self-compassion plays an important role in its ability to buffer against anxiety.

Another study required people to imagine being in potentially embarrassing situations: being on a sports team and blowing a big game, for instance, or performing in a play and forgetting one's lines. How would participants feel if something like this happened to them? Self-compassionate participants were less likely to feel humiliated or incompetent, or to take it too personally. Instead, they said they would take things in their stride, thinking thoughts like "Everybody goofs up now and then" and "In the long run, this doesn't really matter." Having high self-esteem, however, made little difference. Those with both high *and* low self-esteem were equally likely to have thoughts like "I'm such a loser" or "I wish I could die." Once again, high self-esteem tends to come up empty-handed when the chips are down.

In a different study, participants were asked to make a videotape that would introduce and describe themselves. They were then told that someone would watch their tape and give them feedback in terms of how warm, friendly, intelligent, likable, and mature they appeared (the feedback was bogus, of course). Half the participants received positive feedback, the other neutral feedback. Self-compassionate people were relatively unflustered regardless of whether the feedback was positive or neutral, and they were willing to say the feedback was based on their own personality either way. People with high levels of self-esteem, however, tended to get upset when they received neutral feedback (what, I'm just *average*?). They were also more likely to deny that the neutral feedback was due to their own personality (surely it's because the person who watched my tape was an idiot!). This suggests that self-compassionate people are better able to accept who they are regardless of the degree of praise they receive from others. Self-esteem, on the other hand, only thrives when the reviews are good and may lead to evasive and counterproductive tactics when there's a possibility of facing any unpleasant truths about oneself.

Recently, my colleague Roos Vonk and I investigated the benefits of self-compassion versus self-esteem with more than three thousand people from various walks of life, the largest study to examine this issue so far. First, we examined the stability of positive feelings experienced toward the self over time. Did these feelings tend to go up and down like a yo-yo or were they relatively constant? We hypothesized that self-esteem would be associated with relatively *un*stable feelings of self-worth, since self-esteem tends to be diminished whenever things don't turn out as well as desired. On the other hand, because compassion can be extended to oneself in both good times and bad, we expected the feelings of self-worth associated with self-compassion to remain steadier over time.

To test this idea, we had participants report on how they were feeling toward themselves at the time—for instance, "I feel inferior to others at this moment" or "I feel good about myself"—doing so twelve different times over a period of eight months.

Next, we calculated the degree to which overall levels of self-compassion or self-esteem predicted stability in self-worth over this period. As expected, self-compassion was clearly associated with steadier and more constant feelings of self-worth than self-esteem. We also found that self-compassion was less likely than self-esteem to be contingent on particular outcomes like social approval, competing successfully, or feeling attractive. When our sense of self-worth stems from being a human being intrinsically worthy of respect—rather than being contingent on obtaining certain ideals—our sense of self-worth is much less easily shaken.

We also found that in comparison to self-esteem, self-compassion was associated with less social comparison and less need to retaliate for perceived personal slights. It was also linked to less "need for cognitive closure," which is psych-speak for the need to be right without question. People who invest their self-worth in feeling superior and infallible tend to get angry and defensive when their status is threatened. People who compassionately accept their imperfection, however, no longer need to engage in such unhealthy behaviors to protect their egos. In fact, a striking finding of the study was that people with high self-esteem were much more narcissistic than those with low self-esteem. In contrast, self-compassion was completely unassociated with narcissism. (The reason there wasn't a negative association is because people who lack self-compassion don't tend to be narcissistic, either.)

## Exercise One

### *Identifying the Trickster*

A. List up to ten aspects of yourself that play a significant role in your self-esteem—things that either make you feel good or bad about yourself (job performance, role as parent, weight, etc.).

1. _____
2. _____
3. _____
4. _____
5. _____
6. _____
7. _____
8. _____
9. _____
10. _____

B. Ask yourself the following questions as they relate to each item, and consider whether your answers change how you think about things. Are there ways in which the trickster of self-esteem is leading you astray?

1. Q1. Do I want to feel better than others, or to feel connected?
2. Q2. Does my worth come from being special, or from being human?
3. Q3. Do I want to be perfect, or to be healthy?

## Freedom from the Ego

One might say that with self-compassion, although the ego doesn't completely go away, it moves from the foreground into the background. Instead of evaluating yourself as an isolated individual with boundaries that are clearly defined in contrast to others, you see yourself as part of a greater, interconnected whole. The idea that there is some "separate self" that can be judged independently from the many interacting conditions that created that "self" is an illusion. It is only when we fall into the trap of believing that we are "distinct entities" that the issue of self-esteem even comes into play. Of course we want to experience the happiness that stems from feeling good about ourselves; everyone does. Moreover, this happiness is our birthright. But happiness—real, lasting happiness—can be best experienced when we are engaged in the flow of life—connected to rather than separate from everything else.

When we're mainly filtering our experience through the ego, constantly trying to improve or maintain our high self-esteem, we're denying ourselves the thing we actually want most. To be accepted as we are, an integral part of something much greater than our small selves. Unbounded. Immeasurable. Free.

## Chapter Eight

# MOTIVATION AND
# PERSONAL GROWTH

*The curious paradox is that when I accept myself just as I am,
then I can change.*
  —CARL ROGERS, *On Becoming a Person*

TWO OUTLAWS WERE SITTING IN THE SALOON WHEN ONE SAYS TO the other, "Have you seen Billy the Kid lately?"

"Yep. I had lunch with him the other day."

"Oh?"

"Yep, I was riding my horse over the bridge into town, and there was Billy, with a gun, pointed at me. 'Get down off yer horse,' he says.

"What can I do? He has the gun, so I get down off the horse.

"Billy points at a pile of horse poop. 'See the horse poop? Eat the horse poop.'

"What can I do? He has the gun. I eat the poop.

"Then Billy laughs; he laughs so hard he drops the gun. I grab it.

" 'Hey Billy,' I say. 'Now *I* have the gun. See the horse poop? Eat the horse poop.'

"What can he do? I have the gun. He eats the poop.

"So like I said, we had lunch together the other day."

THIS (ADMITTEDLY SOMEWHAT GRATUITOUS) JOKE HIGHLIGHTS THE widespread belief that we need to put a gun to someone's head to make them do something unpalatable—especially when the someone is us.

The number one reason people give for why they aren't more compassionate to themselves is fear of laziness and self-indulgence. "Spare the rod, spoil the child," the saying goes, revealing the belief that only harsh punishment can keep indolence at bay. Corporal punishment might be less common in families and schools today, but we still cling to this approach with ourselves, believing that self-flagellation (even if only mental) is both useful and effective. It's the old carrot-and-stick approach—self-judgment is the stick and self-esteem is the carrot. If you do what you're supposed to do even though you don't want to, you can avoid being bashed with self-criticism and feel better about yourself.

I had an undergraduate student named Holly who really bought into this. She was convinced that she needed to be tough on herself to keep herself in line, so that she would be the person she wanted to be. Born to a conservative Texas family with incredibly high expectations, she felt it wasn't enough to merely graduate college; she had to earn an MBA. Her parents had never gotten beyond high school: all their hopes and dreams were pinned on their daughter's success. The way she kept up this intense pressure on herself was through constant self-criticism. If she got a worse-than-expected grade on an exam, she would pummel herself with harsh self-talk: "You're so stupid and lame. You'll never get into grad school if you keep messing up like this," and so on. The reward she dangled in front of her nose for working so hard was pride.

Holly wanted her parents to be proud of her, and she wanted to be proud of herself. She believed that the only way she would ever be able to reach her goals was to spur herself on with merciless self-criticism.

This type of thinking is incredibly common, *but is it true?*

## The Demoralizing Whip

First, consider the mind-state that self-criticism engenders. What type of mood do the words "You're such a lazy good-for-nothing, I hate you" put you in? Energized, inspired, ready to take on the world? Go get 'em, champ.

It's even easier to see when we think about motivating other people, such as children. Let's say your ten-year-old daughter comes home with a failing exam grade. What's the best way to encourage her to adopt better study habits so that she can do better next time? Should you fiercely criticize her? Tell her she's useless and send her to bed without any supper? Of course not. Such harsh criticism would emotionally flatten her to the point where she'd have little energy left over to reapply herself to her studies. Sadly, some parents do take this approach, but it's far from ideal. More effective would be to reassure her that these things happen, that she is still loved, and to firmly but compassionately encourage a new study routine, assuring her that she can and will do better.

We all know that positive, reassuring messages create the mind-state most conducive to working hard and reaching one's highest potential. We need to feel calm, secure, and confident in order to do our best. That's why when we try to motivate those we love, we usually bend over backward to let them know we believe in them, that they have our undying loyalty, affection, and support. But for some strange reason, we often take the exact opposite approach with ourselves.

Researchers who study motivation have consistently found that our level of self-confidence has a dramatic impact on our ability to reach our goals. Dozens of studies have confirmed that our beliefs in our own abilities—which research psychologist Albert Bandura terms "self-efficacy" beliefs—are directly related to our ability to achieve our dreams.

For example, one study followed more than two hundred high school wrestlers through the course of one wrestling season. It was found that, independent of their prior success at wrestling, those students who had stronger self-efficacy beliefs won more matches than those who doubted themselves. This was especially apparent in high-pressure overtime situations where the match was tied. Wrestling matches decided in overtime are "sudden death"—where the first wrestler to score wins. They are difficult because both wrestlers are exhausted, and a tie indicates an even match of physical skills. In such cases, the only factor that predicts a win is the wrestler's mental belief in his own ability.

Because self-criticism tends to undermine self-efficacy beliefs, self-criticism may harm rather than help our ability to do our best. By constantly putting ourselves down we eventually begin to lose faith in ourselves, meaning we aren't able to go as far as we're capable of going. Self-criticism is also strongly associated with depression, and a depressive mind-set is not exactly conducive to a "get-up-and-go" attitude.

Of course, self-criticism must be *somewhat* effective as a motivator, otherwise so many people wouldn't do it. If self-criticism works at all, however, it is only for one reason: *fear*. Because it is so unpleasant to be harshly criticized by ourselves when we fail, we become motivated by the desire to escape our own self-judgment. It's like we're putting our own heads on the chopping block, constantly threatening the worst, knowing that the terror of our own harsh self-criticism will prevent us from being complacent.

This approach works to a certain degree, but it has some serious drawbacks. One of the biggest problems with using fear as a motivator is that anxiety itself can undermine performance. Whether it's public speaking anxiety, test anxiety, writer's block, or stage fright, we know that fear of being negatively judged can be pretty debilitating. Anxiety distracts people from the task at hand, interfering with their ability to focus and give their best.

Not only does self-criticism create anxiety, it can also lead to psychological tricks designed to prevent self-blame in the case of failure, which in turn makes failure more likely. The tendency to undermine your performance in ways that create a plausible excuse for failing is known as "self-handicapping." One common form of self-handicapping is simply not trying very hard. If I don't practice ahead of time for my neighborhood tennis match, I can blame losing the match on my lack of practice rather than on being a bad tennis player. Another common strategy is procrastination. If I mess up on a work assignment that I didn't start preparing for until the last minute, I can blame my failure on lack of preparation rather than incompetence.

Research indicates that self-critics are less likely to achieve their goals because of these sorts of self-handicapping strategies. In one study, for instance, college students were asked to describe their various academic, social, and health-related goals, and then to report on how much progress they had made toward these goals. Self-critics made significantly less progress toward their goals than others and also reported that they procrastinated more often. So, instead of being a useful motivational tool, self-criticism may actually cause us to shoot ourselves in the foot.

Jim was one of the worst procrastinators I'd ever met. Everything he did was done at the last minute. Whenever he felt insecure about his ability to pull off an important task, he'd procrastinate so that if he messed up he would have a ready excuse—"I ran out of time." When he took his GRE exam to try to get into grad school, for instance, he didn't start studying until a few days before. When he got his score back, which was okay but not fantastic, he told me, "Well, it's actually not that bad considering I hardly studied." When it came time to get an internship as part of his master's program in social work, he waited until the last minute to send out his applications. Not surprisingly, the only internship he ended up being offered was the one no one else wanted. His response? "Well, most of the positions were already filled by the time I sent in my application. At least I got something."

The worst, however, was his wedding day. Jim's fiancée, Naomi, made all the arrangements for the big event herself, hoping that the ceremony—held in the beautiful nineteenth-century church her family had attended when she was a child—would be perfect. Naomi picked out matching dresses for her bridesmaids and tuxedos for Jim and his groomsmen. The one thing she asked Jim to do was buy a pair of black dress shoes for his tux. The wedding was Sunday at noon, so Jim thought he was doing great by hitting the shopping mall at 9:00 A.M. He'd have plenty of time to buy the shoes and show up at the church vestibule at 11:00 A.M. as instructed.

What he forgot, of course, was that the mall didn't open until noon on Sunday. There were *no* shoe stores in the local area that opened before noon. Jim didn't own a pair of dress shoes; all he had were two pairs of colored high-top sneakers and a grungy pair of leather sandals. He was screwed. Luckily, he remembered that the local dollar store opened at 10:00 A.M. and that they had a small shoe collection. He could pick up something there. The only shoes they had in black, however, were some cheap Croc rip-offs. They would have to do. Naomi didn't see Jim's shoes until he was walking down the aisle, and although her face registered a brief look of shock and horror, she quite rightly decided to ignore the issue for the time being and focus on what was most important— their wedding vows. Afterward at the reception, however, I saw them having a pretty tense exchange. While trying not to eavesdrop (okay, maybe I was eavesdropping a little), I heard Jim say: "Well, considering I didn't go shopping until this morning, they aren't so bad. And they're pretty comfortable . . ."

Although it's true that Jim somehow managed to squeak by with his last-minute efforts, and saved himself from harsh self-criticism by always having a ready excuse at hand when he messed up, Jim never reached his full potential. He could have gotten into a better grad school, one where his intelligence could really shine, if he had started studying for his GREs earlier. He could have gotten a better internship, one that gave him experience in the area of social work that most appealed to him, if he had sent out his applications in a timely manner. He could have prevented the fight he had with his new bride on his wedding day if he'd just gone to the mall a day earlier. If Jim was more comfortable with the fact that he *might* fail even when he did his best, he wouldn't have to self-sabotage in order to save his ego when he *did* fail. And failure of some sort is inevitable when we only make a halfhearted effort.

## Because You Care

So why is self-compassion a more effective motivator than self-criticism? *Because its driving force is love not fear.* Love allows us to feel confident and secure (in part by pumping up our oxytocin), while fear makes us feel insecure and jittery (sending our amygdala into overdrive and flooding our systems with cortisol). When we trust ourselves to be understanding and compassionate when we fail, we won't cause ourselves unnecessary stress and anxiety. We can relax knowing that we'll be accepted regardless of how well or how poorly we do. But if that's true, why should we try working hard at all? Why not just kick up our feet eating pizza and watching TV reruns all day?

Many people assume that self-compassion is just a feel-good warm fuzzy—a way to coddle ourselves and nothing more. But healing and growth are not served by such superficial treatment. Unlike self-criticism, which asks if you're good enough, self-compassion asks *what's good for you?* Self-compassion taps into your inner desire to be healthy and happy. If you care about yourself, you'll do what you need to do to in order to learn and grow. You'll *want* to change unhelpful patterns of behavior, even if that means giving up certain things you like for a while. Caring parents don't constantly feed their children candy just because their kids love candy. Indulging your child's every whim is not a sign of good parenting. Being nurturing toward those we care about means sometimes saying no.

In the same way, self-compassion involves valuing yourself in a deep way, making choices that lead to well-being in the long term. Self-compassion wants to heal dysfunctions, not perpetuate them. There's nothing wrong with occasionally indulging yourself, of course. Sometimes eating that piece of lemon cheesecake is actually a form of self-care. But overindulgence (i.e., eating the whole cheesecake) doesn't feel good. It's counterproductive because it prevents us from getting what we really want: to reach our highest potential.

The Buddha referred to the motivational quality of self-compassion as "right effort." From this point of view, wrong effort comes from concern with the ego, with proving oneself, with the desire for control. This type of effort actually increases suffering, because it makes you feel separate and disconnected from the rest of the world and sets up the expectation that things should always be as we want them to be. Right effort, on the other hand, comes from the natural desire to heal suffering. As the Buddha said, "It is like perceiving one's hair being on fire." The actions that are spurred when we see our hair go up in smoke, like grabbing a wet towel or jumping in the shower, stem from wanting to solve the problem, to escape from the danger of being burned. They don't come from the desire to prove ourselves (see what an excellent fire-putter-outer I am?). In the same way, the effort that comes from self-compassion is not the result of egoistic striving, but the natural desire to ameliorate suffering.

If we want to prosper, we need to face up to ways we might be harming ourselves and figure out how to make things better. We don't have to be cruel to ourselves in this process, however. We can be kind and supportive while engaging in the difficult work of change. We can recognize that life is hard, that challenges are part of the human experience. Luckily, kindness and encouragement feel pretty good, and they sure help the medicine go down.

## Exercise One

### *Identifying What We Really Want*

1. Think about the ways that you use self-criticism as a motivator. Is there any personal trait that you criticize yourself for (such as being moody, lazy, overweight, etc.) because you think being hard on yourself will help you change? If so, first try to get in touch with the emotional pain that your self-criticism causes, giving yourself compassion for the experience of feeling so judged.

2. Next, see if you can think of a kinder, more caring way to motivate yourself to make a change if needed. What language would a wise and nurturing friend, parent, teacher, or mentor use to gently point out how your behavior is unproductive, while simultaneously encouraging you to do something different? What is the most supportive message you can think of that's in line with your underlying wish to be healthy and happy?

3. Every time you catch yourself being judgmental about your unwanted trait in the future, first notice the pain of your self-judgment and give yourself compassion. Then try to reframe your inner dialogue so that it is more encouraging and supportive. Remember that if you really want to motivate yourself, love is more powerful than fear.

# Self-Compassion, Learning, and Personal Growth

Many people are afraid they won't be ambitious enough if they're compassionate with themselves. Research suggests otherwise. In one study, for example, we examined how people reacted when they failed to meet their standards, and also how high their standards were in the first place. We found that self-compassionate people were just as likely to have high standards for themselves as those who lacked self-compassion, but they were much *less* likely to be hard on themselves on the occasions when they didn't meet those standards. We've also found that self-compassionate people are more oriented toward personal growth than those who continually criticize themselves. They're more likely to formulate specific plans for reaching their goals, and for making their lives more balanced. Self-compassion in no way lowers where you set your sites in life. It does, however, soften how you react when you don't do as well as you hoped, which actually helps you achieve your goals in the long run.

The ability to realize our potential depends partly on where our motivation comes from. Is it intrinsic or extrinsic? Intrinsic motivation occurs when we're driven to do something because we want to learn, grow, or because the activity is just plain interesting. Extrinsic motivation occurs when we're driven to do something in order to gain a reward or escape a punishment. Even when rewards and punishments come from within, like the reward of self-esteem or the punishment of self-criticism, our motivation is still extrinsic because we're engaging in an activity for ulterior motives.

Research psychologist Carol Dweck, author of *Mindset,* distinguishes two main reasons why people want to achieve their goals. People with *learning* goals are intrinsically motivated by curiosity and the desire to develop new skills. They want to achieve because they want to gain knowledge, and most important, they view making mistakes as a part of the learning process. Those with *performance* goals, on the other hand, are extrinsically motivated to defend or enhance their self-esteem.

They want to do well so that others will approve of them and tend to avoid failure at all costs. This means that instead of challenging themselves they take the safe road. You know the type. People who just want the easy A and don't really care how much they learn in the process. Research shows that in the long run, learning goals are more effective than performance goals. Learning goals propel people to try harder for longer, because they enjoy what they do. They also enable people to ask for the help and guidance they need, because they're less worried about looking incompetent for not already knowing the right answer.

Take Kate and Danielle, for example. Twin sisters who both loved animals as young girls, they had dozens of pictures of lions, zebras, rhinos, giraffes, and other exotic animals plastered all over their bedroom walls while growing up. They used to dream about being zookeepers one day. They ended up going to the same local university and enrolled in an upper-level zoology course their junior year. The course was extremely difficult, and both actually failed their first exam. Danielle had always thought of herself as a good student and couldn't stand the thought that she might get a failing grade in the course. So she dropped out. Kate didn't care. She was learning about animals, and that was what was most important. She went to the teaching assistant's office hours almost every week and ended up getting a B in the course. After graduation, Danielle got an entry-level management position at a large corporation. The job was well paid, and she was able to impress all her friends by buying a new car after only a few months of employment. The job was relatively easy and secure, but also pretty boring. Kate, on the other hand, saved up enough money working as a waitress to go to Botswana for a month, where she had the best time of her life. She decided that she wanted to open her own safari business one day, and after various low-paid and demanding internships learning the ropes, eventually did. Kate and Danielle were both intelligent, hardworking young women, but it was Kate who challenged herself and ended up fulfilling a lifelong dream.

As you might suspect, our research finds that self-compassionate people are more likely to have learning rather than performance goals. Because their motivation stems from the desire to learn and grow, rather than from the desire to escape self-criticism, they are more willing to take learning risks. This is largely because they're not so afraid of failure. Among a group of undergraduates who had recently failed a midterm exam, for example, we found that self-compassionate students were more likely to reinterpret their failure as a growth opportunity rather than as a condemnation of self-worth. When you can trust that failure will be greeted with understanding rather than judgment, it no longer becomes the boogeyman lurking in the closet. Instead, failure can be recognized as the master teacher that it is.

Research also indicates that failure is less likely to damage the overall self-efficacy beliefs of self-compassionate people. Because they aren't so hard on themselves when they fall down, they retain enough confidence in their abilities to pick themselves up and try again. In fact, a recent study found that when self-compassionate people are forced to give up on a goal that's important to them—an inevitability at some point in life—they tend to refocus their energy on a new and different goal. Self-critics, on the other hand, are more likely to throw in the towel. Self-compassionate people have also been found to procrastinate less than those lacking self-compassion. This is partly because they report being less worried about how others view their performances, and thus don't require a plausible excuse for failing.

So it's definitely *not* the case that self-compassion leads to complacency and inertia. Quite the opposite. By losing our fear of failure, we become free to challenge ourselves to a far greater degree than would otherwise be possible. At the same time, by acknowledging the limitations of being human, we are better able to recognize which goals are working for us and which are not, and when it's time to take a new approach. Far from being a form of self-indulgence, self-compassion and real achievement go hand in hand. Self-compassion inspires us to pursue our dreams and creates the brave, confident, curious, and resilient mind-set that allows us to actually achieve them.

## Exercise Two

### *Self-Compassion and Procrastination*

We procrastinate for different reasons. Sometimes we just don't want to do an unpleasant task. Sometimes we procrastinate because we're afraid of failing. Luckily, self-compassion can help deal with procrastination so that it becomes less of a hindrance.

#### Unpleasantness

It's very common to keep putting off unpleasant tasks, like doing our taxes or writing up those incredibly boring notes for work. Or even if the chore isn't particularly unpleasant, like folding and putting away laundry, sometimes we just don't feel like getting off our butts. This isn't surprising, given that it's natural to want to relax and avoid unpleasantness. And putting off these types of tasks is not necessarily a problem unless it ends up causing you more stress in your life because you aren't getting the needful done. If you find that you habitually procrastinate when faced with doing things you don't want to do, it can help to go to the emotion underlying your resistance itself. We often avoid thinking about unwanted tasks because it makes us feel uncomfortable. Another approach, however, is to give yourself compassion for the very human reactions of displeasure and avoidance. Allow yourself to fully dive into the sensation of dread or lethargy or whatever is coming up for you when you think about the task. Can you feel the emotions in your body, holding them in nonjudgmental, mindful awareness? Recognize that these are moments of suffering, even if on a small scale. All our emotions are worthy of being felt and validated. Once you give yourself the sense of comfort you want, you'll probably find yourself less resistant to getting started.

### FEAR OF FAILURE

Sometimes the emotions underlying our habitual procrastination run deeper. If the task is an important one, like starting a big work project, we are often daunted by the possibility of failure. The feelings of fear that come up when thinking about taking on the project, and the feelings of unworthiness that come up when we think about possibly blowing it, can be overwhelming. Again, when we don't want to experience unpleasant emotions, procrastination is a very common way to tune out. And sometimes our unconscious tries to sabotage us so that if we do fail, we can avoid feeling unworthy by blaming our failure on not having enough time to do the job well. If this pattern is habitual, it could seriously limit the extent to which you reach your full potential.

If you suspect your procrastination is due to fear of failure, it's a good time to revisit much of what has been discussed in this book. Remember that all people fail sometimes; it's part of the human condition. And every failure is an incredibly powerful learning opportunity. Promise yourself that if you do fail, you'll be kind, gentle, and understanding with yourself rather than harshly self-critical. Comfort the scared little child inside of you who doesn't want to venture into the dark unknown, assuring him or her that you'll be there to provide support along the way. And then see if you can take the plunge. As we all know from experience, the worst part of dealing with a difficult task is often drawing up the courage to start.

## Searching for True Happiness

The types of dreams inspired by self-compassion are more likely to yield true happiness than those motivated by self-criticism. Our research indicates that self-compassionate people tend to be more authentic and autonomous in their lives, whereas those who lack self-compassion tend to be more conformist because they don't want to risk social judgment or rejection. Authenticity and autonomy are crucial for happiness, of course, because without them life can feel like meaningless drudgery.

Holly, the undergraduate student I talked about earlier in the chapter, learned this lesson eventually. After studying the concept of self-compassion in one of my classes, she began to see that being so critical of herself was only causing her harm. She was getting migraine headaches, which the doctor told her was from stress. Self-induced stress. The headaches got so bad she was having trouble studying. She had to do something. So she decided to give self-compassion a proper try. She set the timer on her cell phone to go off at various intervals throughout the day, and whenever it beeped she asked herself the question—what would be the most healthy and most self-compassionate thing for me to do right now? (As you can see, Holly did everything in a very methodical and determined manner!)

After about a month we met to talk about how her experiment was going. To her surprise, she said that she didn't find herself studying any less frequently or working any less hard by being kinder to herself. In fact, whenever she stopped to ask what would be the healthiest thing to do in the moment, the answer was often focused on her school work.

However, she did start taking naps if she had stayed up late studying the night before, so as a result she was more alert when she worked. She also tried to use gentler, more supportive language with herself whenever she had difficulties or got stuck. This seemed to help her get unstuck more quickly. In fact, when she was having a particularly hard time with one paper, she actually stopped by the professor's office to ask for assistance. She never would have done that before, she said, out of fear of seeming stupid. But she eventually realized that it was only human to need help, and she ended up doing a much better job on the paper than she would have done otherwise.

About a year later, Holly stopped by my office again to say hello and to see whether I would write her a letter of recommendation for graduate school. Holly had been a business major and had always planned on getting her MBA. This was certainly what her parents wanted and expected. But instead, she was applying to a school of special education. She had been volunteering for a local nonprofit that worked with disabled kids (to make her résumé look good, she admitted) and said she unexpectedly found her calling. Her time as a volunteer was the happiest she had ever been, and she wanted her professional life to make a difference in the world. Despite her parents' protestations, Holly realized she wanted to be happy in her life, to do what personally fulfilled her. So Holly got a master's degree in special education, and at last report was thriving as a special needs teacher in a local elementary school. Self-compassion might lead us to make unconventional choices for ourselves, but these will be the right choices made for the right reasons—the desire to follow our hearts.

## Self-Compassion and Our Bodies

Much of my discussion of self-compassion and motivation has focused on the realm of learning, probably because I'm a university professor and I deal with these issues every day. But self-compassion is a powerful motivator in many different domains. One area in which self-compassion plays a particularly strong role is in the epic struggle to accept our bodies. We often tear ourselves to shreds with self-criticism when we don't look the way we think we're supposed to. We stare at the superthin, aerobicized models on the covers of magazines and, understandably, don't feel we measure up. Even the cover girls don't feel they measure up, since most images are digitally enhanced.

Given the value placed on beauty in our society, it's not surprising that perceived attractiveness is one of the most important areas in which people invest their sense of self-worth. This holds true for both genders, but especially for females. If you want to know why teen girls often have self-esteem issues, you need only consider their perceived attractiveness. Research shows that boys' perceptions of their attractiveness tends to remain relatively stable during the child and adolescent years: third grade—looking good; seventh grade—looking good; eleventh grade—still looking good. Girls, on the other hand, feel more insecure about their looks as they grow older: third grade—looking good; seventh grade—not so sure anymore; eleventh grade—I'm so ugly! What's wrong with this picture? Are guys really more attractive than girls are? I think not.

The problem is that standards for female beauty are so much higher than those for males, especially when it comes to weight. Women are supposed to be rail thin but also super curvy, a nearly impossible ideal to achieve without plastic surgery and constant dieting. We may think it's mainly the rich and famous who cling to such unrealistic ideals, as jokes like this one attest: "A beggar walked up to a well-dressed woman shopping on Rodeo Drive and said to her, 'I haven't eaten anything in four days.' She looked at him and said, 'God, I wish I had your willpower.' " In fact, research indicates that four out of five American women are dissatisfied with the way they look, and over half are on a diet at any one time. Almost 50 percent of all girls between first and third grade say they want to be thinner, and by age eighteen fully 80 percent of girls report that they have dieted at some point in their life.

For some, the obsession with thinness leads to eating disorders such as anorexia or bulimia. Anorexia involves undereating to the point of near starvation. Bulimia entails eating unusually large amounts of food in one sitting (binging), then getting rid of the calories afterward (purging) either by vomiting, abusing laxatives, or overexercising. Despite the strong cultural emphasis on thinness and dieting, however, the most prevalent eating disorder is actually binge eating—which occurs when people overeat past the point of fullness but *don't purge* afterward.

Psychologists agree that when people binge eat they are often trying to satiate an internal emotional hunger. Stuffing yourself numbs painful feelings. It's a way of medicating yourself with food. Indulging in the pleasures of food is also an easy way to make yourself happy, at least in the short term. The long-term impact of overeating, however, is not pleasant. Fully one-third of all Americans are classified as obese, and it's estimated that about half of all people who are obese suffer from binge-eating disorder. This causes major health problems in society and costs the medical system billions of dollars each year. Not to mention the emotional pain and self-loathing experienced by people who are obese. People with binge eating disorder are caught in an unfortunate downward spiral—depression fuels overeating, which leads to obesity, which leads to further depression.

So why is being overweight so common at the same time that most people are trying to diet? Because as almost everyone knows from personal experience, diets don't work. People start diets because they hate the way they look, but when they break their diet—as everyone eventually does—they're likely to gain back more than they lost in the first place. After overeating at an office party, for instance, the inner dialogue may go like this: *I can't believe I ate so much. I'm so disgusted with myself. I guess I might as well finish off that bowl of chips since I'm clearly a lost cause.* And, of course, criticizing yourself in this way will probably make you eat even more as a means of self-comfort—eating to feel better because you feel bad about eating. It's a vicious cycle that's hard to stop and is one of the reasons why the pattern of yo-yo dieting is so common.

A self-compassionate response to breaking one's diet looks radically different. First, self-compassion involves forgiving yourself for your lapses. If your ultimate goal is to be healthy, then it doesn't really matter if you fall off your diet from time to time. We are not machines whose dial can simply be turned to "reduce calorie input." Most people fluctuate in their ability to stay focused on their eating goals. Two steps forward, one step back seems to be the natural way of things. By having compassion for yourself when you fall off your diet, you'll be less driven to overeat as a way to make you feel better afterward.

A recent study supports this claim. Female undergraduate students were asked to eat a doughnut as part of a research study—they were given the cover story that they were taking part in a study of eating habits while watching television. After eating the doughnut, half the participants were given instructions to help them feel more compassionate about indulging in the sweet treat: "Several people have told me that they feel bad about eating doughnuts in this study, so I hope you won't be hard on yourself. Everyone eats unhealthily sometimes, and everyone in this study eats this stuff, so I don't think there's any reason to feel really bad about it." The other half in the control group weren't told anything. Researchers found that among women who were on a diet, those in the control group reported feeling more guilty and ashamed after eating the doughnut. And later on, when they were given the opportunity to eat as much candy as they wanted as part of a supposed "taste-testing " session, they actually ate *more* candy than those who weren't on a diet. In contrast, dieting women who were encouraged to be self-compassionate about the doughnut were much less distraught. They also didn't overeat in the taste-testing session afterward, meaning that they were better able to stick to their weight-loss goals despite momentarily falling off the wagon.

Exercise is also an important part of being healthy, and research suggests that self-compassionate people tend to exercise for the right reasons. For instance, self-compassionate women tend to have intrinsic rather than extrinsic motivation to exercise. This means they play sports or work out because they find it fulfilling and worthwhile and not because they think they're supposed to. Research also shows that self-compassionate people are more comfortable with their bodies and aren't as obsessed with physical appearance as those who are more self-critical. They're also less likely to worry about how they look to other people.

Oprah, whose weight-loss efforts have been the focus of intense media attention, is a good role model for how to deal with body issues compassionately. In a memorable 1988 episode of her show, she wheeled out a wagon loaded with fat to represent the sixty-seven pounds she had shed. Shortly afterward she gained the weight back. She dropped the weight again in 2005 through a well-chronicled diet and exercise program. She eventually gained much of it back. Despite the ups and downs, Oprah remains focused on what's most important: "My goal isn't to be thin. My goal is for my body to be the weight it can hold—to be strong and healthy and fit, to be itself. My goal is to learn to embrace this body and to be grateful every day for what it has given me."

When you don't need to be perfect in order to feel good about yourself, you can drop the obsessive fixation with being thin enough or pretty enough and accept yourself as you are, even revel in who you are. Being comfortable in your own skin allows you to focus on what's really important, being healthy—and that always looks good.

## Exercise Three

### Self-Compassion and Our Bodies

Having compassion for the imperfection of our bodies can be especially challenging in a culture that is obsessed with physical attractiveness. We need to learn to love and accept our bodies as they are, not in comparison to unrealistic media images of beauty. At the same time, many people don't take good care of their bodies. The stress of life often leads us to eat and drink more than we should, and our bodies can suffer due to a lack of exercise and time outdoors. The middle way involves accepting our imperfection, recognizing that beauty comes in all different shapes and sizes, at the same time that we nurture our physical health and well-being.

1. Start by taking a pen and paper and making a kind but honest assessment of your body. First list all the features of your body that you like. Maybe you have great hair or a lovely smile. Don't overlook things that may not normally factor into your self-image: the fact that you have strong hands, or the fact that your stomach digests food well (not something to be taken for granted!). Let yourself fully appreciate the aspects of your body that you're happy with.

2. Now list all the features of your body that you don't like so well. Maybe you have blemished skin, or think your hips are too wide, or you're out of shape and get tired easily. Give yourself compassion for the difficulty of being an imperfect human. Everyone has aspects of their body they're unhappy with. Almost no one reaches their physical ideal. At the same time, make sure you're making a balanced assessment of your deficits. Is the fact that your hair is turning gray really such a problem? Are those extra ten pounds really an issue in terms of feeling good and healthy in your body? Don't try to minimize your flaws, but don't blow them out of proportion either.

3. Now give yourself compassion for your imperfections, remembering how difficult it is to feel such strong societal pressure to look a certain way. Try to be kind, supportive, and

understanding toward yourself as you confront the suffering you face—the suffering that most people face—because you're dissatisfied with your body.

4. Finally, try to think if there are any steps you want to take that will help you feel better in your body. Forgetting about what other people think, is there anything *you* would like to change because you care about yourself? Would you feel better if you lost some weight or exercised more, or if you got highlights in your hair to hide the gray? If so, go for it! As you chart out the changes you want to make, make sure that you motivate yourself with kindness rather than self-criticism. Remember that what's most important is your desire to be healthy and happy.

## Self-Clarity and Self-Improvement

Not only does self-compassion provide a powerful motivational engine for change, it also provides the clarity needed to know what needs changing in the first place. Research indicates that people who suffer from shame and self-judgment are more likely to blame others for their moral failures. Who wants to admit their inadequacies when it means facing the attack dogs of self-criticism? It's easier to sweep things under the rug or point your finger at someone else.

Men are especially vulnerable to this pattern, given that the ideal man in our culture is supposed to be strong and infallible. When faced with his inadequacies, men often use anger as a way to deflect responsibility. Anger allows a man to feel temporarily tough and powerful, covering up any feelings of weakness stemming from personal failure. By blaming others he can also feel like a victim (of his wife's erratic moods or sharp tongue, for example), which in turn justifies his feelings of righteous anger. It's a vicious cycle that can lead to truly vicious behavior.

Steven Stosny, the well-known author of *Love Without Hurt*, has created a program for emotionally and physically abusive men that centers on the development of self-compassion. In three-day workshops he calls "boot camps," men with severe anger issues are taught to clearly see and understand the feelings of vulnerability underlying their rage, so that the cycle of blame and anger can end. When men start to relate to their deficiencies with compassion rather than shame, they no longer need to deny personal responsibility in order to defend their egos. This allows them to focus on their true desire: fostering loving, mutually supportive relationships with others. Stosny's anger-management boot camps are some of the most successful in the country and attest to the power of self-compassion to foster self-clarity and change.

A recent research study also supports the notion that self-compassion makes it easier to admit to needed areas of improvement. Participants were asked to recall a previous failure, rejection, or loss that made them feel bad about themselves. They were then told to write about the event, what led up to the event, who was present, precisely what happened, and how they felt and behaved at the time. Afterward, researchers gave one group of participants exercises designed to help them have compassion for the event. For instance, they were asked to list ways that others have had similar experiences, and to write a paragraph expressing feelings of kindness, concern, and understanding for what had happened. Another group was simply asked to write about the event with no particular instructions. The group who were encouraged to have self-compassion had fewer negative emotions such as anger, anxiety, or sadness when writing about what happened than those in the other group. At the same time, they also took more personal responsibility for the event.

Self-compassion doesn't just amount to letting ourselves off the hook. Rather, by softening the blow of self-judgment and recognizing our imperfect humanity, we can see ourselves with much greater honesty and clarity. Maybe we do tend to overreact, to be irresponsible, to be passive, to be controlling, and so on. In order to work on these patterns and help ourselves (and others) suffer less because of them, we need to acknowledge our shortcomings. We need to recognize how we have harmed others in order to heal the wounds we have caused. By self-compassionately accepting the fact that all people make mistakes and act in ways they regret, we can more easily admit our wrongdoings and try to make things right again. If we're consumed with feelings of shame and inadequacy because of what we've done, we are actually being self-absorbed. We aren't focusing our attention and concern where it's most needed—on the person we've hurt. Self-compassion provides the emotional safety needed to take responsibility for our actions, consider their impact on others, and sincerely apologize for our behavior.

## My Story: Still Trying After All These Years

After studying self-compassion for almost fifteen years now, guess what: I don't always practice what I preach. I have a tendency to be irritable when I'm stressed—and as I alluded at the start of this book—I often take this out on my husband, Rupert. Let's say I'm in a bad mood and notice that Rupert hasn't done the dishes when it's his turn. I might have a very negative reaction that's out of all proportion to the event. I'll then tend to exaggerate the seriousness of his offense to justify my overly negative emotions. "You never run the dishwasher and always just leave the dirty dishes to rot" (even though it actually doesn't happen all that often, and sometimes I do the exact same thing). "You're so irresponsible" (completely ignoring the fact that he's under an intense work deadline that's taking up all his attention). Before I started my practice of self-compassion, I would use all my mental ingenuity to convince Rupert that my reactions were his fault, not my own. If he accused me of being unfair, I could find ten reasons why actually my response was perfectly appropriate given his actions. It's painful to admit that sometimes one just gets in a foul mood and—for whatever reason—feels compelled to take it out on other people, usually those we love.

One fruit of my self-compassion practice, however, is that I'm now much more able to see myself clearly and admit my mistakes. If I'm irritable and make some cutting comment, I usually apologize before even hearing the words "That's unfair!" come out of Rupert's mouth. It's funny, but I don't take my negative moods so personally anymore. For whatever reason—my wiring, hormonal cycle, the weather?—sometimes I'm just plain tetchy. Not always, not usually, just sometimes. It happens to be an Achilles heel, but in no way does it define me.

By being self-compassionate when this mood arises, I can more easily admit when I'm out of line and focus on how to remedy the situation. This usually involves explaining to Rupert that I'm in a negative mood that has nothing to do with him, which then allows him to be understanding, even sympathetic, rather than defensive. Then I try to find ways to change my mood. Asking for a hug is a great remedy, and one that's only possible after an apology. And after the apology and hug, guess what? He usually apologizes right back—spats are often a two-way street. Although my irritable moods still come up, I don't take them out on Rupert nearly as often as I used to.

So when you make mistakes or fall short of your expectations, you can throw away that rawhide whip and instead throw a cozy blanket of compassion around your shoulders. You will be more motivated to learn, grow, and make the much-needed changes in your life, while also having more clarity to see where you are now and where you'd like to go next. You'll have the security needed to go after what you really want as well as the support and encouragement necessary to fulfill your dreams.

*Part Four*

## SELF-COMPASSION IN RELATION TO OTHERS

## Chapter Nine

# COMPASSION FOR OTHERS

*If one is cruel to himself, how can we expect him to be compassionate with others?*
—Hasdai Ibn Shaprut (10th c. Jewish scholar)

THE WOMAN WAS IN HER MID-FORTIES, WITH BLOND HAIR, GRAY eyes, and a kind face. We were at a dinner party, taking turns at the carrots and hummus dip, when she asked me what I did for a living. "I study self-compassion," I said. She cocked her head slightly to one side. "*Self*-compassion? But I thought compassion, by definition, was something you had for *other* people. How can you have compassion for yourself?" I explained that compassion was simply a way of relating to suffering, either your own or someone else's. I could see her digesting the idea. "Hmm. I guess that makes sense. So," she asked, "does having more self-compassion mean that you also have more compassion for other people?" "Well," I ventured, "yes and no . . ."

People ask me this question all the time. The answer is actually a bit complicated. In the first study I ever conducted on self-compassion, I asked people the following question: "Do you tend to be kinder to your-self or to others?" I found that people who were low in self-compassion tended to say that they were kinder to others than themselves, whereas those high in self-compassion said they were equally kind to others and themselves. In other words, everyone said they were kind to others, but only self-compassionate people were *also* kind to themselves.

In other research, my colleagues and I have found that self-compassionate people score no higher on general measures of compas-sionate love, empathy, or altruism—which all tap into concern for others' well-being—than those who lack self-compassion. This is because indi-viduals who lack self-compassion, who constantly judge themselves, are still often very caring toward other people.

Take the woman I met at that party, for instance. An experienced geriatric nurse, Sharon was a model of compassion. She often made home visits to her elderly patients, bringing little treats like cookies or flowers from her garden to make them feel special and cared for. She was constantly cracking jokes to keep their spirits up: "You know you're old when getting lucky means finding your car in the parking lot." When she had to help her patients with an embarrassing task, such as changing an adult diaper, she bent over backward to make sure they didn't feel embarrassed or ashamed. "Happens to everyone at some point, nothing to fret about."

Though Sharon found it easy to be kind and understanding toward the elderly in her care, she was extremely hard on herself. If she was late for an appointment, or forgot to do something on her daily checklist, she would eviscerate herself with self-criticism. "What a moron! These people depend on you! When are you going to grow up?" I asked Sharon if she would ever talk to the patients she cared for in the same way she talked to herself. "Of course not!" Why, then, did she treat herself so? "I don't know," she said with a puzzled look on her face. "I guess I feel like I should?"

People like Sharon are everywhere, especially in the West, where religious and cultural traditions tend to extol self-sacrifice. Particularly for women. Our research shows that women tend to have slightly lower levels of self-compassion than men do, largely because they tend to judge and criticize themselves more often. At the same time, there is ample research evidence showing that women tend to be more caring, empathetic, and giving toward others than men. Women are socialized to be caregivers, to selflessly open their hearts to their husbands, children, friends, and elderly parents, but they aren't taught to care for themselves. As forever seared into the public imagination by the 1970s film *The Stepford Wives,* the ideal woman is supposed to fulfill her role as cook, maid, lover, and nanny without complaint. She is not supposed to have needs and concerns of her own.

Although the feminist revolution has helped expand the roles available to women, and we now see more female leaders in business and politics than ever before, the idea that women should be selfless caregivers hasn't really gone away. It's just that women are now supposed to be successful at their careers *in addition to* being the loving wife and ultimate nurturer at home. Dana Crowley Jack's book *Silencing the Self* opens with a quote that captures the experience of many:

> *Even though I can objectively say, okay, I am above average in looks, I have been very successful with my art, I have been very successful at singing, I'm gregarious, I make friends easily. I can say all that, and still there is this, 'You are no good, what's the use.' I always feel the failure of my marriage was my fault, because I wanted a career, and didn't know how to manage being a professional with being a wife.*

Rather than being compassionate toward herself, realizing that she is only human and can only do so much, women such as this one tend to judge themselves relentlessly in the belief that they *should* be doing more. As a result, many women have a deep-seated feeling that they're not entitled to be the recipients of self-care. To understand why compassion for oneself and others do not necessarily go together, therefore, we need only to look to the self-sacrificing women who have cared for us all our lives.

## Putting Things into Perspective

Having said all this, there's also evidence that having compassion for yourself *is* related to having compassion for others in certain contexts. For instance, a recent study found that self-compassionate individuals have different goals in their friendships than those who lack self-compassion. They are more likely to focus on helping and encouraging their friends, as well as being compassionate toward their friends' mistakes and weaknesses. They are also more willing to admit their own mistakes and weaknesses to their friends. In sum, the study found that self-compassionate people are better able to create close, authentic, and mutually supportive friendships than those who are self-critical. (As the next chapter will discuss, research also shows that self-compassionate people tend to be more supportive, accepting, and caring with romantic partners.) Because we are so emotionally vulnerable in close relationships, because our inner selves are laid so bare, we often feel insecure about whether others are judging us. When we stop judging and evaluating ourselves, however, we don't need to worry so much about others' approval and can instead focus on meeting the emotional needs of others.

Although compassion involves feelings of care and concern for others, it also involves taking the perspective of those who are suffering— walking a mile in their shoes, so to speak. (Though perhaps not in the way meant by Scottish comedian Billy Connolly, who once said: "Before you judge a man, walk a mile in his shoes. After that who cares? . . . He's a mile away and you've got his shoes!") Rather than making quick and easy judgments of those who make mistakes, compassion considers what it must feel like to be the person making the mistake. It looks at things from the inside rather than the outside. To feel compassion for the public figure who has just made a blooper (like Dan Quayle when he exclaimed "Republicans understand the importance of bondage between a mother and child"), you must take on his perspective. Rather than merely seeing things from your own point of view (how amusing) you also see things from his point of view (how embarrassing).

We also have to engage in perspective taking when we give *ourselves* compassion. Rather than merely focusing on our own point of view in painful situations—I feel humiliated, afraid, inadequate, and so on— we take the perspective of an "other" toward ourselves. We respond with kindness and concern to our own human limitations, just as a kind friend or loving parent would. By seeing our flawed self from an outsider's perspective, self-compassion allows us to stop judging ourselves so harshly. Our research shows that people with higher levels of self-compassion are also more likely to engage in perspective taking when contemplating the failures and weaknesses of other people. They are more likely to say things like: "Before criticizing somebody, I try to imagine how *I* would feel if I were in their place." By its very nature, compassion is relational, stepping back and forth between various perspectives to see the mutuality of the human condition.

Though important for social harmony, taking the perspective of others does have one downside. It can be overwhelming, especially when others are really hurting. When we see images of hurricane survivors on TV, for instance, we may fear that by letting just a drop of their pain into our hearts we will ourselves be deluged. So to protect ourselves we shut down, or switch the channel. Instead of tuning out, however, we have another option. Our research shows that self-compassion allows us to feel others' pain without becoming overwhelmed by it. In other words, when we recognize how difficult it is sometimes to be there for people who are struggling, and comfort *ourselves* in the process, we are able to be stronger, more stable, and resilient when supporting others in their suffering. This is an especially important skill for those who deal with others' problems for a living.

## Compassion Fatigue

Focusing a lot of our energy on helping others can lead to "compassion fatigue," a syndrome that frequently occurs with therapists, nurses, and other caregivers. Compassion fatigue is a type of exhaustion and burnout experienced as a result of continually dealing with traumatized patients. When listening to tales of abuse or horror, or when tending to bodies that have been ravaged by sickness or violence, caregivers often relive their patients' trauma. For this reason, compassion fatigue is also known by the name "secondary traumatic stress." The symptoms of secondary traumatic stress can resemble those of posttraumatic stress disorder, such as nightmares, emotional numbing, and an exaggerated startle response. Secondary stress may also lead to decreased feelings of safety, increased cynicism, and disconnection from loved ones.

Caregivers who are the most empathic and sensitive tend to be the most at risk, given that they feel the pain of their patients most deeply. It's been estimated that about one-quarter of professionals who work with traumatized patients experience some kind of compassion fatigue. Among those working with survivors of extreme situations such as the Oklahoma City bombing, the figure is almost three times that. Although we do not know how many skilled caregivers quit as a result, the numbers are surely high.

Research suggests that caregivers who have been trained in self-compassion are less likely to experience compassion fatigue—because they have the skills needed to avoid getting overly stressed or burned out when interacting with their patients. It also suggests that self-compassion leads to more "compassion satisfaction"—feeling energized, happy, and grateful that one is able to make a difference in the world.

When you're not so overwhelmed by your caregiving duties, you can focus more easily on the fruits of your efforts.

When caregivers have self-compassion, they are also more likely to engage in concrete acts of self-care such as taking time off, sleeping more, and eating well. They'll stop to care for their own emotional needs, recognizing how difficult it is to deal with such a high level of suffering on a daily basis. The hardships of being a caregiver are just as valid and worthy of compassion as the hardships of being a trauma victim. Certainly there are differences in how debilitating and intense the pain is, but all pain deserves to be held in the warm embrace of compassion, so that healing can occur.

Self-compassion is a way of emotionally recharging our batteries. Rather than becoming drained by helping others, self-compassion allows us to fill up our internal reserves, so that we have more to give to those who need us. It's like those little videos they always show on planes before takeoff, which tell adults to put on their own oxygen mask before helping children to put on theirs. We need to have a steady supply of compassion available to ourselves in order to have adequate resources to share with others. If we're knocked flat on our backs because our own resources are depleted, what use are we to those who rely on us? In many ways, then, self-compassion is an altruistic act, because it puts us into the optimal mental and emotional mind-set to help others in a sustainable, long-lasting way.

## Exercise One

### Taking Care of the Caregiver

If you work in a caregiving profession (and that includes being a family member), you'll need to recharge your batteries so you have enough energy available to give to others. Give yourself permission to meet your own needs, recognizing that this will not only enhance your quality of life, it will also enhance your ability to be there for those who rely on you. Here are some ideas:

- Get a massage, a pedicure, or other form of pampering.
- Take a nap in the middle of the day.
- Go to a comedy club; laughter provides a great release of tension.
- Listen to a soothing song. (I like the Beatles' "Let It Be." Paul McCartney allegedly wrote the song when he was going through a particularly hard time and dreamed about his deceased mother, Mary, who tried to comfort him with the words "let it be.")
- Stretch or do yoga for a half hour.
- Take a walk in nature.
- Lie on the floor, stomach-side down, while someone gently rocks your lower back from side to side. It's incredibly relaxing without requiring too much effort from your partner.
- Go dancing. If you don't want to go to a club or take formal dance lessons, do an Internet search on "five rhythms," "free-form," or "expressive" dance in your area.
- Do the compassionate body scan (see page 133).
- If you decide to have that oh-so-compassionate glass of red wine to help you relax at the end of the day, drink a large glass of water as well so you don't become dehydrated. Or, if you want to cut down on alcohol, have some dark red juice (cranberry, pomegranate, or cherry) mixed with sparkling water in a wineglass. Often just the sight of dark red liquid in a wineglass will trigger a relaxation response.

## Self-Compassion and Forgiveness

Having compassion for others doesn't just involve being responsive to their suffering—it also involves forgiving those who have hurt us. Forgiveness happens when we stop holding a grudge and let go of our right to resentment for being mistreated. It means turning the other cheek— doing unto others as we *would have* others do unto us, not as they *did* do unto us. Forgiveness doesn't mean we stop protecting ourselves, of course, but it does mean we let go of tit-for-tat retaliation. This includes the emotional retaliation of anger and bitterness, which only hurts *ourselves* in the long run. Self-compassion makes it easier to forgive, partly because it gives us the ability to heal the emotional wounds caused by others. My colleagues and I conducted one study that directly examined the link between self-compassion and forgiveness. The propensity to forgive was assessed by agreement with statements such as "When someone disappoints me, I can eventually move past it" and disagreement with statements like "I continue to punish a person who has done something that I think is wrong." We found that self-compassionate people were significantly more likely to forgive others for their transgressions than those who lacked self-compassion.

One of the main ways that self-compassion translates into forgiveness is through the recognition of our common humanity. As discussed in chapter 4, when we see people as separate individuals who are in complete control of their thoughts and deeds, it's natural to blame those who hurt us, just as we blame ourselves when we screw up. But when we gain insight into interconnectedness, we see that innumerable factors continually influence who we are and what we do. We begin to see how impossible it is to completely blame any one individual for anything—ourselves included. Each conscious being rests at the nexus of a vast number of interwoven causes and conditions that influence their behavior. This insight is often the key that allows us to forgive ourselves and others, letting go of anger and resentment and engendering compassion for all.

## My Story: To Forgive Is Divine

I know that for me, forgiving myself for betraying and leaving my first husband and forgiving my father for leaving and neglecting me were closely interwoven. Before my first marriage fell apart, I had a tremendous amount of judgment and anger toward my father. I would roll my eyes whenever talking about him to close friends, making sarcastic comments about the casual way he abandoned me and my brother. "Free love, baby, no strings attached. That's the hippie way." But I had never directly let my father know how angry I was. Our relationship hung on such a tenuous thread that I felt it couldn't withstand the merest tug. On our very occasional visits, I typically put on my "sweet daughter" face to preserve what little sliver of a father-daughter relationship we had. I would then just criticize him behind his back as soon as he walked out the door. It wasn't a healthy dynamic, but it was all I could do to cope with my complicated feelings of hurt, anger, and rejection at the time.

And then I ended up leaving John for Peter. Not out of malice, not out of a lack of caring, but because part of me was desperately unhappy and wanted—needed—to break free. I ended up doing what I thought *I* would never do, hurting and abandoning someone I loved. After learning about self-compassion at my local meditation center, however, I started to gain insight into my behavior and the pain that drove it. I started to forgive myself for leaving John, just as I started to forgive Peter for *not* leaving his wife for me. My understanding of the heart, of the complications and limitations of being human, began to grow and mature. This had a paradoxical effect on my relationship with my father. I started to get even more angry at him.

A few months before I was to marry Rupert, I remember talking on the phone with my dad. Somehow I found the courage to bring up the truth of how hurt I was that he had left me as a child. The equanimity I had started to gain due to my meditation practice had given me courage. My father didn't take this newfound honesty well, however. He immediately started to get agitated and defensive. "It's just our karma, everything happens for a reason." "Screw karma!" I shouted as I hung up the phone on him, collapsing into tears.

Rupert tried to comfort me, but to no avail. I needed to fully experience my rage, anger, and hurt. Devastating feelings of abandonment and rejection welled up, threatening to destroy me (or so it felt at the time). I entered a very dark place, knowing that the time had come to fully acknowledge my feelings of pain and grief.

At the same time, I was also processing the grief and pain I had caused John. This came to a head after bumping into him at a party thrown by mutual friends. His look of withering reproach stopped me dead in my tracks. I quickly left the party, shame permeating my every pore. My first reaction was to meekly accept John's reaction as just deserts for my abominable behavior, and to become even more depressed. Luckily Rupert, who had been learning about self-compassion with me each week, was able to pull my head above water long enough for me to take a few deep breaths. He reminded me that one of the reasons I had married the wrong man was because of the insecurity created by my father's abandonment. I had just continued a cycle of bad decisions based on an intricate web of pain. He encouraged me to have compassion for my mistakes and to stop judging myself. I had done the best I could at the time.

This led me to think about what had driven my father's actions, and to be less judgmental and more forgiving toward *him* as well. My father was raised by incredibly cold and disconnected parents who were also rigid authoritarians. He never really felt loved, but instead always felt like a burden, a mouth to feed and not much more. His parents didn't even bother to attend his wedding to my mother, for instance, although they lived locally, because they felt too uncomfortable in social situations. His parents also had no idea how to handle conflict. After my grandmother got in a fight with her other son over some laundry, for example, they didn't speak again for thirty years. In terms of my grandparents' relationship with me, there was none. They never once visited me as a child after my father left, even though they lived less than an hour away. They just felt too awkward. To put it mildly, my father's parents were completely shut down.

But then I had to think about my grandfather's story. He came to the United States as an economic refugee from Greece at the turn of the twentieth century, traveling through Ellis Island with his parents. (My last name, Neff, is actually a shortened version of the Greek name Nefferados.) He was the eldest of eight brothers and sisters and excelled in the American academic system. He won prestigious prizes in both scholastics and sports, and when he graduated from high school, he had scholarship offers from a number of colleges. The American dream was about to come true. On the day of his high school graduation, however, his father left to go back home to Greece, telling my grandfather that since he was an adult now, he must take on the responsibility of caring for his mother and seven brothers and sisters. He was forced to abandon his dreams of college, of achieving a better life, and instead got a job at a gas station to support his family. He worked in a gas station his whole life, even though he eventually owned the station himself. My grandfather never got over this disappointment, and it destroyed him emotionally.

And so it goes. Pain and dysfunction get passed down from generation to generation. A mixture of genetic inheritance and environmental circumstance ensures that our lives unfold according to a complex web of conditions that is infinitely larger than ourselves. The only way to stop the vicious cycle of reacting to pain by causing more pain is to step out of the system. We need to let our hearts fill with compassion, and forgive ourselves and others.

This was, in fact, what I was finally able to do with my father. After he got over the shock of my anger, and was able to regroup, we actually started to have an honest relationship with each other for the first time ever. A year or two after that angry phone call, during one of our rare visits, my father gave me a heartfelt apology. His love for me had never wavered, he assured me, but he just wasn't capable of giving me what I needed. When he realized that my mother wasn't the right woman for him, and that he had got himself stuck in a life that was making him deeply unhappy, he couldn't deal with it maturely. He had never had a good example of how to talk through a problem, let alone how to make compromises that balanced his own needs with those of others. He saw himself getting trapped into a life he didn't want, just as his father had gotten trapped into a life he didn't want, and he bolted. He didn't present this as an excuse for his behavior, just as an explanation. I could clearly see how grieved he was about the deep pain he had caused me. Luckily by that point I had already done a lot of forgiving of myself and my father (and his father and *his* father), as I had delved more deeply into the practice of compassion. What was important was that the chain had been broken, and that we were now ready to start relating to each other in a new way.

It's important to remember that forgiveness doesn't mean condoning bad behavior, or that we need to interact with people who have hurt us. Discriminating wisdom clearly sees when an action is harmful or maladaptive, and when we need to protect ourselves from those with bad intentions. However, it also understands that all people are imperfect, that we all make mistakes. It understands that people often act out of ignorance, immaturity, fear, or irrational impulse, and that we shouldn't judge people for their actions as if they had full conscious control over them. And even in those cases where people are cognizant of the harm they are causing, the question still needs to be asked—what happened to make them lose touch with their hearts? What wound occurred to lead to such cold and callous behavior? What's *their* story?

Being human involves doing wrong at times. This means that to judge one person is to judge all the world. But to forgive one person is to forgive all the world—ourselves included.

## Exercise Two

### *Forgiving Someone Who Has Hurt Us*

Think of someone you've harbored anger and resentment toward for a long while, and whom you now want to forgive. If you don't feel ready to forgive yet, don't. Forgiveness comes in its own time and shouldn't be rushed. But when you are ready, one of the best ways to forgive someone is to recognize the causes and conditions leading the person to act as they did. Our thoughts, emotions, and behaviors are the product of innumerable interconnected factors, many of which are outside of our control. Understanding interconnectedness can therefore help facilitate the process of forgiveness.

1. When considering the person's harmful actions, see if you can identify any precipitating factors or events. Was the person feeling fear, confusion, lust, anger, or other powerful emotions? Was the person having a stressful life experience, like financial insecurity or some other setback? What demons might this person have been dealing with?

2. Now consider why the person didn't stop themselves anyway. Clearly, the factors necessary to enable self-control (emotional maturity, empathy, ability to delay gratification, etc.) weren't present. Why not? Did the person have poor role models growing up, so that he or she never developed these skills?

3. If it comes down to the fact that this person was just plain mean or selfish—think about what could have created this personality type. Insecure attachment, social isolation, life history, genetically inherited traits?

4. Once you have a better understanding of the causes and conditions leading this person to act as he or she did,

see if it's a bit easier to let go of your anger and resentment. This was a limited, fallible human being, and humans sometimes act in ways they shouldn't. Can you forgive this person? Doing so doesn't necessarily mean you should interact with this person again. It may not be wise. But by freeing yourself from the corrosive effects of anger and blame, you'll help create more peace and contentment in your own mind.

## Cultivating Loving-Kindness

One of the wonderful things about self-compassion is that it allows you to open your heart—and once it's open, it's open. Compassion engages our capacity for love, wisdom, and generosity. It's a beautiful mental and emotional state that is boundless, directionless. By being more understanding and accepting toward ourselves, we can also be more understanding and accepting toward others. By honoring the limitations of our own human imperfection, we can be more forgiving of others' mistakes. By soothing and comforting ourselves when feelings of insecurity arise, we provide ourselves with the sense of safety needed to explore the emotionally complex world inhabited by other people.

One of the traditional Buddhist practices designed to develop goodwill toward ourselves and others is called "loving-kindness meditation." In this practice, phrases that invoke benevolent feelings are repeated silently and are aimed at various targets. Traditionally, the phrases are first directed toward oneself, and the goal is to *personally experience* the loving-kindness being generated. Different versions of the phrases are used, but one set is as follows: *May I be safe, May I be peaceful, May I be healthy, May I live with ease.* The phrases are then directed to a mentor/benefactor, to a dear friend, to a neutral person, to a mildly difficult person, and finally to all conscious beings: *May you be safe, May you be peaceful, May you be healthy, May you live with ease.*

When loving-kindness practice was first brought to the West, teachers often found that people had a hard time generating feelings of loving-kindness for themselves given our culture's emphasis on self-criticism. For this reason, many now switch the order of targets so that one first directs the loving-kindness phrases toward a mentor or benefactor. The idea is to choose someone with whom we have an unconditionally positive relationship, so that feelings of loving-kindness are easy to access. (This someone might even be a beloved pet.) Only then are the phrases directed toward oneself, after the loving-kindness juices have started flowing.

Note that traditional loving-kindness phrases are designed to cultivate feelings of goodwill, not necessarily compassion. Feelings of goodwill are relevant in all situations, happy or otherwise, whereas compassion only arises in response to suffering. To target the feeling of compassion more directly, Chris Germer and I give people a variant of the traditional loving-kindness phrases in our Mindful Self-Compassion workshops. They're designed to help people generate greater self-compassion when they are experiencing feelings of personal inadequacy: *May I be safe, May I be peaceful, May I be kind to myself, May I accept myself as I am.* Or if the suffering stems from external circumstances, the last phrase can be changed to *May I accept my life as it is.* We find that the self-compassion variant of the traditional loving-kindness phrases tends to be more powerful when people are struggling and in need of compassionate care.

There is no one "right" way to do loving-kindness practice. Many people change the wording of the phrases to feel more natural. For instance, some people don't like saying "May I" at the beginning of each phrase. It feels too much like prayer, or like asking permission from an authority figure ("May I go to the bathroom please, Mrs. Smith?"). Alternatives are "I'd like," "I hope," or "I want." Sometimes, people want the phrases to sound more realistic by adding "as possible" to the end. For example, *May I be as safe as possible.*

Finally, it's important to realize that loving-kindness practice works on the level of intention. We nourish the desire for health and happiness—for ourselves and others—as a way to open our hearts. This is not an exercise in wishful thinking, nor are we ignoring the reality that suffering exists. Rather, the idea is that by cultivating the intention for ourselves and others to experience well-being, corresponding feelings of love, concern, and compassion will eventually arise. This in turn translates into more concrete acts of kindness and care.

## Exercise Three

### *Directing Loving-Kindness Toward Our Suffering*

(Also available as a guided meditation in MP3 format at www.self-compassion.org)

If you're grappling with self-judgment, or if you find yourself in the midst of difficult or stressful times, see if you can take fifteen to twenty minutes out of your day to cultivate feelings of loving-kindness and compassion for yourself. To start the practice, sit in a quiet, comfortable place where you won't be disturbed, or else take a solitary walk in a quiet spot. Take a few deep breaths to settle into your body and the present moment. You are right here, right now.

- First, gently get in touch with the source of your suffering. Are you feeling scared, lonely, angry, worthless, frustrated? See if you can just be with the emotions as they are, without doing too much thinking about the story line driving the emotions (what you did, what he didn't do, etc.). Whatever you are feeling is okay. All visitors are welcome. No need to cling to anything or to push it away.

- Now see if you can sense the emotions in your body. Let's say you feel sad. What does sadness feel like? Is there dullness, a pulling sensation at the corner of your eyes, tenseness between your eyebrows, and so on? By locating your emotions in your body, it's easier to feel them without getting lost in thought, and instead be with your present moment experience as it is.
- Now place your hand on your heart, and set your intention to offer yourself kindness, understanding, and compassion for the suffering you're experiencing right now. Remember that what you're feeling is an integral part of the human experience. You are not alone in your suffering.
- Now repeat the following phrases to yourself, softly and gently:

> *May I be safe.*
> *May I be peaceful.*
> *May I be kind to myself.*
> *May I accept myself as I am.*

Or if it feels more appropriate, change the last phrase to:

> *May I accept my life as it is.*

- Keep repeating the phrases, refreshing their emotional content by either getting in touch with the painful emotions in your body, or else feeling the gentle and comforting pressure of your hand on your heart.
- When you notice that your mind has wandered, return to the phrases, or to the experience of your emotions in your body, or to the feeling of your hand on your heart. And start again.

- If you are ever overwhelmed with emotion, you can always return to your breathing as a way of soothing and calming yourself. Then, when you're comfortable, return to the phrases.
- Finally, take a few breaths and just be still for a few moments. If the feeling of compassion is arising for you, allow yourself to savor this sweet feeling. If few or no feelings of compassion are arising, this is the equally beautiful truth of the present moment. Allow yourself to savor your goodwill and intention to care for yourself. This is what matters most.
- When you're ready, slowly resume your normal activities, knowing that you can return to the phrases anytime you wish.

A recent study by Richie Davidson and colleagues confirms the power of loving-kindness. Researchers trained a group of people to do loving-kindness meditation for thirty minutes a day for two weeks. As a point of comparison, they trained another group of people to think more constructively about difficult situations in their lives. In other words, they taught one group to change their hearts, the other to change their heads. Only the loving-kindness group showed significant increases in self-compassion. They also did brain scans of study participants while showing them images of suffering, such as a child with an eye tumor. Those trained in loving-kindness meditation felt significantly more empathy (as evidenced by increased activity in the insula) than those trained merely to change their thinking patterns. Moreover, the larger the increases in self-compassion, the higher the level of insula activation, supporting the idea that self-compassion increases one's capacity for perspective taking. At the end of the experiment, researchers asked participants if they wanted to donate some of their $165 honorarium to a charitable cause or keep the money for themselves. Those in the loving-kindness group donated more money. Even a brief training period in loving-kindness meditation, therefore, can lead to increases in compassion for self and others, as well as demonstrable acts of care and generosity.

The wonderful thing about loving-kindness practice is that it does not necessarily have to be done on the meditation cushion. We can generate feelings of kindness and compassion toward ourselves and others while driving to work, shopping at the grocery store, or waiting in the dentist's office. What's happening is that we are *training our brains* to react to suffering in a caring manner. By focusing on our deepest desire—for all beings to be happy, peaceful, and healthy—we can actually improve our lives and those of others. The Bible teaches that what you sow, so shall you reap. By planting seeds of loving-kindness into our hearts and minds, we can transform our own mental and emotional landscape into something beautiful beyond measure.

There is a famous story of a Tibetan monk held in jail for years by Chinese prison guards, who later made it to India and had an audience with the Dalai Lama. When asked about his time in the prison, the monk said he faced danger a few times. "What danger?" the Dalai Lama asked. "Of losing compassion toward the Chinese," the monk replied. From a Buddhist perspective, having compassion toward those who have hurt us allows us to have peace of mind even in the most hostile surroundings, which in turn prevents that hurt from destroying us. Compassion toward others is really a gift for ourselves, because it nourishes us with benevolent feelings and allows us to feel more secure by recognizing our inherent interconnectedness. With the equanimity of an open heart, the slings and arrows of our difficult and frustrating lives find less purchase, and suffering becomes a doorway into love.

*Chapter Ten*

# SELF-COMPASSIONATE PARENTING

*For only as we ourselves, as adults, actually move and have our being in the state of love, can we be appropriate models and guides for our children. What we are teaches the child far more than what we say, so we must be what we want our children to become.*

—Joseph Chilton Pearce, introduction to *Teaching Children to Love* by Doc Lew Childre

SELF-COMPASSION IS ESSENTIAL FOR GOOD PARENTING. BY TEACHING our children to have self-compassion, we can help them deal with the inevitable pain and imperfection of life. By being compassionate to ourselves, we can better handle the frustrations and difficulties of parenting, so that the world's toughest profession—and let's face it, parenting *is* a profession, just an unpaid one—isn't quite so tough.

## Compassion for Our Imperfect Parenting

Carol was running late. The babysitter was arriving soon to watch her two kids while she went out to a concert with some friends. She put some spaghetti in the pot to boil while she styled her hair and put on makeup. When she returned to the kitchen, she realized the timer had been going off for almost ten minutes. "Mom, I'm starving!" her young son complained. "When will dinner be ready?" The overcooked spaghetti, once drained, was the consistency of mushy mashed potatoes. She poured on extra sauce hoping her kids wouldn't notice, but that was like hoping they wouldn't notice if she served oatmeal rather than Cap'n Crunch for breakfast. "Disgusting!" her eldest complained, frowning and turning up her nose. "You expect us to eat this? Why can't you make nice food like Jan does?" This was an especially spiteful comment. Jan was her ex-husband's new wife, who—among her many other talents—was a gourmet chef.

Carol's first instinct was to accept the blow. To feel horrible for never getting anything right, for being an inadequate mother, for losing her husband to a superior woman. But luckily she caught herself in time. Carol had been trying to be kinder to herself lately and realized that this was a perfect opportunity to be more self-compassionate. She reminded herself that motherhood involved juggling multiple balls in the air, and it was inevitable that one would occasionally drop. And overcooking spaghetti was not exactly a sign of a fatally flawed character. "I'm sorry I ruined dinner, but it's not the end of the world. How about I order in some pizza?" Needless to say her kids were in favor of this idea. She even overheard her daughter whisper to her son, "Cool—Jan never lets us have pizza!" As writer Peter de Vries once commented, "There are times when parenthood seems nothing more than feeding the hand that bites you."

Of course, we don't always handle difficult situations with our children in an ideal way. Our lovable little darlings can drive us absolutely batty, and there's no parent on the planet who hasn't lost it occasionally. We snap at our kids when they annoy us, ignore them when they try to get our attention, or yell at them when we're angry. Everyone gets it wrong at one time or another. When we have compassion for this fact, however, we can more easily admit our imperfections as parents and apologize for our behavior. This not only helps our children feel loved and cared for, it also lets them know that even Mommy and Daddy are fallible human beings who sometimes make mistakes—and that mistakes aren't the end of the world.

Although it's important to apologize to our children when we're out of line, it's equally important not to be overly critical of ourselves either. *Especially* in front of our children. "I forgot to get gas even though the car's almost on empty! How stupid of me! I'm so irresponsible!" This communicates the idea that self-criticism is a valued and appropriate response when we fall short of our ideals. But do you really want your children to suffer at the hands of self-judgment the way you have? This is something parents often overlook. Perhaps you're very careful to be nurturing and supportive toward your children when they've taken a misstep. But if you tear yourself to shreds whenever *you* mess up, you'll send them the wrong message. If, however, you clearly but compassionately acknowledge your limitations in front of your children, you'll provide a much better example. "How annoying! I forgot to fill up the car, and I'm almost on empty. I've been pretty busy at work lately, so I guess it's not surprising that it slipped my mind. I probably have enough gas to get to the station regardless." Modeling self-compassion in front of your children is one of the most powerful ways to help them develop this skill for themselves.

## Exercise One

### *Having Compassion for Our Mistakes as Parents*

At the end of each day, think about any mistakes you made as a parent. Anything you wish you had (or hadn't) done. Try to be as honest as possible, knowing that it's okay to be human and imperfect. Try to be as kind and understanding toward yourself as you would be to a good friend in a similar situation.

Then, think about whether there is anything you can do to help repair the situation. Offer your kids an apology? Promise you'll make it up to them (and really do so)? By modeling the process of making then repairing mistakes, you'll teach your children an invaluable lesson.

Next, try to determine if any difficult emotions underlie your behavior, such as stress, frustration, exhaustion. If so, give yourself compassion for your emotional pain. It's hard to be a parent! Do you think you need to make any changes to help ease your stress, like taking more time for yourself?

Decide on a couple of the self-care activities suggested in the first exercise of chapter 9 (or else make up some of your own), then *really do them*! It's easy as a parent to say "Yeah, I should take the time to do that for myself" while never actually getting around to it. Yes, you're pressed for time, but you'll actually be a more effective and supportive parent by taking your own needs more seriously. It's a win-win situation all around.

## Correcting Your Child While Encouraging Self-Compassion

Many parents wonder how to go about disciplining their children when they step out of line, while at the same time helping them to be more self-compassionate. First and foremost, it's crucial that you don't harshly criticize children or make them feel ashamed for not living up to your expectations. (Besides, it might backfire. As actor Jack Nicholson once commented, "My mother never saw the irony in calling me a son of a bitch.") Our research shows that continual parental criticism can cause some serious problems: children of critical parents are more likely to lack self-compassion and suffer from anxiety and depression in adulthood. As discussed in chapter 2, children often internalize a parent's critical voice, and then carry it with them throughout their lives. Although no parent wants his or her child to suffer, many believe that discipline must be hard-hitting in order to work.

Although it's true that laissez-faire parenting in which children are never reprimanded can hinder a child's growth and development, you *can* set clear boundaries and correct problem behaviors in a kind, compassionate way. This will let children understand why it's important for them to change their ways without making them feel bad about themselves because they messed up.

One key to compassionately responding to our children's misdeeds is to focus on their actual behavior, rather than on their general character. You want to emphasize that we are not defined by our failures and shortcomings but are instead all of us works in progress, in a continual state of learning. It's also important to validate the emotions underlying your child's misbehavior before trying to correct it. Let's say your son Neil tells his younger sister Mary to "shut up" while he's playing his favorite video game. Instead of snapping "You are so rude, Neil! Why can't you be nicer to Mary?," you can try saying "I realize you were irritated by having your game interrupted but you hurt Mary's feelings when you told her to shut up." Or let's say your daughter leaves a honey jar open on the kitchen counter after she takes a call from a friend. Instead of exclaiming "You're such a slob!," you can say something like "I know you were distracted by your phone call, but we can't have bugs crawling everywhere." A little humor might work even better here— "Do you really want our kitchen to look like a scene from *Attack of the Killer Ants*?" If children feel understood rather than attacked, they'll be much more likely to listen to you.

The main thing is to convey to your children that it's okay to make mistakes, and that imperfection is part of life. Statements like "it's only human," "it's only natural to get frustrated," and so on, are good ways to provide this validation.

It's not just what you say that matters, however. Equally important is your tone of voice. Even as preverbal infants, we unconsciously register the emotional meaning conveyed by parents' tone of voice— loving, fearful, angry, and so on. If your tone conveys negative judgment even though your words are neutral, your child is still likely to feel inadequate and ashamed. This may then trigger an angry or defensive reaction. Who wants to feel bad about themselves when it's so much easier to blame someone else? If you make it safe for your child to take personal responsibility for his actions by using compassionate language combined with a kind and caring tone, however, he will find it much easier to acknowledge his problem behavior and work on changing it.

One thing that's also worth considering before correcting your child is whether or not your own reactions are at all ego defensive. Are you identifying with your child, so that you feel his or her subpar behavior reflects poorly on you? When your daughter is fidgeting and can't sit still in a restaurant, is the problem really the fidgeting, or other people's judgments that you must be a bad parent because your child isn't well behaved? Unless you can admit this to yourself, and give yourself compassion for this very human reaction, you're likely to handle the situation poorly. When you are compassionate toward yourself, however, you'll be in a better position to respond compassionately to your child.

## Parenting Young Children

Raising infants and toddlers, with their constant need for supervision, picky food habits, tantrums, not to mention dirty diapers, has to be one of the most challenging jobs around. As humorist Erma Bombeck commented, "When my kids become wild and unruly, I use a nice, safe playpen. When they're finished, I climb out." Parents of young children need all the help they can get. Luckily, when you give yourself compassion, help is always at hand.

Dr. Rebecca Coleman, a clinical psychologist in Australia, has developed a program that teaches mindfulness and self-compassion skills to parents of children under five. The program is called MAP, which stands for Mindful Awareness Parenting. The goal of the program is to help parents improve their ability to make wise decisions in difficult parenting situations. In other words, how to keep sane when little Johnny has just poured a whole bottle of dishwashing soap into the bath you're running, and little Suzy is tugging on your leg and whining for you to braid her hair while you're trying to clean up the mess.

MAP promotes parental sensitivity by teaching parents to have empathy for their kids, increasing their ability to be aware of and nurture their children's relationship needs. Sometimes when children act in difficult or tiresome ways, they are actually sending the message that they need their parents' emotional support. It may not be attention that children are seeking but connection. As discussed in chapter 3, children are physiologically designed to form close attachment bonds with their parents, using them as a secure base from which to explore their world. When children feel frightened or are unsure of themselves, they naturally turn to parents as their primary source of reassurance and comfort. Once they feel safe, they can then engage in the important process of play, discovery, and learning.

Coleman points out that one of the key ways that parents help their children feel safe is through the process of "affective attunement," which involves matching or mirroring the emotion of the child. When a child is upset, parents mirror their child's emotions by making sad noises and expressions, but then they alter their child's emotions by adopting a more soothing face and tone. For instance, a mother may rock her infant and smile gently when he cries, softly repeating "It's okay darling, it's okay." Eventually the child is reassured and calms down. Parents tend to do this instinctively and are not consciously aware that they're regulating their child's emotions.

If a mother with a crying infant feels overwhelmed by her *own* emotions, however—"why can't the damn kid shut up, he's driving me crazy!"—she won't be able to help her son calm down. Instead, she'll just make him more upset, as the child mirrors his parent's agitation. When parents respond to their own frustration with self-compassion, however, they're able to quiet their own turbulent emotions and are therefore in a better position to then help their child become calm and peaceful as well.

Consider a situation that one of my graduate students, Pittman, encountered several months ago. He and his wife, Merilee, recently had a baby girl, and as a result their three-year-old son, Finn, started displaying some "challenging behaviors." One day when returning home from an errand, Pittman found his supposedly toilet-trained son peeing on the living-room wall. When confronted about this, Finn just turned toward his dad, flashed an evil grin, and said, "I hate you."

Thank God for Pittman's self-compassion practice! Though anyone would have understood if he had lost it, he managed to stay centered, take a few deep breaths, and give himself compassion for how difficult and challenging the moment was. This helped him to refocus and remember that—outward signs to the contrary—Finn was not simply being naughty. He was actually suffering from the very human emotion of jealousy, and at three was ill equipped to deal with it effectively. Instead of getting angry at Finn, therefore, he sat down and put his arm around his shoulder. First, he acknowledged Finn's feelings of frustration at the change in the household routine. "I know this is hard for you right now because your baby sister is taking up so much of our attention. But your mom and I love you more than ever . . ." Finn's unhappy mood started to lift almost instantly, as did Pittman's. He even started to see the humor of the situation, knowing he'd have a good story to dine out on for years. The more Finn feels reassured of his parents' love and support as he adjusts to the new member of his family—*especially* when he acts out—the more he'll realize that his parents' love is unshakable (even though their walls may be a little stained).

## Exercise Two

### *Taking a "Time-In" with Your Child*

This excercise is adapted from Dr. Rebecca Coleman's MAP protocol (for more information, go to www.maplinc.com.au).

Young children often express "big feelings" (i.e., crying, tantrums) when they feel misunderstood, ignored, or limited by a parent saying no. When your child is expressing big feelings or is out of control, you can take a "time-in" to help her get back on track. While your child's behavior may look like something that is being done on purpose, it is often really an issue of needing to reconnect and handle overwhelming emotions in a safe way. Your child may need your help to do this.

Before beginning a time-in, make sure that you are calm enough to be sensitive to your child's needs and to help her feel secure. If you need to soothe your own emotions first, try sending yourself compassion for your difficult emotions, or practice some mindful breathing. You may need to tell your child that you need ten seconds of private time while you calm yourself down—just make sure you're back when you said you'd be.

- Choose a specific time-in spot. It's best if this is a neutral place, for example, a chair or a cushion that can be moved so as to not disturb other family members.
- The time-in place is where you and your child can sit together and watch feelings begin to change.
- Invite your child to the time-in place. (If he is emotionally out of control and presents a danger to others, he may need help getting there.)
- Maintain a firm, reassuring, and kind tone of voice.
- Watch your child closely. Observe her behavior. Try to guess the meaning and feelings behind her behavior. What's really happening?
- Time-in allows your child's feelings to "be felt" and accepted. It shows your child that you are willing to help him and that your love means you will be welcoming and accepting of his emotions—even difficult ones.
- Stay in charge in a sympathetic and connected way. Stay present and sensitive. This has a calming effect on young children.
- It may take a while for your child to calm down if she is overwhelmed by her emotions.
- When your child is calm enough, help her to describe her feelings. You might say: "You look like you are struggling with this . . ." or "This looks hard for you; are you angry/afraid/sad?"
- Wait for the answer. Listen well. Acknowledge and accept the answer (or lack of answer).

- Then talk about *your* feelings. Use sentences like: "When you did _____ , I felt _____ (name the emotion) _____ arising in me." Don't expect an apology, just communicate your feelings with a matter-of-fact, nonblaming tone.
- When your child is connected and calm enough, help him find another activity to change the mood, or simply go ahead with your plans for the day as normal (bedtime, preschool, eating a meal, etc.).

## Parenting Adolescents

Although all children benefit from having self-compassion, it's an especially important skill to teach in the teen years. One of the cognitive advances of adolescence is increased perspective-taking ability, meaning teens are better able to see themselves from the viewpoint of others. This ability means that adolescence is often a time of intense self-evaluation and social comparison. Adolescents ask themselves "What do other people think of me?" or "Am I as good as everyone else?" This process occurs as teens attempt to establish their identity and place in the social hierarchy. The intense pressures faced by most adolescents—stress over academic performance, the need to "fit in" with the right peer crowd, concerns with sexual attractiveness—means that the self-evaluations of teens are often unfavorable.

To make things worse, the introspection of the teen years often leads to what is called "the personal fable," a cognitive fallacy leading adolescents to believe that their experiences are unique and that others cannot possibly understand what they are going through. Remember the first time you fell in love? I bet you couldn't possibly imagine that your parents had ever felt anything remotely similar. Adolescents have a hard time understanding the shared human experience, because they haven't yet had enough close relationships to realize that their own thoughts and feelings aren't in fact unique. They also tend to overestimate how much they know and how little others know because, well, *what* they know is *all* they know. As Mark Twain said, "When I was fourteen, my father was so stupid that I could hardly stand to be around the old man. When I turned twenty-one, I was simply amazed at what this elderly gentleman had learned in only seven short years." Our research shows that teens who are under the sway of the personal fable tend to be less self-compassionate, because they don't recognize that their difficulties and failings are merely a normal part of what it means to be human.

For all these reasons, teaching teens about self-compassion can be immensely valuable. Of course, teens are sometimes resistant to the idea of self-compassion at first given that it sounds a bit hearts and flowers-y. Not cool when your favorite band is Napalm Ghost Slayer. However, when you explain that self-compassion is not the same as complaining, self-pity, or self-indulgence, most teens become much more open to the concept. (After all, the lead singer of Napalm Ghost Slayer had to learn self-compassion when he went into rehab, right?) It can also be useful to talk about the difference between self-esteem and self-compassion. Given teens' daily experience with the horrors of school lunchroom dynamics, they can readily grasp the problem with striving to feel special and above average all the time. By explaining that self-compassion is a way to feel good about yourself that doesn't require feeling superior to others, you can help teens more easily understand why self-compassion is a healthier way to relate to themselves.

## My Story: Parenting Rowan

While Rupert and I certainly suffered in the early years of Rowan's autism, our commitment to self-compassion made a huge difference. First, we helped each other to be self-compassionate toward all the mistakes we made as parents, and there were many. When I would snap in anger at Rowan after a particularly frustrating day, for instance, and feel horribly guilty as a result, Rupert would help me remember that I couldn't be expected to deal with things perfectly all the time. I could then more easily get over my frustration, apologize and comfort Rowan if he was still upset, and start over.

Perhaps most important, Rupert and I made sure that we didn't get so lost in our roles as caregivers that we stopped meeting our own needs. We realized that we both required regular time off from being a parent of a child with autism. Unfortunately, both our parents lived out of town. and we couldn't find a babysitter who could handle Rowan's tantrums and incontinence, so we made a policy of babysitting for each other. One night a week I was free to do whatever I wanted, go to a meditation or dance class, have a drink with friends, or see a music show; and one night a week, Rupert did the same. We made sure we were giving attention to our own needs, which helped us stay refreshed and relaxed when dealing with the challenges of parenting Rowan and supporting each other.

Now that Rowan is getting older (he's eight at the time of writing), I'm starting to model the process of self-compassion for him, and he's slowly taking it on board. One feature of autism is "echolalia," which refers to the tendency to directly repeat phrases that others say. I've treated Rowan's echolalia as an opportunity to shape his internal dialogue, so the words he uses when he becomes upset are soothing, self-compassionate ones. Autistic children have an extremely hard time dealing with frustration. If Rowan spills a glass of water on his clothes, for instance, it can cause a level of suffering and anxiety that's way out of proportion to the actual incident. And once that distress train gets rolling, it's hard to stop.

In such situations, I try to model how to respond in an accepting, compassionate way. "Poor darling, you spilled the water and got all wet. It's okay to be upset and frustrated. This is really hard for you right now, isn't it?" This helps him learn to accept and validate his emotions in the present moment. Then I try to model steps to help him move on emotionally in the next moment, rather than continuing to obsess about what went wrong. "I know you're feeling bad, but we've changed your clothes and everything is okay now. There's really no need for you to cry about it anymore, and I'm worried that you're making yourself unhappy. Do you want to be sad or do you want to be happy?"

Sometimes when I ask this, Rowan says he wants to be sad, in which case I hold and comfort him while he feels his sadness. "These things happen, it's okay to be upset." Sometimes, however, he says, "I want to be happy." In this case, I try to help him find things to be happy about. "Can you tell me something that's good right now? Like the fact that we're together, or that you have two cool leopard geckos called Gary I and Gary II?"

Although he still has trouble getting beyond his distressed moods, a compassionate approach does seem to help them pass more quickly. I also know that he's begun to take this way of talking to himself on board. The other day he got upset because his DVD was stuck, for instance, and I overheard him say, "It's okay. Things break sometimes."

The time I really knew that he had "gotten it," however, was when we went to the zoo together. I had had several frustrating experiences that morning (traffic, trouble parking, etc.) and was in a foul mood. After a few minutes of huffing and stamping at the African wildlife exhibit (me, not the wildebeests), Rowan turned and said, "It's okay, Mommy. Do you want to be sad or happy?" And I thought *I* was supposed to be the wise, mature grown-up! Though taken aback at first, I realized he was right! It was a beautiful day, and here I was being comforted and helped by my beloved son. The message of self-compassion had come full circle.

## Chapter Eleven

# LOVE AND SEX

*Love is fed by the imagination, by which we become wiser than we know, better than we feel, nobler than we are: by which we can see Life as a whole: by which, and by which alone, we can understand others in their real as in their ideal relations.*
—OSCAR WILDE, *De Profundis*

SELF-COMPASSION NOT ONLY HELPS US BE BETTER PARENTS AND caregivers, it also enhances our love and sex lives. When we let go of egoistic striving—ending our obsession with evaluating ourselves positively—our love and desire for others only intensifies. By embracing life as it is, allowing the life force to flow through us freely, our passion can reach new, more wonderful heights.

## Love and Romance

One of the challenges of finding a romantic relationship that meets our deepest needs is just that—our reliance on a relationship to meet our deepest needs. The reason it's so blissful to fall in love is partly because it allows us to feel truly valued, accepted, and understood by another. Our partner loves us warts and all, which means that maybe our warts aren't so bad. And of course there is much truth to this. It's a wonderful gift to see one's own beauty reflected in the eyes of another. But if we exclusively rely on our partner's good opinion of us to feel okay about ourselves, some time or another we're going to get a rude awakening. Eventually the stardust starts to thin in even the best of romances, and not only are our partners going to see things about us they don't like— they're going to let us know it. On our wedding day, Rupert's father told us "Don't worry, the first forty years of marriage are tricky, but after that it's plain sailing." Okay, he was exaggerating for comedic effect, but there's no denying that relationships are difficult.

We can't always rely on our partners to make us feel good about ourselves because at the end of the day, for acceptance to truly penetrate our hearts, it has to come from within. Although feeling loved and accepted by our partner certainly helps, it's too easy to dismiss the approval of others as misplaced "niceness." Yes, my partner loves me, you might say to yourself, but he doesn't see the *real* me. He doesn't hear the nasty, petty thoughts that constantly go on inside my head. If he saw the real me, he wouldn't think I was so great anymore.

I had a colleague named Diane who suffered greatly from this pattern. Her live-in boyfriend, Eric, thought the world of her, and in many ways Eric's love and support was what kept her going. But Diane thought Eric's good opinion of her was mainly because he didn't *really* know her. She constantly judged and criticized herself and assumed that if she revealed her true self to Eric, he would judge her too. The thing Diane disliked about herself the most was that she had a strong tendency to be controlling and just couldn't seem to loosen up.

Diane adored Eric, and she tried to appear as relaxed as possible around him because she didn't want him to realize she was actually an "anal-retentive tyrant," as she put it. Eric was a laid-back guy, which is one of the things Diane loved about him. The irony, of course, was that Eric's relaxed nature was constantly pushing Diane's desire-for-control buttons. He was always forgetting to do small things like stopping by the grocery store to pick up the quart of milk she asked for, or closing the toilet seat lid after going to the bathroom, or mowing the lawn before it started to resemble a tropical jungle. Eric was a dreamer whose behavior tended toward the scattered and distracted, and this drove her absolutely crazy.

After about two years of living together, Diane and Eric were arguing more and more often. Instead of just being annoyed at Eric's forgetfulness, she was becoming increasingly angry and mean toward him. She started to call him names like irresponsible, lazy, and immature. If Eric hadn't been so in love, he probably would have gotten fed up with the constant criticism and left. Instead, he wanted to understand what was going on.

After many long conversations, it soon became clear that Diane's desire to control really stemmed from fear. Shortly after she got her driver's license at age sixteen, Diane was driving some friends to the beach, overcorrected on a curve, and flipped the car three times. One of her best friends almost died. She was so freaked out that she wanted to make sure nothing bad would ever happen again. By attempting to control everything in her life, Diane felt safer, as if she could counter the unpredictability of existence. Instead of having compassion for her controlling tendencies, however, her first instinct was either to criticize herself for being so rigid, or else criticize Eric for being so careless—often both.

Once Eric understood what was causing her behavior, he was able to help her deal with her emotions more productively. Eric had dabbled in Buddhism and other Eastern traditions and understood the value of self-compassion. He realized that this was what Diane needed most. Whenever he saw Diane getting stressed or angry, therefore, even when she was attacking him with a barrage of criticism, he would remind her to get in touch with the feelings underlying her reaction. "Are you upset because you feel afraid and out of control? Why don't you take a moment to give yourself some compassion, *then* we can talk about what happened."

While this did feel odd at first, Diane started to practice being self-compassionate more and more, using her angry feelings as a reminder that she needed to be kind, gentle, and understanding with herself. Whenever she felt the desire to control rise up, she would comfort herself with caring, soothing words. "I know you feel this way because you were so frightened when your best friend almost died. This situation is triggering your fear, which is understandable. This is really hard for you right now." As soon as she changed her attitude toward herself, she found that her feelings of agitation would start to quiet. She would become more trusting and relaxed.

After a few months of this new pattern, Diane and Eric were arguing much less often. Diane finally allowed herself to realize that Eric *did* love the real her, and that she was worthy of his love. Eric, for his part, started to be a little more responsible—he didn't want to cause Diane any unnecessary pain. While they're still a work in progress, their relationship is better than it's ever been. They've even broached the subject of getting married at some point (though if they do, they'll definitely leave the wedding arrangements up to Diane!).

## Exercise One

### *Identifying Your Relationship Patterns*

Think about your current or most recent romantic relationship. What are your strongest emotional buttons? Do you get hurt easily, immediately jumping to the conclusion your partner doesn't care? Do you get anxious, assuming your partner will leave? Almost all people have core issues that cause them to overreact in relationships. It's as if a whole boatload of extra "stuff" gets added on to what our partner says or does, causing things to quickly spiral out of control. Our patterns are scars, vestiges from previous relationships gone wrong. Although a loving, supportive partner can help us heal these patterns, the most direct source of healing comes from within.

The next time a button gets pushed in your relationship, try to get clarity about what is actually happening. Rather than immediately blaming your partner for how you feel, try to assess the extent to which it's just your old pattern reasserting itself, and take the opportunity to give yourself compassion. If you feel hurt, for example, try to become mindful of this feeling, fully accepting your overreaction. Actively focus on soothing and calming your pain with self-kindness, recognizing that all humans have emotional wounds of one sort or another. (Your self-compassion mantra might come in handy here.)

Rather than relying on your partner to give you exactly what you need, try meeting your own needs first. Identify what you're craving (validation, care, support, etc.) and see if self-compassion can help give it to you. This will help take the pressure off your partner to be a mind reader and react in the exact manner you want. As you learn to rely more on self-compassion to deal with your patterns when they arise, you'll eventually find that they have less hold over you. Wounds do heal, as long as they are given the care and attention they need.

## Relationship Dynamics

Research psychologist John Gottman is one of the world's leading experts on understanding what makes a romantic relationship work. He claims he can tell whether or not a couple is going to split up with 91 percent accuracy based on a brief observation of how they interact in conflict situations. They key is not *whether* a couple has conflicts (show me the couple who doesn't), but *how* they have conflicts. There are four main problem behaviors in conflicts that typically indicate a doomed relationship—what Gottman calls the "four horsemen of the apocalypse." They are, in order of importance: criticism, contempt, defensiveness, and stonewalling. If people harshly criticize their partners while fighting, show disgust or contempt (eye rolling, sarcasm, etc.), are overly defensive and blame problems on their partners, or engage in stonewalling (ignoring partners and shutting down communication), the prognosis is bleak. Luckily, Gottman has also identified factors that predict happy, stable relationships. If a couple shows any sort of positive emotion during a conflict—a kind look, a small gesture of affection, an apology, laughter—these relationships are likely to last.

Self-compassion tends to inspire positive rather than destructive emotions during relationship conflicts. When we're upset over a relationship issue, self-compassion allows us to soothe and calm the intensity of our feelings, meaning that we're better able to rein in the four horsemen. We're less likely to be harshly critical, show contempt, or be ego defensive during an argument if we experience the emotional safety needed to acknowledge our own role in the dispute. Self-compassion also provides the equanimity needed for talking through difficult relationship issues, meaning that it can reduce stonewalling. Self-compassion tends to soften our hearts, making it easier to get in touch with the affection we feel for our partners, and facilitating the expression of positive emotions during conflicts. And because self-compassion lets us take our egos less seriously, we can sometimes even find humor in our overreactions.

I remember once when I was having a fight with Rupert, the line "give me a break!" came out of my mouth in the exact same sarcastic voice of my mother, who often spouts this line when she's angry. We both looked at each other and burst out laughing, silently acknowledging that we come by our bad habits honestly. Needless to say, the conflict was much easier to resolve afterward.

There's another way that self-compassion can help in conflict situations. Often fights between partners stem from each person wanting their own point of view to be validated at the same time. If I talk about the way I see a relationship problem, and Rupert doesn't acknowledge how I feel but merely states his differing view, I won't feel heard. Let's say I'm upset because Rupert has spent three weekends in a row riding horses with friends (horses are his passion), and I ask him not to ride next weekend because I want to spend more time with him. Instead of acknowledging the fact that I'm upset, he tells me how he sees things. "But you know how much I love riding and you're not being very generous, especially since the weather is so good for riding right now." Because I don't feel that Rupert has taken my feelings seriously, my reaction will start becoming more extreme as if to say, "See? I'm justified in feeling this way!" For instance, I might say, "But we never spend time together as a family anymore!" (Even though we actually just spent a weeklong family vacation together last month.) This just causes him to ramp things up from his end. "You always exaggerate. And you never consider what I want or need!" The tone of anger and blame in both our voices will then make it even less likely for us to come to a point of mutual understanding.

The wise advice of relationship counselors is for each partner to validate the emotions of the other partner before presenting his or her own point of view. "I know that you love riding and want to do it as much as possible before the hot and humid weather begins, but I get lonely when you're away and would like to spend more of next weekend with you." Or "I can understand that you feel left out when I spend the weekend riding with my friends, but this is really important to me and I won't be gone nearly as often once the heat sets in." Sometimes, however, in the thick of things, it's hard for people to break out of their own reactions to really listen to their partners and validate their emotions. If I wait for my partner to give me what I need while he's waiting for me to give him what he needs, we might both be waiting a long time. This is where self-compassion can come in handy.

If you can compassionately validate *your own* feelings, gently reminding yourself that it's only natural for you to feel the way you do, you won't have to speak louder and louder in order to feel heard. You can tell yourself what you really want to hear in the moment, "I'm so sorry you're feeling hurt and frustrated right now, what can I do to help?" Then, once you begin to feel accepted and cared for, you'll be in a better place to listen to what your partner is saying and see things from his or her point of view. Less fuel will be added to the fire, and the conflict will hopefully start to cool down.

## The Relationship Benefits of Self-Compassion

Research demonstrates that self-compassion really does improve the quality of romantic relationships. We recently conducted a study with more than a hundred couples, measuring each partner's self-compassion level and asking them to tell us how happy and satisfied they were in their relationship. We also asked each participant to describe their partner's relationship behavior. Were they caring and sensitive or controlling and demanding? Did they get angry at the drop of a hat or could they talk things out? This enabled us to see if highly self-compassionate people would report having better romantic relationships, and if they would be described as being more loving, supportive, and considerate by their partners.

We also assessed participants' self-esteem levels, but we didn't think that people with high self-esteem would necessarily have better relationships than those who lacked self-esteem. People often become angry, jealous, and defensive when their self-esteem is threatened by partners, a pattern that's at the root of many relationship problems. When self-esteem comes in the form of narcissism, moreover, it often leads to selfishness and game playing in romantic relationships—not exactly keys to lasting happiness.

The results of our study indicated that self-compassionate people *did* in fact have happier and more satisfying romantic relationships than those who lacked self-compassion. This is largely because self-compassionate participants were described by their partners as being more accepting and nonjudgmental than those who lacked self-compassion. Rather than trying to change their partners, self-compassionate people tended to respect their partners' opinions and consider their point of view. They were also described as being more caring, connected, affectionate, intimate, and willing to talk over relationship problems than those who lacked self-compassion. At the same time, self-compassionate men and women were described as giving their partners more freedom and autonomy in their relationships. They tended to encourage partners to make their own decisions and to follow their own interests. In contrast, people who lacked self-compassion were described as being less affectionate and more critical toward their partners. They were more controlling, trying to order their partners around and dominate them. They were also described as being more self-centered, inflexibly wanting everything their own way.

High self-esteem, it should be noted, did not appear to do a whole hell of a lot for couples. Self-esteem was *not* associated with happier, healthier relationships, and people with high self-esteem weren't described by their partners as being any more accepting, caring, or supportive in their relationships than those who lacked self-esteem. In other words, the results of our study suggest that self-compassion plays an important role in fostering good relationships, but that having high self-esteem doesn't necessarily help. Self-compassion fosters feelings of mutuality in relationships so that the needs of self and other are balanced and integrated. Self-esteem, on the other hand, is more ego-focused, magnifying a sense of separation and competition between the needs of each partner.

To have the type of close, connected relationships you really want with others, you first need to feel close and connected to *yourself*. By being caring and supportive when you confront the limitations of living a human life, you'll have the emotional resources needed to act in a caring and supportive way with your significant other. By meeting your own needs for love and acceptance, you'll be less needy and clingy. And by accepting the fact neither you nor your relationship is going to be perfect, you'll be able to enjoy your relationship more for what it is rather than comparing it to some notion of how a romance is *supposed* to be—a Cinderella meets Prince Charming fairy tale that doesn't exist in real life (and which would be too one-dimensional to hold anyone's interest for long anyway). Self-compassion embraces imperfection with love, providing the fertile soil needed for romance to truly flourish.

## My Story: And I Promise to Help You Have Compassion for Yourself

As I mentioned earlier, when Rupert and I got married we included in our vows the promise to help each other be more self-compassionate. This was not an empty promise, but a commitment to a way of being with ourselves and each other that radically transformed our relationship. Moreover, we took some concrete steps to help us become more self-compassionate when relating to each other. One practice we found to be particularly effective was to take "self-compassion breaks" during arguments. Such breaks provide a space in which we can not only cool down, but also give ourselves compassion for the difficult situation in which we have landed ourselves. This practice is helpful for a variety of reasons. For one thing, it helps us to both soothe our bruised egos, a useful tool given that many of the fights couples have stem from the need to protect one's self-esteem.

As a typical example, I remember once when Rupert got irritated with me because I kept interjecting into a discussion he was having with a friend. It was when the British government was proposing to ban foxhunting (which they subsequently did in 2004). Rupert, an avid equestrian, grew up with the sport, while I'm a vegetarian. Needless to say we had vastly different opinions on the ethical nature of galloping across the countryside following hounds chasing down a fox. The problem wasn't that I was expressing my opinion; it was that I kept cutting Rupert off mid-sentence so he couldn't properly express his own point of view. After the friend went home, Rupert mildly rebuked me for continually butting in on his conversation. Instead of gracefully apologizing, I merely upped the ante by suggesting that Rupert's opinion on foxhunting was thickheaded and needed to be corrected. In hindsight, I could see that I was too ashamed to admit that I was indeed out of line by continually interrupting him, even if I *did* believe foxhunting was cruel. So to salvage my self-esteem I tried to change the subject to a more self-flattering topic: the fact that I was right and Rupert was wrong. This just exacerbated things, of course, as Rupert now had the double whammy of feeling humiliated in front of his friend while also being insulted by his wife. Things started to heat up from there.

Fortunately, before things spun too far out of control, I somehow managed to squeak out "self-compassion break!" between the rounds of machine-gun fire. We both took a few minutes to close our eyes and send ourselves compassion. I realized that it was only human of me to want to express my opinion on a topic that I felt passionately about. I wasn't trying to shut Rupert up, I was just carried away by my enthusiasm. Once my defensive posture softened and I forgave myself for stepping out of line, I was able to properly apologize to Rupert. "You know, you're right. It was really rude of me to keep cutting you off and it must have been terribly frustrating for you. I apologize. Even though I still don't agree with your opinion, to be fair, you were making some very valid points that I wasn't open to considering."

Rupert, for his part, had been giving himself compassion for how frustrated he felt, so when I validated his feelings and his point of view he was ready to accept my apology. He didn't feel he had to defend himself any longer and was in a more receptive frame of mind after being soothed and comforted by his own compassion. In fact, he admitted that many of my points were also valid, and we ended up having a really productive discussion about the evils *and* merits of foxhunting, enabling us to come to more agreement and consensus about the issue than I had thought possible. Rupert did give up foxhunting later that year, in fact, but not in order to placate me. Rather, his own compassionate sense allowed him to feel more for the fox than for the culture he grew up with. (He still jumps horses over fences across country, but without the moral quandary of having to hunt an animal in order to do so.)

Sometimes when Rupert and I are having a conflict, of course, the issues go deeper than mere bruised egos, or an abstract moral concept such as whether or not it's okay to foxhunt. Most people develop patterns of reacting in relationships that are unhelpful, patterns that are typically formed in response to early childhood traumas. My pattern, for instance, I call "hurt little girl." Because I felt abandoned by my father at an early age, feelings of hurt and abandonment come up quite easily in my relationships with men. This pattern was especially strong in the early years of my relationship with Rupert. As mentioned earlier, I met Rupert while conducting my dissertation research in India. Rupert, for his part, was a travel guidebook writer who was gathering information for a guide to South India. After we got married, Rupert continued to largely earn his living by writing articles for travel magazines. Even though I knew that Rupert's job required him, by definition, to be away from home a lot, I would still sometimes act as if he were abandoning me when he went off on a new assignment. I would pout when Rupert left and sulk when he returned, the feeling of being hurt and abandoned coloring my every expression.

Rupert's childhood pattern, in contrast, he calls "unfairly treated little boy." A lot of his early childhood pain stemmed from being harshly treated by the British teachers at the private school he attended, who were supposed to have his best interests at heart. When he got a poor grade in his math class, for instance, they responded by publicly humiliating him and making him drop his favorite course in history—even though he really excelled in this subject—as punishment. And with the teacher persecution came bullying from other kids, who got the message that it was okay to pick on him. The stress of such unfair treatment was so bad that he actually suffered a nervous breakdown at age eleven and spent three months in bed. When I acted hurt every time Rupert had to take a business trip—work that was necessary to help support us as a couple—it quickly pressed his "that's unfair!" button. Rather than being able to alleviate my insecurities, therefore, Rupert would tend to become angry and upset when I acted hurt. From his point of view, my reactions were a direct criticism of him—a criticism that was grossly unjust given that he had done nothing wrong. His feelings, like mine, were experienced in an exaggerated manner, our overreactions stemming from a well of pain that ran much deeper than the pain of the particular circumstances at hand.

Luckily, because Rupert and I had made a commitment to self-compassion, we were eventually able to break free of the grip of our childhood conditioning. This was challenging because our complementary patterns meant that we both tended to be simultaneously under their irrational sway. Still, as long as one of us remembered to start the self-compassion process during a conflict, the engine driving our negative reactions would start to run out of steam. My hurt little girl would get her needs met by feeling cared for and accepted, so that I could recognize that I wasn't really being abandoned. Similarly, Rupert's unfairly treated little boy would start to feel assuaged, so he could let go of his anger and realize that my reactions were not actually a personal criticism. Once we were able to treat our childhood patterns with compassion, we could focus on what was actually happening here and now, and our conflict would unravel more easily. The vow we made to help each other be more self-compassionate was one of the best things we ever did.

## Exercise Two

### *Take a Self-Compassion Break*

The next time you're in a heated argument with your partner, try taking a self-compassion break. It's best if you have both agreed to do this, but even if your partner isn't on board, taking a brief "time-out" to give yourself compassion during a conflict can be incredibly useful. The hardest thing is mustering up enough awareness to remember to take a break. Often we're so involved in the story line of what's driving the conflict that nothing else enters our awareness. With practice, however, you can use the pain involved in a conflict to remind yourself that what you need in the moment is self-compassion.

During the break, you should go to a place where you can be alone for a few minutes (even the bathroom if need be). The first thing to do is to put the "story" of what the fight is about on hold. Your task now is just to soothe your upset state by validating your emotions. Tell yourself "this is really hard right now" (once again, your self-compassion mantra will probably be useful here). One of the key causes of suffering when in conflict is that each person is trying so hard to make their point that the other person doesn't feel heard or validated. Also, each feels unloved and rejected by the other's angry tone. So hear and validate yourself first. Accept and care for yourself first. This will help de-escalate your emotional reactivity and put you in a more peaceful frame of mind.

Once the break is over, you'll be able to engage with your partner more constructively. If you can, try to express at least one positive emotion to your partner—a laugh, a smile, a kind word, or a statement that you understand what your partner is saying. This can help shift the dynamics of the conflict considerably and help to transform it into a productive discussion.

Self-compassion gives incredible strength to romantic relationships. When we stop depending on our partners to meet all our emotional needs—giving *ourselves* the love and acceptance we want—we become less clingy, needy, and dependent. When we remember that we're only human, we can admit our mistakes and talk things through with greater calm and clarity. And by being gentle and warm with ourselves, we'll be in a better emotional space to be there for the person we love.

## Self-Compassion in the Bedroom

Not only can self-compassion lead to satisfying and mutually validating romantic relationships—it can also improve our sex lives. Bonus. Sex is an amazing way to feel alive, passionate, and connected. It's also one of the most pleasurable activities we can engage in as adults. So why is our society so conflicted when it comes to sex? Even though sexual images are everywhere, people have a hard time dealing with sex in an open, honest way. There can be incredible shame associated with sexuality, especially for women. Even for those raised after the sexual revolution of the 1960s, society sends the message that a woman's value and self-worth lies in her ability to keep herself sexually pure. A woman who outright enjoys sex and—God forbid—wants a lot of it is called . . . well, we know what she's called.

It's not nearly as bad as it used to be, of course. Women are no longer required to be virgins when they marry, but there's still a huge double standard. Men who have multiple sexual partners are praised for being studs, while women are condemned for the exact same thing. There are few role models of women who are proud and unapologetic about their sexuality. The character Samantha from *Sex in the City* is a good example. Her views on when to have sex with a man she's just started dating? "Don't play 'hard to get' with a man who's hard to get." The reason Samantha is so funny, of course, is because she is brave enough to celebrate something that is usually so frowned upon.

On the other hand, a woman who has sex with a man on their first date mainly because she wants him to like her, not because it reflects her authentic sexuality, *is* in fact devaluing herself. If a woman derives her sense of self-worth primarily based on how many catcalls she gets while walking in her stilettos (Jimmy Choos or not), she's selling herself short because her self-worth is dependent on how the outside world views her rather than coming from within. Using sex as a means to get self-esteem may lead to poor decisions about who to have sex with and can also make you emotionally vulnerable. "Why didn't he call me back? Wasn't I good enough?"

Teen girls face an especially daunting challenge when it comes to sexuality and self-worth. On the one hand, adolescence is becoming more and more sexualized in our society. Take a stroll in any suburban shopping mall and you'll see girls with thongs peeking out of their low-cut jeans, their lacy push-up bras clearly visible underneath paper-thin T-shirts. And not just teens. According to Diane Levin and Jean Kilbourne, the authors of the book *So Sexy, So Soon,* even prepubescent girls are wearing miniskirts, thongs, and padded bras. The message?

Your value lies in what you got, and if you got it, flaunt it. The music young people listen to reinforces the notion that girls are primarily sex objects. Approximately two-thirds of the popular songs that focus on sex have lyrics that are degrading toward women. Like this song from the Ying Yang Twins: "They say a closed mouth don't get fed. So I don't mind asking for head. You heard what I said, we need to make our way to the bed." The average teen listens to about two and a half hours of music per day.

For some young women, sex itself is becoming less meaningful. In her book *Unhooked,* Laura Sessions Stepp documents how "hookups" are the norm in many high schools and college campuses, and that it is no longer considered cool to want sex in the context of a long-term, emotionally intimate relationship. In reaction to rampant misogyny, some girls are responding in kind. As one put it, "Sometimes you just want to screw them before they screw you." Stepp recounts the story of a girl named Nicole who had sex with a guy in his room after he sent her a text asking to meet up. "Several hours later, as she prepared to leave, he asked her, 'What do we do about this?' . . . 'We do nothing,' she said. 'I got what I wanted.'"

At the same time that sexual norms appear to be getting looser, the opposite trend is also occurring. If you look closely, you'll see that many of the young girls in the mall wearing thigh-high boots and cutoff tops are also sporting purity rings. Almost one-quarter of teen girls (and about one-sixth of teen boys) have taken a pledge to remain sexually abstinent until marriage. Some have made successful careers out of being virgins, like Britney Spears, Jessica Simpson, or Brooke Shields. These young stars largely became popular for showing as much skin as possible, posing provocatively for the camera, and waxing lyrical about the importance of chastity. Such conflicting messages about sex are not without their consequences. Several large-scale studies have found that young people who make virginity pledges are just as likely to have premarital sex as those who don't take the pledge, but are *less* likely to use condoms and *more* likely to have anal and oral sex. (Like, technically it doesn't count.)

It's no wonder that girls and women in our society have such a hard time relating to their sexuality in a healthy way. We are either made to feel ashamed for being too sexual, or else for not being sexual enough.

Self-compassion can help us develop a healthier, more authentic way of relating to sex. First and foremost, by being supportive and nurturing toward our sexuality—whatever shape or form it comes in—we can stop being victims of sexual shame. We don't need to judge ourselves according to society's mixed-up sexual norms. Some people are straight, some homosexual, some bisexual, others trysexual (as in "I'll try anything"). Some people want sex all the time, others only occasionally. Some people choose to remain virgins until they're married, others don't. Some people want lifelong celibacy, others monogamy, others serial monogamy, others polyamory. Some married couples are basically platonic and don't have sex at all. There is no right or wrong when it comes to sex, only what's healthy or unhealthy for each individual or couple. When we deny our human nature—and sexual desire certainly lies at the very core of human nature—we will not have healthy sexual relationships. And therefore we will not have healthy romantic relationships either. Well-being cannot be nurtured in a lie.

When we give ourselves compassion, however, when we care for and look after ourselves, we can start to let go of society's narrow definitions of how men and women are supposed to be sexually. We can start to love and accept ourselves exactly as we are and can express our sexuality in the way that most fulfills us. In his book *The Soul Beneath the Skin: The Unseen Hearts and Habits of Gay Men,* author David Nimmons argues that gay men are probably the most liberated on this front. Because they've had to buck societal convention anyway, they are more likely to find support in their communities for sexual authenticity in whatever form it takes.

What's most important is to honor the passionate aliveness that results when two human souls join together. What is right for one person may not be right for another, so it's unreasonable to expect that all people should follow one "acceptable" pattern of sexuality and one pattern only. Our sexual decisions should stem from our inner desire for happiness, not from the pressure to mold ourselves into a particular form to get societal approval, or even approval from our partner.

## Exercise Three

### *Releasing Sexual Shame*

Take a good, honest look at your sexual self. Are you fully accepting of your sexual feelings, whatever they may be? Is there anything you feel ashamed about, or judge yourself for? First, give yourself compassion for the self-judgment you are experiencing. Realize that almost all people have sexual thoughts and feelings they are ashamed of, and have compassion for this shared aspect of the human experience. Try to let go of your self-blame, and instead give yourself compassion for the difficulty of being a sexual being in our sexually conflicted, confused society.

Then, it's important to ask yourself whether the negative feelings you have about your sexuality come from the fact that you're harming yourself in some way, or if they stem primarily from societal conventions. Do you feel ashamed mainly because the larger culture tells you you're not supposed to be the way you are? Or do you feel there is in fact an unhealthy aspect to your sexuality, that you're harming yourself or someone else by acting out sexual urges in a way you truly regret? As you think about your sexual self, try to determine what's authentic for you. Remember that all human beings are different sexually, but there is one thing we share—most of us suffer at some point in our lives because our sexuality comes into conflict with societal dictates. If you want to make changes in your sex life, make sure your decisions are driven by your desire to be healthy and happy. Authentic sexuality means you accept and validate all your sexual feelings, and fulfill your desires in a way that helps you to grow and flourish.

When we accept ourselves, our bodies, and our sexuality—embracing ourselves with kindness—we may also be directly enhancing our sexual responsiveness. Although this is a new area of research, some evidence suggests that self-compassionate women are more in touch with their bodies. One study assigned a group of female undergraduates to a fifteen-week mindfulness training course, or else to a control group. Researchers found that the mindfulness group increased their levels of self-compassion compared to controls—a finding consistent with other research. However, results also showed that increased self-compassion was associated with faster recognition of sexual feelings. When presented with erotic images, self-compassionate women were quicker to notice when they had become aroused. This suggests that self-compassion can help women become more attuned to their bodies and more comfortable with their sexuality.

Self-compassion can also improve our sex lives in another way. It can help heal the childhood wounds that spill over into the bedroom. Again, this issue can be especially salient for women. Given that half of all marriages end in divorce, and that most children from divorced homes are raised by single mothers, a huge number of girls are deprived of their fathers' love and attention while growing up. The "hurt little girl" pattern caused by this deprivation is incredibly common, and I know I'm not at all unusual in suffering from it. I also know, however, that the pattern can interfere with sexual intimacy. Because sex opens us up psychologically and spiritually, it also tends to open up old wounds having to do with not feeling loved enough. This creates a neediness and craving for validation that is about as sexy as a cold, wet blanket.

## My Story: Sexual Healing

I remember early on in my relationship with Rupert, I'd sometimes find myself inexplicably switching from sex goddess to wounded little girl in the blink of an eye, sighs of passion suddenly devolving into sobs of sadness without warning. This was disconcerting for Rupert, to say the least. It was as if by receiving the love and intimacy I had always wanted, old patterns of feeling unloved and rejected felt safe enough to break through to conscious awareness. Because of our commitment to self-compassion, we'd try to use these occasions as opportunities for healing. Instead of being ashamed of my decidedly *un*sexy behavior, with Rupert's encouragement I was able to focus on the suffering I was experiencing in the moment, and the desire to ameliorate that suffering. Both of us would concentrate all our attention on soothing the emotions of my wounded self, having compassion for the deep scars still imbedded in my psyche. There was a several-month period where this was happening frequently, and Rupert, bless him, was completely supportive.

What happened may sound strange, and can be interpreted on a metaphoric level, but while we were focusing on healing "hurt little girl" as we made love, it felt as if we were also healing the wounds of countless women who had gone before me. I got clear mental images of women passing through my body and being released, and I felt deeply in touch with the pain caused to women throughout history. Repressed, suppressed, used, abused, devalued, disempowered, and abandoned: so many souls in need of healing. As we focused our intention on releasing these wounded souls, Rupert and I fell into a sort of trance, transforming suffering through the power of compassion—my own and that of innumerable others. After a few months of consciously dedicating our lovemaking in this way, I stopped seeing these mental images of hurt women. The cycle seemed to be over, the healing complete. And amazingly, hurt little girl never asserted herself in the bedroom again, assured that she *was and is* loved. (Luckily, sex goddess still likes to make an appearance now and then.)

*Part five*

## THE JOY OF
## SELF-COMPASSION

*Chapter Twelve*

# THE BUTTERFLY EMERGES

*The deeper that sorrow carves into your being the more
joy you can contain.
Is not the cup that holds your wine the very cup that
was burned in the potter's oven?*
—KAHLIL GIBRAN, *The Prophet*

SELF-COMPASSION HAS THE POWER TO RADICALLY TRANSFORM OUR mental and emotional reality. Just like the alchemists of old, who sought to use the philosopher's stone to transmute lead into gold, we can use self-compassion to transmute suffering into joy. By changing the way we relate to our own imperfection and pain, we can actually change our experience of living. Try as we may, we can't control life so that it goes exactly as we want it to. The unexpected and undesired do happen, every day. Yet when we wrap our suffering in the cocoon of compassion, something new emerges. Something wonderful, exquisite, beautiful.

# Openheartedness

When we give ourselves compassion, we are opening our hearts in a way that transforms our lives. What does it mean to be openhearted? It's a phrase we use all the time, but what does it actually mean? Openheartedness is a state of emotional receptivity in which even unpleasant or negative experiences are held with caring concern. When we kiss the boo-boo on a child's hurt finger or listen empathetically to a dear friend telling us their woes—when we feel compassion, in other words—we experience an inner warmth spreading out from the center of our chest. This feeling is what lets us know that our hearts are open. And how does it feel to have an open heart? Pretty damn good! When compassion is flowing through our veins, we feel at our vibrant best—connected, alive, "plugged in." When we unlock our hearts, new experiences are free to emerge—experiences of love, courage, and unlimited possibility.

When our hearts are closed, however, we remain unmoved by life's sorrows. As we shut out the pain, we also shut ourselves down. Our fear of being overwhelmed by negative emotions leads us to tune out, so that we feel only constriction in the center of our chest. The price paid for protecting our hearts is to cut off our very lifeblood. We feel cold, empty, unhappy, and deeply unsatisfied. And the time when our hearts are most likely to close is when our pain is caused by negative self-judgment, when we feel we aren't good enough in some way. We're often incredibly callous when relating to our own inadequacies and imperfections, meaning that much of the time we're slamming the door of our heart right in our own face.

Fortunately, when we decide to hold our flawed humanity with compassion, everything changes. By responding to our own pain with a sense of kindness and connection, by soothing and comforting ourselves when faced with the imperfection of ourselves or our lives, we are creating new positive emotions that weren't there a moment earlier. Instead of just feeling inadequate, we now feel both inadequate *and connected in remembering this shared aspect of the human experience.* Instead of just feeling sadness, we now feel both sadness *and the sweet tenderness of concern for a wound that needs healing.* Instead of just feeling frightened, we now feel both frightened *and comforted by our own kindness and caring.* By relating to ourselves with compassion, we are holding our negative emotions in the warm embrace of good feeling.

This means that hidden within every moment of anguish lies the potential for contentment. Pain can become the doorway to happiness, because feeling loved, cared for, and connected is what makes us truly happy.

I remember the first time the penny dropped for me that self-compassion had the power to transform difficult, painful experiences into pleasurable ones. It was in my last year of graduate school at Berkeley, a couple months after learning about self-compassion in my weekly meditation group. I was in a particularly bad mood. My soon-to-be-ex-husband John had just called me up on the phone to tell me what a horrible, disgusting person I was, so that I had to hang up on him mid-harangue. Rupert was out of town on a work assignment, and we had argued the morning he departed so things had been left on a sour note between us. The deadline for submitting the final draft of my dissertation was fast approaching. I was behind in my work and seriously wondering if I really had what it took to make it as an academic. Would I ever get a "real" job, would I ever have a happy, uncomplicated life? I was rolled up into a tight black ball of insecurity, fear, and self-loathing.

And then I remembered self-compassion. *What did the teacher say again?* I thought to myself. *Oh yeah, that's right, first just be mindful of what you're experiencing. Observe each thought and emotion as it arises and describe it gently, without trying to resist it or push it away. Okay I think I can do that. Let's see. Shame, tightness in my throat, pressure, pain in my stomach. Heaviness, sinking, sinking. Fear, pressure in the back of my head, heart beating fast, hard to breathe . . . All right, now try giving yourself compassion for how hard it is to feel this way right now. Hmm. Can't feel anything. I'll try giving myself a little hug . . . Warmth. Warm tingles rising up my arms. Softness.* And then the tears came. Deep wells of grief as I allowed myself to really feel how hard it was at the moment. *It's okay, it's okay. Life is hard sometimes, it's okay. Everyone has these moments. I'm here for you, I care about you. It's not so bad, it will pass. Softening in my chest and throat. Little waves of contentment spreading from the center of my face. Quieting. Quieting. Quiet.*

Each time a new painful feeling arose, I would hold it in my awareness like this, describe it mentally, and send myself compassion for feeling it. And then I would hold the feeling of compassion in my awareness, describing it and feeling it in my body, savoring how good it felt to be cared for. After things quieted down, another painful feeling would soon rise up, and round I'd go through the whole cycle again. It went on like this for about an hour.

Yet after a while, I realized that my predominant experience was no longer an unpleasant one. Change was afoot. Instead of being stuck in the pain, my awareness was increasingly resting in the feelings of love, kindness, and connectedness that held the pain. As it did, the pain itself started to soften, the worry to lift, and I began to feel a lightness in my body. It was perhaps the first time I had really opened my heart to myself, and I started to feel almost giddy, like I had drunk a glass of champagne for the first time. Or perhaps it was more like drinking a glass of vintage red wine—the flavors were rich, deep, spicy, and complex. I felt centered, stable, at peace. I realized that these beautiful sensations I was experiencing weren't contingent on things going the way I wanted them to. They didn't depend on receiving praise, or being successful, or having a perfect relationship. I realized that my own heart was a deep well I could drink from at any time, and that ironically I would be *most* likely to remember to drink from that well when things were at their most difficult. I had found something that would change my life forever, and I was grateful beyond words.

## Exercise One

### *Transforming Negativity*

The next time you find yourself in the grip of negative emotions, try generating some positive emotions to go alongside them. You can use the following phrases when you're stuck in negativity, designed to validate your feelings while also focusing on your desire to be happy:

*It's hard to feel (fill in the blank) right now.*
*Feeling (blank) is part of the human experience.*
*What can I do to make myself happier in this moment?*

The first phrase compassionately acknowledges the difficulty of having negative emotions. The second phrase is a reminder that negative emotions are a normal, natural part of being human, and therefore should not be judged. The third phrase helps you get in touch with your desire to be happy. This may enable you to broaden your focus, finding creative ways to reset your buttons. You might take a hot bath, or consider what's good about your present situation (there's almost always *something* good in any given moment). These steps are not taken to resist being in a negative frame of mind, but because you want health and well-being for yourself.

Once you say these phrases, your negative mood may start to lift, replaced by a feeling of calm contentment. You might even be able to have a sense of humor about it all, and nothing lifts a bad mood like a good chuckle. Woody Allen made a career out of laughing at negativity, of course: "What if everything is an illusion and nothing exists? In that case, I definitely overpaid for my carpet."

## Open-Mindedness

Not only does self-compassion open our hearts, it also opens our minds, releasing our perceptions from the tight clamp of negativity. When we're lost in negative judgment, our awareness automatically narrows in on what's wrong with ourselves and our lives. We only see the blemish of imperfection, taking for granted the beauty and wonder of the bigger picture.

The evolutionary purpose of negative emotions is to spur actions that will help us survive, eliciting powerful urges known as *specific action tendencies*. Anger, for instance, creates the urge to attack, fear the urge to escape, shame the urge to hide, and so on. When caught in the grip of negative emotions, it feels like we have one option and one option only. When the bear is charging us, we don't have time to deliberate between choices. We act or we die. This tendency may come in handy when threatened by hairy carnivores, but it's not so useful when our problems are less directly life threatening, like when our new car gets dinged by a stray shopping cart in the grocery store parking lot. Negative emotions narrow our worldview to the point that we can't see other possibilities right under our noses. As Helen Keller said, "When one door of happiness closes, another opens, but often we look so long at the closed door that we do not see the one that has been opened for us."

When we give ourselves compassion, holding our disappointment in kind, connected, mindful awareness, the door opens up again. When we soothe and comfort ourselves, we provide ourselves with a sense of safety, giving us the courage to finally peek out from the rock we've been hiding under and see what's outside. More often than not, things aren't as bad as we feared, and we start noticing things about ourselves and our lives that are actually pretty good.

The calm, hopeful mind-set provided by self-compassion can lead to an upward spiral of positive emotions that helps us break free of fear and greatly improves the quality of our lives. Leading social psychologist Barbara Frederickson, author of the book *Positivity,* has proposed something called broaden-and-build theory to explain how it all works. Frederickson argues that positive emotions allow you to take *advantage* of opportunities rather than merely *avoid* dangers. Positive emotions, rather than narrowing our attention, do just the opposite. Because they help us to feel calm and safe, good feelings increase openness to new experiences, as well as increasing a sense of connectedness and trust in others. As Frederickson says, "Positivity opens us. The first core truth about positive emotions is that they open our hearts and minds, making us more receptive and more creative."

First, let's consider how negative emotions tend to interfere with seeing things clearly and prevent us from making wise decisions. Let's say you're running late for work and still have to walk your dog before leaving for the day. You're stressed and mad at yourself for not getting up earlier. You grab the leash and try to attach it to Fido's collar, leash in one hand, cup of coffee in the other. But in your harried state you keep missing the ring on his collar and it takes you three times longer than it should to hook the leash on. What's more, you take so long that Fido thinks you're bending down for a cuddle. He excitedly tries to lick your face and ends up spilling your coffee all over the kitchen floor. You curse, wipe up the spill, and roughly pull Fido out the door. You're impatient and grumpy as you take the dog for a walk around the block. *When is he going to do his morning business? I'm fifteen minutes late already.* When he finally does his morning duty, he does so smack-dab in the middle of the sidewalk. You reach into your purse for your disposable dog poop bags, only to find that you forgot to bring the bags in your rush to get out the door. Five minutes, ten leaves, and fifteen grimaces later you manage to clear the mess from the sidewalk. When you finally get home, you wash your hands and go to grab your car key from the front pocket of your purse, where it normally resides. But the key isn't there. You look once, twice, three times, each time getting more and more frustrated. You finally dump all the contents of your purse out only to find that your car key is, in fact, in your back pocket. You had put it there so you could get out the door more quickly after returning home from walking the dog. When you finally get to work, you're a half hour late and have missed the beginning of your work-group's daily meeting. You walk in sheepishly, all eyes staring as you try to find a chair, wishing you were invisible. Your negative mind-set has caused you to be clumsy and inefficient, not to mention landing you in trouble with your boss. And your day is likely to just keep getting worse from there.

Now consider how this scenario might have played out if you had focused on the positive rather than the negative. You're running late for work and have to walk your dog before leaving for the day. Although you slept in a bit too long, you're grateful that you got those few extra minutes of sleep. You pour yourself a cup of coffee, noticing how good it smells. You take a moment to enjoy the first few sips and realize that you should probably put your coffee in a travel mug before you take Fido for his walk. You grab the leash for Fido's collar, leash in one hand, cup of coffee in the other. As you do so, Fido tries to give you a kiss. You put down your coffee (which fortunately was in a spill-proof travel mug), give Fido a scratch behind the ears, and quickly and easily attach his leash. *What a sweet dog, he's such a good companion,* you think to yourself. You calmly walk outside, remembering to pick up the dog poop bags on your way out. You notice what a bright, beautiful morning it is and thoroughly enjoy your brief walk. As soon as Fido finishes his morning business, you clean up and soon arrive back home. You wash your hands and search your purse for your car keys. *Where are they? I always keep them in the front pocket of my purse. Oh yeah. That's right. I put them in my back pocket so I could get out the door more quickly. Guess I'm cleverer than I thought!* You arrive to work only ten minutes late, with five minutes to spare before your work-group's morning meeting starts. Your spirits are high as the meeting begins, especially when your boss approves of the creative solution you offer for a problem he brings up.

Your positive mind-set has helped you to be deft, careful, and efficient in your actions and will likely lead to a day that just keeps getting better.

We've all had many times that have unfolded like the first scenario, and thankfully also many times that have unfolded like the second. It seems that when we're in a negative mind-state, everything that can go wrong *does* go wrong. When we're in a positive frame of mind, however, things seem to go more smoothly. Frederickson's research shows that this process isn't magic. Rather, negative emotions tend to narrow our attention so much that we miss the obvious and make mistakes, meaning that we cause ourselves extra stress and problems. Positive emotions, on the other hand, tend to broaden our attention so that we notice useful details and have creative ideas, meaning that we maximize our thinking, decision-making abilities, and coping skills.

## Exercise Two

### *Take a Pleasure Walk*

Take a fifteen- to thirty-minute pleasure walk outside. It's best if you can take the walk in nature but any outdoor walk will do (e.g., walking from your office to the bus stop). The goal of the walk is to notice as many pleasant things as possible, so that you are generating an upbeat frame of mind. How many happy, beautiful, or inspiring things can you notice while you're walking? Is it a nice day? Or if it's raining, can you focus on the life-giving qualities of the rain? Are there beautiful plants or flowers? Bird song? A squirrel? Are there any pleasant scents? What's good about the experience of walking itself? Can you get in touch with the wonder of being able to walk, of feeling the earth underneath your feet?

And how about any people you pass? Are there two lovers holding hands, friends laughing, a mother with her small child? If you're smiling at this point (and you probably will be after generating such positive emotions), are you getting any smiles back? Perhaps even a hello? So much of our mental state depends on our intention to notice the good, an intention that will water the seeds of happiness.

Fredrickson and her colleagues have recently become interested in how feelings of compassion help to cultivate positive emotions. They conducted a study in which participants were taught how to do the loving-kindness meditation described in chapter 9. Five days a week, for eight weeks, participants generated feelings of loving-kindness for themselves, close others, acquaintances, strangers, and finally to all living beings.

Compared with a control group (who had signed up for the meditation course but hadn't yet taken it), participants who practiced loving-kindness meditation reported feeling more positive emotions such as love, joy, gratitude, contentment, hope, pride, interest, amusement, and awe on a daily basis. They also reported feeling greater self-acceptance, as well as more positive relationships with other people in their lives. Interestingly, participants also experienced better physical health, reporting fewer symptoms of illness such as headaches, congestion, or weakness.

Similarly, an fMRI study by Richie Davidson examined the brain functioning of experienced Buddhist monks and novice student volunteers who meditated on unconditional compassion for all beings, the self included. Results indicated that while meditating, both groups had higher levels of brain activation in the left prefrontal cortex, the brain region associated with joy and optimism. The monks, in fact, had the highest levels of activation ever recorded by Western scientists. (Those were some happy monks!)

## Self-Compassion and Positive Psychology

Over the past decade, eminent psychologists such as Martin Seligman and Mihaly Csikzentmihalyi have become increasingly interested in the way that positive emotions like love, joy, curiosity, and hope can help to maximize health and well-being. Generally known as the "positive psychology" movement, its focus is on understanding the factors that lead to mental health rather than mental illness—on cultivating strengths rather than eliminating weaknesses. Our research shows that self-compassionate people experience more positive emotions in their lives—such as enthusiasm, interest, inspiration, and excitement—than those who are self-critical. They also report being much happier. Ironically, even though self-compassion arises during experiences of suffering, it tends to create joyous mind-states. Again, self-compassion doesn't erase negative feelings, it *embraces* them with care and kindness. This sets off the "broaden-and-build cycle" mentioned earlier. Because self-compassion makes us feel safe, centered, and connected, we can delight in what's wonderful about our lives rather than dwelling solely on problems and limitations. We can start to pursue our dreams rather than merely ward off dangers.

Accordingly, our research shows that self-compassionate people are much more optimistic than those who lack self-compassion. Optimism refers to the belief that things are going to be okay, that the future holds good things. Unlike pessimists, who often don't bother trying because they assume that everything is going to hell in a handbasket (as the saying goes, you should always borrow money from a pessimist—they don't expect it back), optimists usually work diligently toward their goals, secure in the assumption that their efforts will bear fruit. Self-compassionate people are more optimistic because they know that if problems occur, they can deal with them. They have the emotional strength needed to cope with whatever arises. If you're able to comfort yourself every time something painful happens, staying centered and not running away with reactivity, you can start to *trust* yourself. You can more easily find inner courage when hard times hit, knowing that you can get through almost anything with the help of your own compassionate support.

Similarly, we've also found that self-compassionate people tend to be more curious about life than others. Curiosity is the engine of growth, spurring us on to explore, discover, and take risks, even when we feel anxious or uncomfortable. Self-compassion provides us with the sense of safety and equanimity needed to remain open as we take leaps into the unknown. It allows us to take refuge in interest and discovery when we have no idea what's going to unfold from one moment to the next.

People with self-compassion also tend to be more satisfied with their lives than those who lack self-compassion, a finding we've demonstrated among people living in both Eastern and Western cultures. Life satisfaction refers to an overall sense of contentment with how one's life has developed, the feeling that one's life has meaning and value. When you apply the soothing balm of self-compassion to your broken bits—your failures and disappointments—you can integrate your sorrow into a deep, rich, and satisfying acceptance of what it means to live a human life.

## Celebrating the Human Experience

We know that self-compassion generates positive feelings that maximize health and well-being. What is truly wondrous, however, is the fact that these positive emotions do not require you to *pretend* that reality is anything other than what it is. Instead, self-compassion allows you to widen your outlook so that you can fully appreciate and acknowledge all aspects of life, the bad as well as the good.

A truly satisfying, enjoyable life is varied and diverse—polyphone, not monotone. Imagine if the only songs you ever heard were your top ten favorites, and that was it. Forever and ever. You'd soon want to jump out of a window due to the relentless boredom. To keep things interesting we need contrast and variety in our lives. The Doris Day ideal of a constantly sunny disposition is just that—a Hollywood ideal. A cardboard cutout of a real person that ultimately leaves one wanting more. Hollywood lore has it that Doris Day turned down the role of Mrs. Robinson in the film *The Graduate* because it clashed with her usual goodie-two-shoes film persona. Can you imagine how much more interesting her film biography would have been—and how much longer her career would have lasted—if she had accepted the part and run with it?

While we ultimately want happiness in our lives, achieving this state requires feeling all of our emotions—the highs and the lows, the leaps forward as well as the setbacks. Emotions such as sadness, shame, anger, and fear are as necessary and integral to life's drama as joy, pride, love, and courage. As Carl Jung once wrote, "Even a happy life cannot be without a measure of darkness, and the word happy would lose its meaning if it were not balanced by sadness." The key word here is *balance*. We don't want negative feelings to color all of our perceptions, but we don't want to totally exclude them either. As if excluding them was even possible.

When we're compassionate toward our suffering, the pleasures of kindness, connectedness, and mindfulness quickly become blended with our painful feelings. The resulting flavor can be surprisingly satisfying—a little like dark chocolate. Without any pain, the pleasure of life would be too sugary, without any depth or complexity. On the other hand, pain without pleasure would be too bitter, like unsweetened cocoa. But when pain and pleasure are combined, when both are embraced with an open heart, you start to feel whole, full, complete. So next time you're having a hard time, try remembering the words *dark chocolate*. It might just provide the inspiration you need to wrap your bitter pain in the sweet, loving folds of compassion.

## My Story: The Horse Boy

I certainly have firsthand knowledge of the joy that self-compassion can provide. The commitment that Rupert and I made to having open hearts and open minds allowed us to do something crazy—to pursue an impossible dream and have that dream come true.

No one knows what causes autism, it's a mystery. We also don't understand why autism has been increasing at such alarming rates. For parents in the front line, however, the big question isn't what causes autism, but what to do about it? Much of the information on therapies and treatments for autism is conflicting. All of it is expensive. When our son, Rowan, was diagnosed with the disorder, we had no choice but to accept the unknowns and deal with each moment as best we could. Because there were so few answers, we decided we'd try anything to help Rowan that wasn't going to harm him. Little did I know the adventure that decision would take us on.

Autism is exhausting. As I mentioned earlier, Rowan was subject to endless screaming fits caused by his overstimulated nervous system. But out in nature he would calm a little. When the tantrums came, Rupert would often take Rowan out into the woods behind our house. One day, when Rowan was three, he suddenly ran out of the woods and into our neighbor's horse pasture, getting through the fence and in among the horses' hooves before Rupert could stop him.

There he was, flat on his back, five horses milling and stamping around him.

That's when something extraordinary happened. The boss mare—a notoriously grumpy old horse called Betsy—gently nosed the others aside and bent her head to our son in submission. Something amazingly gentle and unfathomable passed between them. Rupert—a lifelong horseman—had assumed that Rowan wasn't safe around horses, but after seeing Betsy's reaction, he immediately got the idea to take Rowan riding on her. I was nervous and begged him to be cautious. But the moment Rupert put him into the saddle and climbed up behind, Rowan began, amazingly, to talk. He began to use meaningful speech for the first time. We were blown away.

That same year, another extraordinary thing happened. Rupert—who works in human rights as well as being a writer—brought a group of San (or Bushmen) tribesmen from Southern Africa to speak at the UN to protest being evicted from their ancestral hunting grounds. The Bushmen have a strong tradition of healing through the use of trance. We joined them for a few days at a gathering of traditional healers outside of Los Angeles, and they offered to "work" on Rowan. Almost immediately Rowan began to point, show his toys to people, engage with others far more than he usually did. For a few days it was almost, tantalizingly, like having a "normal" child. We were ecstatic. Sadly, he fell back into the depths of his negative symptoms as soon as the Bushmen went home. But this sudden, inexplicable leap forward, combined with Rowan's radical, positive reaction to Betsy, had planted an idea in Rupert's mind.

One evening he came in from riding with Rowan and said, as if it was the most natural thing in the world, that he thought it might be a good idea for us to take Rowan to the one place on Earth where horses and healing went together—Mongolia. This is the country where the horse was first domesticated, and where the word *shaman* (meaning "he who knows") comes from. A no-brainer, he said. I disagreed. Strongly.

"Let me get this straight," I said. "You want us to take our autistic son across Mongolia on horseback? That's absurd! It's the *last* thing we need to do. It's hard enough to get through each day, let alone do something crazy like this. I can't believe you'd even seriously suggest it. And I hate horses!"

Maybe hate is too strong a word, but I was never one of those I-want-a-pony girls. Rupert is the horsy one in our family. Growing up in the suburbs of L.A., I had been more about Goth rock and trying to be cool. Rupert had taught me to ride—kind of. But I never had the desire to really impose my will over a horse. And horses know that: I've been run away with and bucked off more times than I can count.

But Rupert had a strong and persistent gut feeling that we needed to take Rowan to Mongolia in order to help him. The feeling in *my* gut when I thought of going to Mongolia wasn't intuition—more like terror. Rupert and I fought about it, and fought hard. Then uncharacteristically—for we're both pretty stubborn—we both backed off, half hoping the other would cave in. Two years passed. Rowan and Rupert rode together almost every day, and the effects of this home-grown equine therapy were clear in terms of Rowan's rapidly developing language. But by age five, Rowan still wasn't toilet trained. We had taken him out of diapers, thinking he'd be so uncomfortable pooping in his underpants that he'd become motivated to use the toilet. But it wasn't working. Nothing worked. And Rowan still suffered from un-fathomable, inconsolable tantrums. He was also cut off from his peers, unable to make friends.

Rupert had been in e-mail contact with a Mongolian travel operator and was tentatively planning the trip despite my reservations. A young filmmaker friend, Michel, wanted to go along to document the journey. He would go without being paid, he said, seeing it as a great filmmaking opportunity. I continued to resist.

Still, I had learned through the years that when Rupert gets a strong gut feeling, it's often right. He had a gut feeling about me, after all, and actually asked me to marry him the first day we met. So I thought about the whole Mongolia thing for a while, and my reaction surprised me. I realized that I didn't want to miss the adventure. That life was provid-ing me with the chance to turn things around, to channel our grief over Rowan's autism into a quest for healing. That I was being offered a choice between love and fear. So I took a deep breath and said yes. I did joke, however, that for me it was a win-win. If the trip was a failure, I'd get to say "I told you so" to Rupert forever, and if it was a success, well, even better.

Rupert, being a writer, had put in a proposal to write a book about the trip called *The Horse Boy,* hoping that he might get a book advance to offset at least some of our costs and lost income while we were away. The proposal had been with Rupert's agent for several months, however, and we hadn't heard anything back. As an act of faith, we decided to go ahead and buy the plane tickets, maxing out our credit cards.

Amazingly, about two weeks later, a bidding war broke out and Rupert got a book advance that exceeded our wildest dreams. Suddenly there was more than enough money to cover all our expenses, to make a proper documentary (also called *The Horse Boy*), and most important, to put money away for Rowan's future. It was as if life was affirming our decision to take the adventure and giving us as much security as possible to do so. We were overwhelmed with gratitude.

So it was in this thankful frame of mind that we found ourselves in August 2007 at the foot of a sacred mountain in Mongolia, where nine shamans had gathered outside the capital city of Ulaanbaatar to conduct a ritual for us. According to our guide Tulga, most had come hundreds of miles just to help Rowan. It was perhaps the most intense afternoon of my life. Rowan hated it at first, screamed and resisted, clearly disoriented and not understanding all the noise and drumming going on around us. (Although I must say, he was not really more distressed than he would have been on a typical visit to the grocery store.)

Then it got really bizarre—the shamans said that a black energy had entered my womb during my pregnancy, and they made me go down to the river to wash my private parts with vodka. Yes, vodka. They also said that a female ancestor on my mother's side, someone with mental illness, was somehow clinging to Rowan. In fact, my maternal grandmother had lost her eight-year-old son in a car crash when my mother was only two. Then—years later—only a few weeks after my mom moved out and got married, my mom's father died of a heart attack. My grandmother went mad with grief and had to be committed. Was this the female ancestor they meant? Bizarre. There was little time to reflect because next thing we knew Rupert and I were being made to kneel, facing the mountain wall while a shaman whipped us (not Rowan, thank God) with rawhide thongs, raising agonizing red welts on our backs, arms, and thighs while Tulga, laughing nervously, told us: "Is important not to cry out."

Childbirth apart, I don't think I've ever experienced anything so painful. As I knelt in the grass, breathing deeply and feeling the rawhide thongs pierce my skin, I sent myself compassion. Compassion for the pain of the whip, compassion for the pain of having an autistic child, compassion for everyone in the world suffering in so many different ways. I knew that the pain the shaman was causing was born from the intention to heal, and that made it bearable.

"Do you forgive your crazy husband?" asked Rupert, once the ritual was done. We hugged, laughing. What else could we do?

And then something beautiful happened. Rowan started laughing, giggling, playing with the shamans. Shortly afterward, to our amazement, Rowan turned to this little boy who'd been standing at the edge of the circle, hugged him, and said, "Mongolian brother."

He'd never done anything like that before.

The little boy was called Tomoo—our guide Tulga's son. Seeing the boys' amazing interaction, Tulga decided to bring Tomoo along on the trip with us. Rowan had made his first friend.

So off into the great interior we went. It started with near disaster. Rowan suffered a sudden loss of confidence during our first day on horseback, completely rejecting the horses so that we had to abandon them and continue on in a 4x4. This was heartbreak for Rupert: horses were the place where he and Rowan connected most. But watching as Rowan's friendship with Tomoo began to flourish during the endless days of travel and the long, impossibly beautiful evenings camped out on the open steppe was pure joy. Something in our son was changing.

We washed ourselves and prayed in the sacred waters of Sharga Lake, a strange, dreamlike place of wild swans and wilder horses, before traveling north into Siberia, land of the mysterious reindeer people. Their healers were, by reputation, the most powerful in the region. Rupert had heard that these nomadic peoples (purportedly the ancestors of the first Native Americans who crossed the Bering Strait tens of thousands of years earlier) could be very difficult to locate, however. Finding them and asking for a healing for Rowan was the final goal of our journey. But there were no roads to their remote settlement. To get there, Rowan would have to accept being on horseback again.

By now I was getting pretty exhausted by the trip. Imagine washing a five-year-old's soiled underwear three times a day with bottles of water filled up at streams (no washers or dryers out on the steppe). I was also sick of the terrible food—especially the rancid alcoholic mare's milk called *airag*, which tastes like vomit. Still, something was drawing us onward.

Rowan did finally get back on a horse again and started enjoying riding once more. So up we went, following our guides up the twelve-thousand-foot pass that had to be crossed to reach the high summer pastures of the reindeer people. Three days' hard riding later, we finally came upon their teepees. Rowan was entranced. The people here—as everywhere in Mongolia—could not have been more welcoming, bringing out tame reindeer for him and Tomoo to ride, letting them cuddle with the impossibly cute baby reindeer before the healings began.

For three days the shaman, an old, intensely charismatic man called Ghoste, worked on Rowan, dancing and drumming in the firelit glow of his teepee while Rowan crawled about, pretending to be a baby elephant.

On the last night I had a strange dream—and I almost never remember my dreams. My late grandmother was with her son who had been killed. Only now he was a grown man, and they were walking away together, hand in hand, happy.

Next morning, Ghoste said it was time for us to go. He also said that the stuff that really drove us crazy—Rowan's incontinence, his tantruming—these would stop now . . . today.

I was guarding my heart—so was Rupert. But the next day, while camped down by the river, Rowan did his first intentional bowel movement and cleaned himself. Two days later, he had his first success in a real toilet—something not even his grannies or paid professionals had been able to achieve. From that point on, we had only a few tantrums of any note. Within weeks of returning home, they had ceased completely. Meanwhile Rowan's circle of friends started to grow. He even began riding Betsy by himself—for Rupert, the fulfillment of a dream.

Was it the shamans, was it some sort of placebo effect, or was it simply the effect of taking him to a radically new environment, pushing him to his limits? I honestly don't know. What I do know, though, is that as a family we took a risk and somehow, through whatever crazy leap of faith, we found healing.

Healing, not cure. Rowan did not get cured of his autism. Rowan is still autistic. But he did get healed of the dysfunctions that went along with his autism. These days Rowan is now so functional that some people have trouble telling that he's "on the spectrum" anymore. But his autism will always be at the core of who he is and how he sees the world, and we wouldn't want it any other way.

The healing that *Rupert and I* received in Mongolia was that we came to truly accept Rowan's autism and stopped fighting against it. By opening up to the mystery of autism, by learning to see it as an adventure rather than a curse, we realized that Rowan's autism was actually the best thing that ever happened to us. We wouldn't be leading such an incredibly interesting life if it weren't for Rowan's autism. Ghoste had told us we needed to take Rowan to a good traditional healer each year until he was nine. It didn't matter from which tradition. So in 2008 we took him to Namibia to see the Bushman healer Rupert is closest to—a powerful shaman named Besa (a measure of their closeness is that

Rowan's full name is Rowan Besa Isaacson). In 2009 we took him to see an amazing Aboriginal healer in Australia. In 2010 we traveled to New Mexico and Arizona to see a Navajo medicine man. Each time we've taken one of these journeys, Rowan has been transformed, and we've been transformed—coming together closer as a family.

We've also been able to share the types of experiences we've had with Rowan with other families. We've started running four-day "Horse Boy" camps for families with autistic children, allowing for a more intense immersion in horses and nature. Several children have had major breakthroughs at the camps, including nonverbal kids who have uttered their first words on horseback, to the astonishment of their parents. I've been talking a lot about self-compassion to the parents at the camps, how crucial it is when trying to cope with the stress of raising an autistic child. The joy, satisfaction, and plain old fun we have doing all this is truly awe inspiring.

Autism is a gift, if you allow it to be. All of Rowan's charm, humor, talent, and intense interest in the natural world is because of his autism, not in spite of it. Why would we ever want to change that? As Rupert likes to remind me: "The old saying is that when life gives you lemons, make lemonade. I say f*** that. When life gives you lemons, make margaritas."

## Exercise Three

### *Find the Silver Lining*

Think of one or two of the biggest challenges you've faced in your life so far, problems that were so difficult you thought you'd never get through them at the time. In hindsight, can you see if anything good came out of the experience? Did you grow as a person, learn something important, find more meaning in your life? If you could, would you go back in time and change what happened, if it meant that you wouldn't be the person you are now because of it?

Next, think about a challenge you're facing right now. Is there any way to see your problem in a different light? Is there anything positive that might come out of your present circumstances? Any learning opportunities, career possibilities, new relationships, a reorganization of your priorities?

If you're finding it difficult to see *anything* positive about your current situation, it's probably a signal you need more self-compassion. Try using the three doorways of kindness, common humanity, and mindfulness to approach your feelings of fear or distress. Silently offer kind, nurturing words of support, as if from a close friend. Maybe even give yourself a little hug if no one's looking. Think about the ways your situation connects you with other people having similar problems—you are not alone. Try taking a few deep breaths, and accepting that the situation *is* happening, even though you don't like it much.

Now look again. What is life trying to teach you right now? Is this an opportunity to open your heart, to open your mind? Is there any way that this seeming curse might actually be a blessing? Margaritas anyone?

*Chapter Thirteen*

# SELF-APPRECIATION

*Our deepest fear is not that we are inadequate. Our deepest fear is that we are powerful beyond measure. It is our light, not our darkness that most frightens us. We ask ourselves, Who am I to be brilliant, gorgeous, talented, fabulous? Actually, who are you not to be? You are a child of God. Your playing small doesn't serve the world. There is nothing enlightened about shrinking so that other people won't feel insecure around you. We are all meant to shine, as children do. We were born to make manifest the glory of God that is within us. It's not just in some of us; it's in everyone. And as we let our own light shine, we unconsciously give other people permission to do the same. As we are liberated from our own fear, our presence automatically liberates others.*
— MARIANNE WILLIAMSON, *A Return to Love*

THIS BOOK HAS LARGELY FOCUSED ON HOW TO RELATE TO OUR FAILures and inadequacies with self-compassion. But the three basic components of self-compassion—kindness, a sense of common humanity, and mindfulness—are not just relevant to what we don't like about ourselves. They are equally relevant to what we *do* like.

## Appreciating Our Good Side

Sometimes it's more difficult to see what's right about ourselves than what's wrong. For those of us who don't want to seem vain, even *thinking* about our positive traits can make us uncomfortable. For this reason, a lot of people have a hard time accepting compliments. You know the type. "Mary, you look great! I like your blouse." "Oh. Thanks, but it would look better on someone who wasn't so flat-chested." Praise can make us squirm, and we often don't know how to respond without self-consciousness.

Flattery feels a lot better than insults, of course, but how many of us really take the praise in? Own it. Delight in it. For a whole host of reasons, it's often trickier than you might think to feel positive about ourselves; most of these stem from fear.

One fear involves setting up overly high expectations. Underplaying our good points means that we're more likely to pleasantly surprise others rather than disappoint them. If you score the winning goal in your weekly soccer match after repeatedly bemoaning what a crap player you are, you're likely to received astonished praise from your teammates. "I didn't know you had it in you! Well done!" At the same time, if you miss that crucial shot at the close of the game, sympathy will still be forthcoming. "Oh well, at least you tried." Appearing proud and confident about your skills, on the other hand, opens you up for attack when things go wrong. "Hey, I thought you said you were one of the best players on your college team. What college was that, the University of Uncoordinated Lame Asses?"

We also fear letting go of the devil we know. If we're in the habit of cutting ourselves down, recognition of our positive qualities will feel alien to us. Our sense of self may be so infused with feelings of inadequacy that it becomes frightening to see ourselves as worthy and valuable. Ironically, this can feel like a sort of death to us, and our negative sense of self will therefore fight hard to survive.

Fear of outshining others is another stumbling block. There's no doubt we live in a competitive culture where we need to feel special and above average to feel okay about ourselves. At the same time, it's lonely at the top. Some part of our psyche recognizes that the climb toward superiority is also a descent into isolation. Although we want high self-esteem, we also intuitively know its potential downsides—feeling separate and disconnected from others. If I acknowledge my greatness, does that mean I'm better than you, and does that in turn mean you and I can no longer relate as equals? The bipolar way in which we both crave and fear high self-esteem makes it hard to be comfortable in our own skin.

Thomas, an accountant at a technology company, felt extremely awkward and uncomfortable when anybody praised him. If he received a compliment on his work performance, for instance, he'd quickly say "thanks" for the sake of politeness but just as quickly change the subject. He felt like a fish out of water and almost nauseated whenever a positive spotlight was turned on him. He had no role model for how to accept a compliment, or how to linger in the warmth of another's praise. Instead, he was frightened to death of turning into his boss, a cigar-smoking slick guy with a swollen head who thought he was the cat's pajamas. He hated his boss's vain imperiousness and was terrified of being anything like him.

There's a reason we always root for the modest, self-effacing hero of the movie rather than his cocky, brash antagonist. Nobody likes a narcissist—except the narcissist. If we acknowledge our positive features and delight in them, doesn't that mean we're egotists? And egotists are unlovable, aren't they? It's a bit of a catch-22. If we admit good things about ourselves, it must mean we're bad, so we focus on what's bad about ourselves in order to feel good. Absurd, isn't it? Yet we all do it.

So how do we celebrate our admirable qualities without falling into the egotism trap? I believe the answer is still self-compassion, though in a different guise. I like to call it "self-appreciation." When we can enjoy what's good about ourselves, acknowledging that all people have strengths as well as weaknesses, we allow ourselves to revel in our goodness without evoking feelings of arrogance, superiority, or overconfidence. William James once wrote that "the deepest principle in human nature is the craving to be appreciated." Luckily, we can meet our deep need to be appreciated without depending on other people to approve of us. We can acknowledge our own beauty. Not because we're better than others, but because we are human beings expressing the beautiful side of human nature.

## Sympathetic Joy

In Buddhism, one of the foundations of well-being is *mudita,* which translates as "sympathetic joy." This state occurs when we are delighted by the good qualities and circumstances of others. An understanding of sympathetic joy can help us better grasp the meaning of self-appreciation, since the two are closely related. The basic sentiment underlying sympathetic joy is kindness and goodwill. If I am concerned for your well-being and want the best for you, I will want you to succeed. I'll be glad that you have gifts and talents that help you be contented in life.

Typically, however, others' good qualities tend to make us feel inadequate. *That woman is gorgeous so I must be ugly. He's intelligent so I must be stupid.* The green-eyed monster causes us to suffer when others shine, which means we suffer a lot. But what if we radically altered our perceptions? What if we took pleasure in others' accomplishments, felt genuinely happy for them? This would increase our odds of feeling happy by the number of people we have the opportunity to feel happy for. Given the latest estimates of the world population, that's about 6.8 billion percent!

An essential ingredient of sympathetic joy is the recognition of our inherent connectedness. When we're part of a larger whole, we can feel glad whenever one of "us" has something to celebrate. I work at the University of Texas at Austin, and we Austinites have serious college football fever. Whenever the Longhorns win a big game, the entire city is elated. Of course, as team supporters we don't personally throw that winning touchdown. It's our sense of oneness with our team that allows us to delight in their success. When we feel connected with others, we can fully revel in their glory. But what would happen if we widened that sense of belonging to include all of humanity, not just our local sports team? Then our side would always win.

We need to be aware of others' positive qualities to fully appreciate them, of course. If I take my husband's intelligence, good looks, creativity, or sense of humor for granted, that means I will stop being consciously aware of his good characteristics. They will morph into the background of the assumed and the expected. I must take note of his strengths and talents to fully appreciate and acknowledge the amazing person he is. For this reason, sympathetic joy also requires mindfulness.

## The Roots of Self-Appreciation

When qualities of kindness, common humanity, and mindfulness are applied toward the suffering of others, they manifest as compassion. When they're applied to our own suffering, they manifest as self-compassion. When they're directed toward others' positive qualities, they manifest as mudita: sympathetic joy. And when they're directed toward our own positive qualities, they manifest as self-appreciation.

Let's first consider the quality of kindness as it applies to self-appreciation. Many of us focus much more on our weaknesses rather than on our strengths. As discussed, we often belittle our positive features because it feels too scary and uncomfortable to acknowledge them. If we are kind to ourselves, however, we can rejoice in our good qualities. Isn't it wonderful that I'm a good father, a hard worker, a faithful friend, a committed environmental activist? Aren't my traits of honesty, patience, diligence, creativity, sensuality, spirituality, and empathy something to be celebrated? It's a great gift of self-kindness to have appreciation for ourselves, and to demonstrate our approval with sincere praise. We don't have to speak this praise aloud, making ourselves and others uncomfortable in the process. But we can quietly give ourselves the inner acknowledgment we deserve—and need.

The sense of common humanity inherent in self-appreciation means that we appreciate ourselves not because we're better than others, but because all people have goodness in them. To appreciate others' goodness while ignoring or deprecating our own creates a false division between us and them. But as a distinctive expression of the universal life force that animates all our experience, we honor everything when we honor ourselves. As the Zen master Thich Nhat Hahn writes, "You are a wonderful manifestation. The whole universe has come together to make your existence possible." If you take the notion of *interbeing* seriously, then celebrating your achievements is no more self-centered than having compassion for your failings. We can't really claim personal responsibility for our gifts and talents. They were born from our ancestral gene pool, the love and nurturing of our parents, the generosity of friends, the guidance of teachers, and the wisdom of our collective culture. A unique nexus of causes and conditions went into creating the ever-evolving person we are. Appreciation for our good qualities, then, is really an expression of gratitude for all that has shaped us both as individuals and as a species. Self-appreciation humbly honors all of creation.

Self-appreciation also requires mindfulness. Just as we need to notice others' good qualities in order to appreciate them, we need to consciously acknowledge our own positive features. Given the discomfort that often arises when we appreciate ourselves, however, we sometimes screen such thoughts from our conscious awareness. We suppress our suspicions that maybe we aren't so bad after all, because we don't know what to do with these novel good feelings. Mindfulness allows us to approach things in a new way, letting go of our habitual tendencies. One of the most powerful habits of the mind, of course, is to focus on the negative rather than the positive, and this tendency is no more apparent than when we think about ourselves. Our instinct tells us to identify problems and fix them so that we can survive. This means we often take our good qualities for granted while obsessing about our weaknesses. *If I could only lose fifteen pounds,* she told herself over and over again, blithely ignoring her youth, good health, intelligence, successful career, and loving boyfriend. By adopting the intention to notice what's good about ourselves, though, we are able to counter this slide toward negativity.

Some may be concerned that if we focus too much on what's right about ourselves we'll ignore much needed areas of growth. This is true only if our focus is, in fact, "too much." If we take a lopsided view of ourselves—"I am perfect and have no flaws whatsoever"—that would certainly be a problem. I don't know why we so often fall into the trap of this kind of either/or thinking, but it doesn't serve us. Every human being has both positive and negative traits. Rather than running away with an exaggerated story line about either, good or bad, we instead need to honor and accept ourselves as we authentically are. No better and no worse. The key is having balance and perspective so that we can see ourselves without distortion. When the sun rises we can appreciate our light, and when the sun sets we can have compassion for our darkness.

## Exercise One

### *Appreciating Yourself*

List ten things about yourself that you really like or appreciate. (These don't have to be qualities you display all of the time, just some of the time.) As you write down each quality, see if you can notice any uncomfortable feelings—embarrassment, fear of vanity, unfamiliarity? If discomfort comes up, remind yourself that you are not claiming you're better than anyone else, or that you're perfect. You're simply noting the good qualities that you sometimes display. Everyone has good features. See if you can acknowledge and enjoy these positive aspects of yourself, lingering over them and really taking them in.

1. _____
2. _____
3. _____
4. _____
5. _____
6. _____
7. _____
8. _____
9. _____
10. _____

## Self-Appreciation Versus Self-Esteem

On the surface, self-appreciation and self-esteem may appear to be quite similar. After all, they both involve an apparent focus on our good qualities, don't they? But though there are certainly many points of overlap between self-appreciation and self-esteem, there are also some important ways in which they differ. One key distinction centers on their acknowledgment of the common human experience. Self-esteem tends to be predicated on separation and comparison, on being *better* than others, and therefore special. Self-appreciation, in contrast, is based on connectedness, on seeing our similarities with others, recognizing that everyone has their strong points.

Another important distinction has to do with the tendency to *define* ourselves as either good or bad. Remember that self-esteem is a judgment of worthiness that operates at the level of representational self-concept. It involves labeling ourselves in an attempt to capture our unique essence (I am thin and wealthy, successful and beautiful, and so on). Self-esteem stems from *thoughts* about who we are, rather than simply *being* who we are. This is why it's so important to paint a positive self-portrait in order to have high self-esteem. Our self-concept becomes confused with our *actual* self. Self-appreciation, on the other hand, is not a judgment or label, nor does it define us. It is a way of *relating* to what is good in us. It recognizes that we are an ever-changing process that can never fully be defined—whether positively or negatively. It does, however, acknowledge our moments of splendor.

There are always wonderful things to appreciate about ourselves, even if they don't make us unique. The fact that I can breathe, walk, eat, make love, hug a friend—these are all magnificent abilities that are definitely to be celebrated, despite the fact that just about everyone shares these abilities—despite the fact that they are beautifully *average*. It's usually only after people lose one of these gifts that they realize how wondrous they actually are. And when we can appreciate those aspects of ourselves that *are* unique, it can be done in the context of recognizing our complex, interconnected nature, not as a way of scoring points over our fellows.

With self-appreciation, we don't need to put others down to feel good about ourselves. I can appreciate my own achievements *at the same time* that I recognize yours. I can rejoice in your talents *while also* celebrating my own. Appreciation involves acknowledging the light in everyone, ourselves included.

## Appreciation for What's Good in Our Lives

Although I've mainly been discussing the importance of appreciating our personal qualities, appreciation can also be extended to our life circumstances in general. Self-appreciation embraces all that is good and wholesome, both internally and externally.

Because the same fears of vanity and egotism aren't generated when we acknowledge our favorable life conditions, we have fewer blocks to this form of self-appreciation. It's not nearly as challenging to appreciate what's good in our lives—our loving family, our supportive friends, our stable job—as it is to appreciate *ourselves*. Having said that, because of the habitual tendency of our minds to focus on the negative, we often take our good fortune for granted. We get so caught up in problem solving and coping with the pain of life that we give insufficient attention to that which gives us pleasure—and so suffer more than we need to. As research is beginning to demonstrate, however, appreciation can radically transform our experience.

In her book *The How of Happiness,* researcher Sonia Lyubomirsky notes that positive life circumstances account for a surprisingly small slice of happiness—explaining only about 10 percent. Even after a grand event like winning the lottery, people tend to settle back to their previous levels of (un)happiness after only a couple of years. For this reason, many psychologists argue that we have a happiness "set point" that is largely genetic. This is only part of the story, however. Research also shows that people can boost their happiness levels significantly simply by changing the way they relate to their lives. In other words, it's not so much *what* happens to you but your *attitude* toward what happens that matters. Lyubomirsky finds that several key factors make a difference in terms of maximizing happiness. Some of the most important are being grateful for what you have, looking at the bright side of difficult situations, not comparing yourself to others, practicing acts of kindness, being mindful, and savoring joy. All of these factors fall nicely within the larger concept of self-appreciation, but we'll focus on two in particular: gratitude and savoring.

## Gratitude and Savoring

### GRATITUDE

Religion has long emphasized the value of gratitude in daily life, typically in the form of giving thanks in prayer. Consider this passage from the Bible's book of Psalms. "Give thanks to Him who spread the earth above the water, who made the heavenly lights, who made the sun to rule by day and the moon and stars to rule by night. For His loving-kindness is ever-lasting" (Psalms 136: 5–9, American Standard Version). Prayers such as these focus attention on celebrating the beauty and wonder of creation. Gratitude pulses at the core of most religions and is considered an important gateway to spiritual fulfillment.

Robert Emmons, one of the foremost researchers on gratitude, has found strong support for the notion that gratitude leads directly to happiness. He defines gratitude as recognizing and acknowledging the gifts we are given, either by other people, God, or by life itself. Studies show that grateful individuals tend to feel more happy, hopeful, vital, and satisfied with their lives, while being less materialistic and envious of others' success. Luckily, research also suggests that gratitude is something that can be learned.

In one study, for instance, researchers asked a group of undergraduate students to give weekly reports on their current life experience over a period of ten weeks. Students were randomly assigned to three different groups. Individuals in Group A had to write about things they felt grateful for (e.g., "the generosity of friends," "wonderful parents," "the Rolling Stones"). Group B students were asked to write about things they found annoying or irritating (e.g., "finding parking," "messy kitchen no one will clean," "stupid people driving"). Group C was a control group; students in this group were simply asked to write about anything that affected them that week, without specifying whether the impact was positive or negative (e.g., "cleaned out my shoe closet"). The researchers found that people in the gratitude group were not only happier than the others, they also reported fewer symptoms of illness and exercised more often than those in the other two conditions. It appears that gratitude changes both our emotional and physical experience for the better.

## Exercise Two

### *Keeping a Gratitude Journal*

Research suggests that keeping a daily gratitude journal is one of the best and most reliable ways to increase happiness. You may want to choose a special notebook for your journal, one that provides a sense of beauty and reverence. It doesn't really matter, however; there's no right way to do it. What's important is that you set aside a specified time to write about the gifts, kindnesses, pleasant surprises, and good moments of each day, as well as the things that give you joy in life more generally.

Make sure you continually try to find new things to be grateful for. Your friends, family, and loved ones will probably be regulars, but don't let the exercise become stale or repetitive. What gifts have you enjoyed that you perhaps took for granted the day before? Sunshine, the rule of law, indoor plumbing? The amazing things that allow us to lead our incredibly leisure-filled lives are endless.

It also helps to be as specific as possible about what we're grateful for, to make it more real and concrete. For instance, instead of saying "I'm grateful for my cat" try "I'm grateful for the way my cat purrs and rubs up against my leg, making me feel loved."

After a relatively short time, keeping a gratitude journal can make a substantial contribution to your level of happiness. Yet another thing to be grateful for!

## SAVORING

The practice of savoring is closely related to gratitude. Savoring refers to the *conscious enjoyment* of that which gives us pleasure; that is, lingering over delightful experiences, swishing them around in our awareness like a glass of good wine. We often think of savoring in terms of a sensual experience: noticing the subtle taste and aroma of our food rather than merely wolfing it down. Smelling, tasting, and caressing our lover's skin rather than merely "doing the deed." But savoring can be applied to all enjoyable experiences—reveling in the lovely sound of a friend's laughter, the beauty of a fallen leaf, the satisfying depth and complexity of a well-written novel.

When we savor an experience, we hold it in mindful awareness, paying conscious attention to the pleasant thoughts, sensations, and emotions arising in the present moment. We can also savor delightful memories, so that we relive joyous experiences and appreciate them all over again—like the day we met our life partner, or first held our newborn child, or took that romantic trip to Prague. Savoring is an intentional act designed to prolong and deepen pleasure, luxuriating in its beauty.

## Exercise Three

### *Savor the Moment*

Pick a food or drink that you find particularly tasty. It could be a piece of dark chocolate, a slice of hot pizza, lobster with butter, a cup of Earl Grey tea, a glass of fine champagne—whatever food or drink reliably gives you pleasure.

As you eat or drink the item, try to savor it as much as possible. Notice all your senses. How does it taste? What subtle flavors are there? Sweet, bitter, salty? How does it smell? What aromas can you detect? How does it feel as you hold it, chew it, swallow it? What textures does it have? How does it look? Does it have interesting colors, or does it catch the light in a particular way? How does it sound? (Okay, this one might be easier if you chose the champagne, but you might notice a satisfying crunch or sizzle . . .) Slow down and fully dive into all the pleasurable sensations of your delicious treat, savoring each sensation fully.

Next, notice how it feels to experience pleasure itself. Do you feel little bubbles of happiness in your throat, a warm feeling in your chest, tingling in your nose? Enjoy the sensation of pleasure as long as possible, and when it fades, let it go. Then take a moment to give thanks and appreciation to one of the great gifts of life—food and drink!

Psychologists have begun to examine the effect of savoring on well-being. Studies indicate that people who are able to savor the pleasant aspects of their lives are happier and less depressed than those who don't. In one study, for instance, people were asked to take a twenty-minute walk once a day for a week. Participants were randomly assigned to one of three conditions. One condition involved a "positive focus" group in which people were instructed to consciously acknowledge as many pleasant things as possible—flowers, sunshine, and so on—and think about what made these things enjoyable. (The pleasure-walk exercise in chapter 12 was inspired by this study.) Another condition involved a "negative focus" group that was instructed to notice as many unpleasant things as possible—trash, traffic noise, and so on—and think about what made these things so disagreeable. The third condition was a control group that was simply told to "go for a walk" with no specific instructions. The people who were asked to savor their positive experiences were significantly happier after the walk compared with the other groups. In follow-up interviews, they also said that they felt a greater sense of appreciation for the world around them.

By simply taking the time to notice and savor the everyday things that give us pleasure, we can dramatically intensify our experience of joy.

## The Gift That Keeps on Giving

Self-appreciation allows us to revel in what's positive about ourselves and our lives. And the amazing thing is that nothing special or out of the ordinary has to happen in order to tap into this wellspring of good feeling. Good feeling can be refreshingly, wonderfully average. You don't need to have something new occur in order to stop and smell the roses. You just need to pay attention to what's in front of your nose. Rather than wandering around in problem-solving mode all day, thinking mainly of what you want to fix about yourself or your life, you can pause for a few moments throughout the day to marvel at *what's not broken.*

You can feel how amazing it is to have a body pulsing with life right now as you read these words. You can consider the wondrous fact that by looking at a few squiggles on a page, you are able to receive and retain the transmission of ideas. Even though you and I have never met, our minds can communicate, all through the sheer power of the written word. Remarkable! You can feel the soft coolness of your breath as it enters and exits your nostrils, fully appreciating the usually-taken-for-granted process that makes your life possible. The wonder of normal day-to-day existence far surpasses our ability to take it all in, but by appreciating it even just a little, we're capable of increasing our happiness to a truly extraordinary degree. As noted by the French writer de la Rochefoucauld, "Happiness does not consist in things themselves but in the relish we have of them."

Self-appreciation is a gift that's there for the taking. All people have aspects of themselves and their lives that are worthy of being appreciated. The good and beautiful is all around us. And within us. Splendor is a human quality and belongs to us all.

## Conclusion

Self-appreciation and self-compassion are really two sides of the same coin. One is focused on what brings us pleasure, the other on what brings us suffering. One celebrates our strengths as humans, the other accepts our weaknesses. What really matters is that our hearts and minds are open. Rather than continually evaluating, comparing, resisting, obsessing, and distorting—we simply open. Open to seeing ourselves and our lives exactly as they are, in all their glory and ignominy. Open to the love of all creation, ourselves included, without exception.

As we walk through the triumphs and tragedies of our lives, we relate to everything with kindness. We feel our interconnectedness with everyone and everything. We become aware of the present moment without judgment. We experience the full spectrum of life without needing to change it.

We don't need to be perfect to feel good about ourselves, and our lives don't need to be any certain way for us to be content. Every one of us has the capacity for resilience, growth, and happiness, simply by relating to our ever-arising experience with both compassion and appreciation. And if you feel you can't change, that it's too hard, that the countervailing forces of our culture are too strong, then have compassion for that feeling and start from there. Each new moment presents an opportunity for a radically different way of being. We can embrace both the joy and the sorrow of being human, and by doing so we can transform our lives.

# NOTES

## CHAPTER 1

PAGE

6 *winning in the game of life* As an example, see Sidney J. Blatt, "Dependency and Self-Criticism: Psychological Dimensions of Depression," *Journal of Consulting and Clinical Psychology* 50 (1982): 113–24.

8 *Although thousands of articles* For example, see Jennifer Crocker and Lora E. Park, "The Costly Pursuit of Self-Esteem," *Psychological Bulletin* 130 (2004): 392–414.

10 *Self-compassion, by definition* Kristin D. Neff, "Self-Compassion: An Alternative Conceptualization of a Healthy Attitude Toward Oneself," *Self and Identity* 2 (2003): 85–102.

12 *"Human beings by nature"* His Holiness Tenzin Gyatso, *Kindness, Clarity, and Insight* (Ithaca, NY: Snow Lion Publications, 1989).
*The research that my colleagues and I* For a review, see Neff, "Self-Compassion," in *Handbook of Individual Differences in Social Behavior,* ed. Mark R. Leary and Rick H. Hoyle (New York: Guilford Press, 2009), 561–73.

15 *You can determine your precise level* Neff, "Development and Validation of a Scale to Measure Self-Compassion," *Self and Identity* 2 (2003): 223–50.

## CHAPTER 2

PAGE

19 *Because human beings tend to live* Paul Gilbert, *Human Nature and Suffering* (Hove, UK: Erlbaum, 1989).
*the phrase "Lake Wobegon effect"* Mark D. Alicke and Olesya Govorun, "The Better-Than-Average Effect," in *The Self in Social Judgment*, ed. Mark D. Alicke, David A. Dunning, and Joachim I. Krueger (New York: Psychology Press, 2005), 85–106.

20 *Even people who've recently caused* Caroline E. Preston and Stanley Harris, "Psychology of Drivers in Traffic Accidents," *Journal of Applied Psychology* 49 (1965): 284–88.
*Ironically, most people also think* Emily Pronin, Thomas Gilovich, and Lee Ross, "Objectivity in the Eye of the Beholder: Divergent Perceptions of Bias in Self Versus Others," *Psychological Review* 111 (2004): 781–99.

20  *Research suggests that all people self-enhance*   For example, see Constantine Sedikides, Lowell Gaertner, and Jack L. Vevea, "Evaluating the Evidence for Pancultural Self-Enhancement," *Asian Journal of Social Psychology* 10 (2007): 201–3.
    *the term "downward social comparison"*   Abraham Tesser, "Toward a Self-Evaluation Maintenance Model of Social Behavior," in *The Self in Social Psychology*, ed. Roy F. Baumeister (New York: Psychology Press, 1999), 446–60.

21  *The movie was actually based on the nonfiction*   Rosalind Wiseman, *Queen Bees and Wannabes: Helping Your Daughter Survive Cliques, Gossip, Boyfriends, and New Realities of Girl World* (New York: Crown, 2002).

24  *Perhaps our behavior becomes more understandable*   Gilbert, "Compassion and Cruelty: A Biopsychosocial Approach," in *Compassion: Conceptualisations, Research and Use in Psychotherapy*, ed. Paul Gilbert (London: Routledge, 2005), 9–74.

25  *research shows that individuals who grow up*   Sidney J. Blatt, *Experiences of Depression: Theoretical, Clinical, and Research Perspectives* (Washington, D.C.: American Psychological Association, 2004).

27  *We recently conducted a study in the United States*   Kristin D. Neff, "Development and Validation of a Scale to Measure Self-Compassion," *Self and Identity* 2 (2003): 223–50.

30  *research shows that highly self-critical people*   Darcy A. Santor and David C. Zuroff, "Interpersonal Responses to Threats to Status and Interpersonal Relatedness: Effects of Dependency and Self-Criticism," *British Journal of Clinical Psychology* 36 (1997): 521–41.
    *"self-verification theory"*   William B. Swann, *Self-Traps: The Elusive Quest for Higher Self-Esteem* (New York: W. H. Freeman, 1996).

33  *externalize and release emotional pain*   Katie Williams, Paul Gilbert, and Kirsten McEwan, "Striving and Competing and Its Relationship to Self-Harm in Young Adults," *International Journal of Cognitive Therapy* 2 (2009): 282–91.
    *A number of large-scale studies*   Blatt, "The Destructiveness of Perfectionism: Implications for the Treatment of Depression," *American Psychologist* 50 (1995): 1003–20.

## CHAPTER 3

PAGE

41  *As I've defined it, self-compassion*   Kristin D. Neff, "Self-Compassion: An Alternative Conceptualization of a Healthy Attitude Toward Oneself," *Self and Identity* 2 (2003): 85–102.

43  *the "tend and befriend" instinct*   Shelley E. Taylor, *The Tending Instinct: How Nurturing Is Essential to Who We Are and How We Live* (New York: Holt, 2002).

44  *The well-known psychologist Harry Harlow*   Harry F. Harlow, "The Nature of Love," *American Psychologist* 13 (1958): 573–685.

45  *John Bowlby, another influential psychologist*   John Bowlby, *Attachment and Loss. Vol. 1: Attachment* (New York: Basic Books, 1969).
    *This creates a pervasive feeling of*   Klaus E. Grossmann, Karin Grossmann, and Everett Waters, eds., *Attachment from Infancy to Adulthood: The Major Longitudinal Studies* (New York: Guilford Press, 2005).
    *It probably comes as no surprise*   Kristin D. Neff and Pittman McGehee, "Self-

Compassion and Psychological Resilience Among Adolescents and Young Adults," *Self and Identity* 9 (2010): 225–40.

46   *A person who is insecurely attached*   Cindy Hazan and Phillip R. Shaver, "Love and Work: An Attachment Theoretical Perspective," *Journal of Personality and Social Psychology* 59 (1990): 270–80.

48   *mother-child bonding after birth*   Ruth Feldman et al., "Evidence for a Neuroendocrinological Foundation of Human Affiliation: Plasma Oxytocin Levels Across Pregnancy and the Postpartum Period Predict Mother-Infant Bonding," *Psychological Science* 18 (2007): 965–70.

   *Research has also shown that increased levels*   A great source for reviewing the oxytocin literature is http://www.oxytocin.org.

   *and also facilitates the ability to feel warmth*   Helen Rockliff et al., "Effects of Intranasal Oxytocin on 'Compassion Focused Imagery'" (submitted).

   *Oxytocin is released in a variety of social*   Julianne Holt-Lunstad, Wendy A. Birmingham, and Kathleen C. Light, "The Influence of a 'Warm Touch' Support Enhancement Intervention Among Married Couples on Ambulatory Blood Pressure, Oxytocin, Alpha Amylase, and Cortisol," *Psychosomatic Medicine* 70 (2008): 976–85.

   *Because thoughts and emotions have the same*   Dacher Keltner, "The Compassionate Instinct," *The Greater Good* 1 (2004): 6–9.

   *Although this system was designed by evolution*   Paul Gilbert, "Compassion and Cruelty: A Biopsychosocial Approach," in *Compassion: Conceptualisations, Research and Use in Psychotherapy,* ed. Paul Gilbert (London: Routledge, 2005), 9–74.

   *Over time increased cortisol levels*   Richard J. Davidson et al., "Depression: Perspectives from Affective Neuroscience," *Annual Review of Psychology* 53 (2002): 545–74.

   *A recent study examined reactions to personal*   Olivia Longe et al., "Having a Word with Yourself: Neural Correlates of Self-Criticism and Self-Reassurance," *Neuroimage* 49 (2009): 1849–56.

49   *Research indicates that physical touch*   To see a great video by one of the leading researchers into the science of touch, go to http://www.greatergoodscience.org, select "Videos and Podcasts," select "The Science of a Meaningful Life Video Series," and watch the video presentation by Dr. Dacher Keltner.

51   *Marshall Rosenberg, author of bestselling*   Marshall Rosenberg, *Nonviolent Communication: A Language of Life* (Encinitas, CA: PuddleDancer Press, 2003).

54   *The healing power of self-kindness*   Allison C. Kelly, David C. Zuroff, and Leah B. Shapira, "Soothing Oneself and Resisting Self-Attacks: The Treatment of Two Intrapersonal Deficits in Depression Vulnerability," *Cognitive Therapy Research* 33 (2009): 301–13.

## CHAPTER 4

Page

62   *Rather than framing their imperfection*   Kristin D. Neff, "Development and Validation of a Scale to Measure Self-Compassion," *Self and Identity* 2 (2003): 223–50.

63   *the more separate and vulnerable we feel*   Tara Brach, *Radical Acceptance: Embracing Your Life with the Heart of a Buddha* (New York: Bantam Books, 2003).

   *Abraham Maslow was a well-known*   Abraham Maslow, *Motivation and Personality* (New York: Harper, 1954).

64 *Similarly, psychoanalyst Heinz Kohut* Heinz Kohut, *The Analysis of the Self* (New York: International Universities Press, 1971).

*Loneliness stems from the feeling* Roy F. Baumeister and Mark R. Leary, "The Need to Belong: Desire for Interpersonal Attachments as a Fundamental Human Motivation," *Psychological Bulletin* 117 (1995): 497–529.

*Research indicates that social isolation* For example, see Lisa F. Berkman, "The Role of Social Relations in Health Promotion," *Psychosomatic Medicine* 57 (1995): 245–54.

*involvement in a support group lessens* David Spiegel et al., "Effect of Psychosocial Treatment on Survival of Patients with Metastatic Breast Cancer," *Lancet* 9 (1989): 888–91.

66 *When we're deeply invested in seeing* Abraham Tesser, "Toward a Self-Evaluation Maintenance Model of Social Behavior," in *Advances in Experimental Social Psychology*, vol. 21, ed. Leonard Berkowitz (New York: Academic Press, 1988), 181–227.

*One of the saddest consequences* Robert Pleban and Abraham Tesser, "The Effects of Relevance and Quality of Another's Performance on Interpersonal Closeness," *Social Psychology Quarterly* 44 (1981): 278–85.

67 *According to Henri Tajfel's social identity theory* Henri Tajfel, "Social Identity and Intergroup Behaviour," *Social Science Information* 13 (1974): 65–93.

68 *Tajfel's research showed* Tajfel, "Experiments in Intergroup Discrimination," *Scientific American* 223 (1970): 96–102.

*One study illustrates this point quite well* Michael J. A. Wohl and Nyla R. Branscombe, "Forgiveness and Collective Guilt Assignment to Historical Perpetrator Groups Depend on Level of Social Category Inclusiveness," *Journal of Personality and Social Psychology* 88 (2005): 288–303.

69 *There's a wonderful program* For information, see http://www.challengeday.org. You can also see a video clip of the exercise that is described by doing a search on "The Teen Files—Part 2: Lines That Divide Us" at http://www.youtube.com.

71 *Research indicates that perfectionists* Gordon L. Flett and Paul L. Hewitt, *Perfectionism: Theory, Research, and Treatment* (Washington, D.C.: American Psychological Association, 2002).

*The popular YouTube character Kelly* The video, by Liam Sullivan, is called "Let Me Borrow That Top" and can be seen by doing a search on the title at http://www.youtube.com.

72 *"If you are a poet"* Thich Nhat Hahn, *Being Peace* (Berkeley, CA: Parallax Press, 1987).

73 *It's useful here to draw a distinction* Joseph Goldstein and Jack Kornfield, *Seeking the Heart of Wisdom: The Path of Insight Meditation* (Boston: Shambhala, 1987).

## CHAPTER 5

PAGE

98 *Many hundreds of studies have now shown* Kirk W. Brown and Richard M. Ryan, "The Benefits of Being Present: Mindfulness and Its Role in Psychological Well-Being," *Journal of Personality and Social Psychology* 84 (2003): 822–48.

98  *For instance, brain scans using fMRI*  J. David Creswell et al., "Neural Correlates of Dispositional Mindfulness During Affect Labeling," *Psychosomatic Medicine* 69 (2007): 560–65.

99  *Jon Kabat-Zinn's Mindfulness-Based Stress Reduction*  Jon Kabat-Zinn, *Full Catastrophe Living: Using the Wisdom of Your Body and Mind to Face Stress, Pain, and Illness* (New York: Dell Publishing, 1991).
*Research has shown that learning to be*  Alberto Chiesa and Alessandro Serretti, "Mindfulness-Based Stress Reduction for Stress Management in Healthy People: A Review and Meta-Analysis," *Journal of Alternative and Complementary Medicine* 15 (2009): 593–600.
*MBSR also helps people cope with chronic pain*  Kabat-Zinn, "An Outpatient Program in Behavioral Medicine for Chronic Pain Patients on the Practice of Mindfulness Meditation: Theoretical Considerations and Preliminary Results," *General Hospital Psychiatry* 4 (1982): 33–47.

101  *MBSR course increases self-compassion levels*  Shauna L. Shapiro, Kirk W. Brown, and Gina Biegel, "Teaching Self-Care to Caregivers: Effects of Mindfulness-Based Stress Reduction on the Mental Health of Therapists in Training," *Training and Education in Professional Psychology* 1 (2007): 105–15.
*more self-compassion than those who are*  Kevin M. Orzech et al., "Intensive Mindfulness Training-Related Changes in Cognitive and Emotional Experience," *Journal of Positive Psychology* 4 (2009): 212–22.

103  *Journaling is an effective way*  Joshua M. Smyth, "Written Emotional Expression: Effect Sizes, Outcome Types, and Moderating Variables," *Journal of Consulting and Clinical Psychology* 66 (1998): 174–84.

## CHAPTER 6

PAGE

110  *One of the most robust and consistent*  Kristin D. Neff, "Self-Compassion," in *Handbook of Individual Differences in Social Behavior,* ed. Mark R. Leary and Rick H. Hoyle (New York: Guilford Press, 2009), 561–73.
*Research has demonstrated that our brains*  Tiffany A. Ito et al., "Negative Information Weighs More Heavily on the Brain: The Negativity Bias in Evaluative Categorizations," *Journal of Personality and Social Psychology* 75 (1998): 887–900.

111  *can cause both depression and anxiety*  Jay K. Brinker and David J. A. Dozois, "Ruminative Thought Style and Depressed Mood," *Journal of Clinical Psychology* 65 (2009): 1–19.
*Research indicates that women are much more*  Susan Nolen-Hoeksema, "Responses to Depression and Their Effects on the Duration of Depressive Episodes," *Journal of Abnormal Psychology* 100 (1991): 569–82.

112  *self-compassionate people tend to experience*  Kristin D. Neff, Stephanie S. Rude, and Kristin L. Kirkpatrick, "An Examination of Self-Compassion in Relation to Positive Psychological Functioning and Personality Traits," *Journal of Research in Personality* 41 (2007): 908–16.
*self-compassionate people have been found*  Neff, "Development and Validation of a Scale to Measure Self-Compassion," *Self and Identity* 2 (2003): 223–50.

114  *researchers asked participants to identify*  Martina Di Simplicio et al., "Oxytocin En-

hances Processing of Positive Versus Negative Emotional Information in Healthy Male Volunteers," *Journal of Psychopharmacology* 23 (2009): 241–48.

116 *In one classic study* Daniel M. Wegner et al., "Paradoxical Effects of Thought Suppression," *Journal of Personality and Social Psychology* 53 (1987): 5–13.

117 *Research shows that people with higher levels* Neff, "Development and Validation."

122 *As defined in Daniel Goleman's influential book* Daniel Goleman, *Emotional Intelligence: Why It Can Matter More Than IQ* (New York: Bantam Books, 1995).

123 *people who are more self-compassionate have* Neff, "Development and Validation."
*people's reactions to an awkward* Mark R. Leary et al., "Self-Compassion and Reactions to Unpleasant Self-Relevant Events: The Implications of Treating Oneself Kindly," *Journal of Personality and Social Psychology* 92 (2007): 887–904.
*report on problems experienced* Ibid.
*Researchers measured cortisol levels* Helen Rockliff et al, "A Pilot Exploration of Heart Rate Variability and Salivary Cortisol Responses to Compassion-Focused Imagery," *Clinical Neuropsychiatry* 5 (2008): 132–39.

124 *PTSD is a severe and ongoing emotional reaction* American Psychiatric Association, *Diagnostic and Statistical Manual of Mental Disorders: DSM-IV* (Washington, D.C.: American Psychiatric Association, 1994).
*in one study of college students who showed* Brian L. Thompson and Jennifer Waltz, "Self-Compassion and PTSD Symptom Severity," *Journal of Traumatic Stress* 21 (2008): 556–58.

128 *Paul Gilbert, a clinician at the University of Derby* Paul Gilbert, *The Compassionate Mind* (London: Constable, 2009).
*This fear of compassion then acts as a roadblock* Gilbert et al., "Fear of Compassion: Development of a Self-Report Measure," *Psychology and Psychotherapy: Theory, Research and Practice* (forthcoming).

129 *In a study of the effectiveness of CMT* Paul Gilbert and Sue Procter, "Compassionate Mind Training for People with High Shame and Self-Criticism: Overview and Pilot Study of a Group Therapy Approach," *Clinical Psychology & Psychotherapy* 13 (2006): 353–79.

131 *He wrote the wonderful book* Christopher K. Germer, *The Mindful Path to Self-Compassion* (New York: Guilford Press, 2009).

## CHAPTER 7

PAGE

136 *Of course, this didn't stop the Task Force* Andrew M. Mecca, Neil J. Smelser, and John Vasconcellos, eds., *The Social Importance of Self-Esteem* (Berkeley: University of California Press, 1989).

137 *In one influential review of the self-esteem literature* Roy F. Baumeister et al., "Does High Self-Esteem Cause Better Performance, Interpersonal Success, Happiness, or Healthier Lifestyles?," *Psychological Science in the Public Interest* 4 (2003): 1–44.
*worse than average on an intelligence test* Todd F. Heatherton and Kathleen D. Vohs, "Interpersonal Evaluations Following Threats to Self: Role of Self-Esteem," *Journal of Personality and Social Psychology* 78 (2000): 725–36.

138 *William James, one of the founding fathers* William James, *Principles of Psychology* (Chicago: Encyclopedia Britannica, 1890).

139 *Charles Horton Cooley, a well-known sociologist* Charles Horton Cooley, *Human Nature and the Social Order* (New York: Charles Scribner, 1902).

*Research shows that self-esteem is more* Susan Harter, *The Construction of the Self: A Developmental Perspective* (New York: Guilford Press, 1999).

140 *researchers examined how college undergraduates* Duane Buhrmester et al., "Five Domains of Interpersonal Competence in Peer Relationships," *Journal of Personality and Social Psychology* 55 (1988): 991–1008.

*high self-esteem people are more confident* Jonathan D. Brown, "Self-Esteem and Self-Evaluation: Feeling Is Believing," in *Psychological Perspectives on the Self*, ed. J. Suls (Hillsdale, NJ: Erlbaum, 1993), 27–58.

142 *Narcissistic Personality Inventory* Robert Raskin and Howard Terry, "A Principal Components Analysis of the Narcissistic Personality Inventory and Further Evidence of Its Construct Validity," *Journal of Personality and Social Psychology* 54 (1988): 890–902.

*But narcissists are actually caught in a social trap* W. Keith Campbell and Laura E. Buffardi, "The Lure of the Noisy Ego: Narcissism as a Social Trap," in *Transcending Self-Interest: Psychological Explorations of the Quiet Ego*, ed. Heidi A. Wayment and Jack J. Bauer (Washington, D.C.: American Psychological Association, 2008), 23–32.

*It turns out that narcissists think they're wonderful* Jean M. Twenge and W. Keith Campbell, *The Narcissism Epidemic: Living in the Age of Entitlement* (New York: Free Press, 2009).

143 *When Paris Hilton claimed* As told to the *Sunday Times* (London), July 16, 2006.

*In one classic study* Brad J. Bushman and Roy F. Baumeister, "Threatened Egotism, Narcissism, Self-Esteem, and Direct and Displaced Aggression: Does Self-Love or Self-Hate Lead to Violence?" *Journal of Personality and Social Psychology* 75 (1998): 219–29.

*This pattern helps explain why clinician* Otto G. Kernberg, *Aggressivity, Narcissism, and Self-Destructiveness in the Psychotherapeutic Relationship: New Developments in the Psychopathology and Psychotherapy of Severe Personality Disorders* (New Haven, CT: Yale University Press, 2004).

145 *The most commonly used measure* Morris Rosenberg, *Society and the Adolescent Self-Image* (Princeton, NJ: Princeton University Press, 1965).

146 *Jean Twenge writes about this trend* Twenge, *Generation Me: Why Today's Young Americans Are More Confident, Assertive, Entitled—and More Miserable Than Ever Before* (New York: Free Press, 2006).

147 *One study found that 48 percent* Linda J. Sax et al., *The American Freshman: National Norms for Fall 2004* (Los Angeles: UCLA, Higher Education Research Institute, 2004).

*Twenge and colleagues examined the scores* Twenge et al., "Egos Inflating Over Time: A Cross-Temporal Meta-analysis of the Narcissistic Personality Inventory," *Journal of Personality* 76 (2008): 875–902.

*"Understanding the narcissism epidemic"* Twenge and Campbell, *The Narcissism Epidemic*.

148 *Because the praise given by teachers* Martin E. Seligman, *The Optimistic Child* (Boston: Houghton Mifflin, 1995).

*Several common areas of contingent self-worth* Jennifer Crocker et al., "Contingencies of Self-Worth in College Students: Theory and Measurement," *Journal of Personality and Social Psychology* 85 (2003): 894–908.

149 *Research shows that the more your overall* Jennifer Crocker, Samuel R. Sommers, and Riia K. Luhtanen, "Hopes Dashed and Dreams Fulfilled: Contingencies of Self-Worth and Admissions to Graduate School," *Personality and Social Psychology Bulletin* 28 (2002): 1275–86.

150 *Psychologists refer to this process as* Philip Brickman and Donald Campbell, "Hedonic Relativism and Planning the Good Society," in *Adaptation Level Theory: A Symposium,* ed. Mortimer H. Apley (New York: Academic Press, 1971), 287–302.

153 *In one study my colleagues and I conducted* Kristin D. Neff, Stephanie S. Rude, and Kristin L. Kirkpatrick, "An Examination of Self-Compassion in Relation to Positive Psychological Functioning and Personality Traits," *Journal of Research in Personality* 41 (2007): 908–16.

154 *Another study required people to imagine* Mark R. Leary et al., "Self-Compassion and Reactions to Unpleasant Self-Relevant Events: The Implications of Treating Oneself Kindly," *Journal of Personality and Social Psychology* 92 (2007): 887–904.

155 *Recently, my colleague Roos Vonk and I* Kristin D. Neff and Roos Vonk, "Self-Compassion Versus Global Self-Esteem: Two Different Ways of Relating to Oneself," *Journal of Personality* 77 (2009): 23–50.

## CHAPTER 8

PAGE

162 *Dozens of studies have confirmed* Albert Bandura, *Self-Efficacy: The Exercise of Control* (New York: Freeman, 1997).
*followed more than two hundred* Thomas D. Kane et al., "Self-Efficacy, Personal Goals, and Wrestlers' Self-Regulation," *Journal of Sport & Exercise Psychology* 18 (1996): 36–48.

163 *report on how much progress they had made* Theodore A. Powers, Richard Koestner, and David C. Zuroff, "Self-Criticism, Goal Motivation, and Goal Progress," *Journal of Social and Clinical Psychology* 26 (2007): 826–40.

166 *The Buddha referred to the motivational quality* Taken from a talk given by Ajahn Brahmavamso at Bodhinyana Monastery, February 7, 2001.

168 *we examined how people reacted* Kristin D. Neff, "Development and Validation of a Scale to Measure Self-Compassion," *Self and Identity* 2 (2003): 223–50.
*We found that self-compassionate people* Kristin D. Neff, Stephanie S. Rude, and Kristin Kirkpatrick, "An Examination of Self-Compassion in Relation to Positive Psychological Functioning and Personality Traits," *Journal of Research in Personality* 41 (2007): 908–16.
*Research psychologist Carol Dweck* Carol S. Dweck, *Mindset* (New York: Random House, 2006).

170 *As you might suspect, our research finds* Kristin D. Neff, Ya-Ping Hseih, and Kullaya Dejittherat, "Self-Compassion, Achievement Goals, and Coping with Academic Failure," *Self and Identity* 4 (2005): 263–87.
*Among a group of undergraduates* Ibid.
*failure is less likely to damage* Ibid.

170 *they tend to refocus their energy* Michelle E. Neely et al., "Self-Kindness When Facing Stress: The Role of Self-Compassion, Goal Regulation, and Support in College Students' Well-Being," *Motivation and Emotion* 33 (2009): 88–97.

*found to procrastinate less than those* Jeannetta G. Williams, Shannon K. Stark, and Erica E. Foster, "Start Today or the Very Last Day? The Relationships Among Self-Compassion, Motivation, and Procrastination," *American Journal of Psychological Research* 4 (2008): 37–44.

173 *self-compassionate people tend to be more authentic* Neff, "Development and Validation."

175 *Research shows that boys' perceptions* Susan Harter, *The Construction of the Self: A Developmental Perspective* (New York: Guilford Press, 1999).

*The problem is that standards for female beauty* April E. Fallon and Paul Rozin, "Sex Differences in Perceptions of Desirable Body Shape," *Journal of Abnormal Psychology* 94 (1985): 102–5.

*research indicates that four out of five* Brenda L. Spitzer, Katherine A. Henderson, and Marilyn T. Zivian, "Gender Differences in Population Versus Media Body Sizes: A Comparison over Four Decades, *Sex Roles* 40 (1999): 545–65.

*Almost 50 percent of all girls* Kristina Thomas, Lina A. Ricciardelli, and Robert J. Williams, "Gender Traits and Self-Concept as Indicators of Problem Eating and Body Dissatisfaction Among Children, *Sex Roles* 43 (2000): 441–58.

176 *For some, the obsession with thinness* Laurie B. Mintz and Nancy E. Betz, "Prevalence and Correlates of Eating Disordered Behaviors Among Undergraduate Women," *Journal of Counseling Psychology* 35 (1988): 463–71.

177 *A recent study supports this claim* Claire E. Adams and Mark R. Leary, "Promoting Self-Compassionate Attitudes Toward Eating Among Restrictive and Guilty Eaters," *Journal of Social and Clinical Psychology* 26 (2007): 1120–44.

178 *self-compassionate women tend to have* Cathy M. R. Magnus, Kent C. Kowalski, and Tara-Leigh F. McHugh, "The Role of Self-Compassion in Women's Self-Determined Motives to Exercise and Exercise-Related Outcomes," *Self and Identity* (forthcoming).

*self-compassionate people are more comfortable* Amber D. Mosewich, "Young Women Athletes' Self-Conscious Emotions and Self-Compassion" (master's thesis, University of Saskatchewan, Saskatoon, Saskatchewan, Canada, 2006).

*They're also less likely to worry* Katie-Ann Berry, Kent C. Kowalski, Leah J. Ferguson, and Tara-Leigh F. McHugh, "An Empirical Phenomenology of Young Adult Women Exercisers' Body Self-Compassion," *Qualitative Research in Sport and Exercise* (forthcoming).

*Oprah remains focused on* http://www.Oprah.com, December 11, 2008.

180 *Research indicates that people who suffer* June P. Tangney et al., "Shamed into Anger? The Relation of Shame and Guilt to Anger and Self-Reported Aggression," *Journal of Personality and Social Psychology* 62 (1992): 669–75.

181 *has created a program for emotionally* For more information on Steven Stosny's anger management programs, go to www.compassionpower.com.

*Participants were asked to recall* Mark R. Leary et al., "Self-Compassion and Reactions to Unpleasant Self-Relevant Events: The Implications of Treating Oneself Kindly," *Journal of Personality and Social Psychology* 92 (2007): 887–904.

## CHAPTER 9

PAGE

187  *In the first study I ever conducted*  Kristin D. Neff, "Development and Validation of a Scale to Measure Self-Compassion," *Self and Identity* 2 (2003): 223–50.

188  *self-compassionate people score no higher*  Kristin D. Neff, Lisa M. Yarnell, and Elizabeth Pommier, *The Relationship Between Self-Compassion and Other-Focused Concern* (submitted for publication).

189  *women tend to have slightly lower levels*  Neff, "Development and Validation."
*women tend to be more caring*  Nancy Eisenberg, "Empathy," in *Encyclopedia of Psychology, Vol. 3,* ed. Alan E. Kazdin (Washington, D.C.: American Psychological Association, 2000), 179–82.
*"Even though I can objectively say"*  Dana Crowley Jack, *Silencing the Self: Women and Depression* (Cambridge, MA: Harvard University Press, 1991).

190  *different goals in their friendships*  Jennifer Crocker and Amy Canevello, "Creating and Undermining Social Support in Communal Relationships: The Role of Compassionate and Self-Image Goals," *Journal of Personality and Social Psychology* 95 (2008): 555–75.

191  *are also more likely to engage in perspective taking*  Neff, Yarnell, and Pommier, *The Relationship Between Self-Compassion and Other-Focused Concern.*
*allows us to feel others' pain without becoming*  Ibid.

192  *Focusing a lot of our energy on helping others*  Charles R. Figley, *Compassion Fatigue: Coping with Secondary Traumatic Stress Disorder in Those Who Treat the Traumatized* (Philadelphia: Brunner/Mazel, 1995).
*It's been estimated that about one-quarter*  Beth H. Stamm, "Work-Related Secondary Traumatic Stress," *PTSD Research Quarterly* 19 (1997): 49–64.
*Among those working with survivors*  David F. Wee and Diane Myers, "Stress Responses of Mental Health Workers Following Disaster: The Oklahoma City Bombing," in *Treating Compassion Fatigue,* ed. Charles R. Figley (New York: Brunner-Routledge, 2002), 57–84.
*caregivers who have been trained*  Shauna L. Shapiro et al., "Mindfulness-Based Stress Reduction for Health Care Professionals: Results from a Randomized Trial," *International Journal of Stress Management* 12 (2005): 164–76.
*self-compassion leads to more*  Ron Ringenbach, "A Comparison between Counselors Who Practice Meditation and Those Who Do Not on Compassion Fatigue, Compassion Satisfaction, Burnout, and Self-Compassion," *Dissertation Abstracts International* (2009) AAT 3361751.

193  *concrete acts of self-care*  Figley, *Compassion Fatigue.*

195  *link between self-compassion and forgiveness*  Neff, Yarnell, and Pommier, *The Relationship Between Self-Compassion and Other-Focused Concern.*

205  *A recent study by Richie Davidson*  Richie Davidson, "Changing the Brain by Transforming the Mind. The Impact of Compassion Training on the Neural Systems of Emotion (paper presented at the Mind and Life Institute Conference, Investigating the Mind, Emory University, Atlanta, GA, October 2007).

## CHAPTER 10

PAGE

211 *Our research shows that continual* Kristin D. Neff and Pittman McGehee, "Self-Compassion and Psychological Resilience Among Adolescents and Young Adults," *Self and Identity* 9 (2010): 225–40.

213 *The program is called MAP* Rebecca Coleman, *Mindful Awareness Parenting (MAP™) Instructor Manual* (Australia: Wiseheart Consulting & Publishing, 2009).

217 *To make things worse, the introspection* Daniel K. Lapsley et al., "Separation-Individuation and the 'New Look' at the Imaginary Audience and Personal Fable: A Test of an Integrative Model," *Journal of Adolescent Research* 4 (1989): 483–505.

218 *Our research shows that teens* Neff and McGehee, "Self-Compassion and Psychological Resilience."

## CHAPTER 11

PAGE

225 *Research psychologist John Gottman* John Gottman, *The Marriage Clinic: A Scientifically Based Marital Therapy* (New York: Norton Press, 1999).

226 *Luckily, Gottman has also identified factors* Gottman et al., "Predicting Marital Happiness and Stability from Newly Wed Interactions," *Journal of Marriage and the Family* 60 (1998): 5–22.

228 *A colleague and I recently conducted a study* Kristin D. Neff and S. Natasha Beretvas, *The Role of Self-Compassion in Healthy Relationship Interactions* (submitted for publication).

*People often become angry* Steven R. H. Beach et al., "Self-Evaluation Maintenance in Marriage: Toward a Performance Ecology of the Marital Relationship," *Journal of Family Psychology* 10 (1996): 379–96.

229 *When self-esteem comes in the form* W. Keith Campbell, Craig A. Foster, and Eli J. Finkel, "Does Self-Love Lead to Love for Others? A Story of Narcissistic Game Playing," *Journal of Personality and Social Psychology* 83 (2002): 340–54.

237 *Approximately two-thirds of the popular songs* Brian A. Primack et al., "Degrading and Nondegrading Sex in Popular Music: A Content Analysis," *Public Health Reports* 123 (2008): 593–600.

*"Several hours later, as she prepared"* Laura S. Stepp, *Unhooked: How Young Women Pursue Sex, Delay Love, and Lose at Both* (New York: Riverhead Books, 2007).

*Almost one-quarter of teen girls* Peter S. Bearman and Hannah Brückner, "Promising the Future: Virginity Pledges and First Intercourse," *American Journal of Sociology* 106 (2001): 859–912.

*Several large-scale studies have found* Janet E. Rosenbaum, "Patient Teenagers? A Comparison of the Sexual Behavior of Virginity Pledgers and Matched Nonpledgers," *Pediatrics* 123 (2009): 110–20.

240   *One study assigned a group*   R. Gina Silverstein and Willoughby B. Britton, "Get Out of Your Mind and Into Your Body: The Role of Mindfulness in the Treatment of Female Sexual Dysfunction" (poster presented at the Sixth World Congress of Behavioral and Cognitive Therapies, Boston, MA, June 2010).

## CHAPTER 12

PAGE

250   specific action tendencies   Richard S. Lazarus, *Emotion and Adaptation* (New York: Oxford University Press, 1991).

251   *broaden-and-build theory*   Barbara L. Fredrickson, "The Role of Positive Emotions in Positive Psychology: The Broaden-and-Build Theory of Positive Emotions," *American Psychologist* 56 (2001): 218–26.
      *"Positivity opens us"*   Fredrickson, *Positivity* (New York: Crown, 2009).

254   *Fredrickson and her colleagues have recently*   Fredrickson et al., "Open Hearts Build Lives: Positive Emotions, Induced Through Meditation, Build Consequential Personal Resources," *Journal of Personality and Social Psychology* 95 (2008): 1045–62.
      *Similarly, an fMRI study by Richie Davidson*   Antoine Lutz et al., "Long-Term Meditators Self-Induce High-Amplitude Gamma Synchrony During Mental Practice," *Proceedings of the National Academy of Sciences, USA* 101 (2004): 16369–73.

255   *can help to maximize health and well-being*   Martin E. Seligman and Mihaly Csikzentmihalyi, "Positive Psychology: An Introduction," *American Psychologist* 55 (2000): 5–14.
      *self-compassionate people experience more positive*   Kristin D. Neff, Stephanie S. Rude, and Kristin Kirkpatrick, "An Examination of Self-Compassion in Relation to Positive Psychological Functioning and Personality Traits," *Journal of Research in Personality* 41 (2007): 908–16.
      *self-compassionate people are much more optimistic*   Ibid.

256   *self-compassionate people tend to be more curious*   Ibid.
      *demonstrated among people living*   Kristin D. Neff, Kasom Pisitsungkagarn, and Ya-Ping Hseih, "Self-Compassion and Self-Construal in the United States, Thailand, and Taiwan," *Journal of Cross-Cultural Psychology* 39 (2008): 267–85.

## CHAPTER 13

PAGE

276   *many psychologists argue that we have*   David T. Lykken, *Happiness: What Studies on Twins Show Us About Nature, Nurture, and the Happiness Set-Point* (New York: Golden Books, 1999).

277   *Lyubomirsky finds that several key factors*   Sonia Lyubomirsky, *The How of Happiness: A New Approach to Getting the Life You Want* (New York: Penguin, 2008).
      *Studies show that grateful individuals*   Robert A. Emmons, *Thanks! How the New Science of Gratitude Can Make You Happier* (New York: Houghton Mifflin, 2007).
      *researchers asked a group of undergraduate students*   Robert A. Emmons and Michael E. McCullough, "Counting Blessings Versus Burdens: An Experimental Investiga-

tion of Gratitude and Subjective Well-Being in Daily Life," *Journal of Personality and Social Psychology* 84 (2003): 377–89.

280  *the effect of savoring on well-being*  Fred B. Bryant, "Savoring Beliefs Inventory (SBI): A Scale for Measuring Beliefs About Savoring," *Journal of Mental Health* 12 (2003): 175–96.

*people were asked to take a twenty-minute walk*  Fred B. Bryant and Joseph Veroff, *Savoring: A New Model of Positive Experiences* (Mahwah, NJ: Lawrence Erlbaum, 2007).

# INDEX

abstinence, 237
acne, healing, 54–55
action tendencies, 250
adolescents, parenting, 217–18
adrenaline, 48
Alcoholics Anonymous, 96
Ali, Muhammad, 20
amygdala, 48, 110, 114
anger:
   and feelings of power, 28, 180–81
   narcissistic, 143
   road rage, 94
   underlying vulnerability in, 181
anorexia, 176
anxiety, 110
attachment system, 43–46
author's story:
   abandoned and unlovable, 31–33
   to err is human, 56–59
   forgiveness, 196–99
   getting through dark times, 105–6
   the horse boy, 258–65
   irritability, 182–83
   parenting, 218–20
   relationships, 230–34
   sexual healing, 241–42
   what's normal?, 76–79
autism:
   author's son's condition, 77–79, 105–6,
      218–20, 264–65
   echolalia in, 219
   gift of, 265
   the horse boy, 258–65
awareness, 85–88

backdraft, 131
Bandura, Albert, 162–63

beauty, standards of, 175–78
belong, need to, 63–65
Bennett-Goleman, Tara, *Emotional Alchemy*, 13
Besa (shaman), 264–65
binge eating, 176
"black goo" mind, 110, 112, 113
blame, 5
body, acceptance of, 174–80
body scan, exercise, 133–34
Bowlby, John, 45
Brach, Tara, *Radical Acceptance*, 63
brain:
   and caring, 44
   and connectedness, 64–65
   self-criticism vs. self-kindness in, 48–49
broaden-and-build theory, 251
Buddhism, 27, 254
   author's experience with, 6–7, 56
   loving-kindness meditation in, 201, 206
   right effort in, 166
   sympathetic joy in, 270
bulimia, 176
Bushmen (San tribesmen), 259, 264

California Task Force on Self-Esteem, 136
Campbell, Keith, 147
caregivers:
   compassion fatigue of, 192–93
   taking care of, 193–94
caregiving system, 43–49
caress, 50–52
celebrating the human experience, 256–57
Challenge Day, 69
Chaplin, Charlie, 84
chastity, 237
Childre, Doc Lew, 207
Chödrön, Pema, *Start Where You Are*, 41

Coleman, Rebecca, 213–14, 215
Columbine High School, 144
common humanity, 41, 61–79, 271
 celebrating the human experience,
  256–57
 Challenge Day, 69
 comparisons, 65–67
 as doorway to self-compassion, 102
 forgiveness in, 195
 illusion of perfection, 70–71
 interconnectedness, 72–75
 interconnectedness exercise, 75–76
 isolation vs., 62–63
 journal, 104
 need to belong, 63–65
 and self-appreciation, 272–73
 suffering, 120
 us against them, 67–69
comparisons, 20, 65–67
compassion:
 for others, 9–10, 187–206, 271
 as our birthright, 12
 for ourselves (see self-compassion)
 satisfaction of, 192
compassionate imagery, exercise, 129–30
Compassionate Mind Training (CMT),
  128–29
compassion fatigue, 192–93
Confucian ideal, 27
connectedness:
 disconnectedness, 62–63
 effects on the brain, 64–65
 interconnectedness, 72–75
Connolly, Billy, 190
conscious enjoyment, 279
consciousness, 88–89
contingent self-worth, 148–50
Cooley, Charles Horton, 139
coping skills, 123–24
cortisol, 48, 123–24
courage, 124
criticism, vs. motivation, 160–65
Csikzentmihalyi, Mihaly, 255
culture, role of, 27

Dalai Lama, 11–12, 27
Dass, Ram, Be Here Now, 85

Davidson, Richie, 205, 254
Day, Doris, 257
death, fear of, 64
Declaration of Independence, U.S., 12
depression, 33–34, 82, 110
de Vries, Peter, 208
disconnectedness, 62–63
distortion, 4–6
Dostoyevsky, Fyodor, 117
downward social comparison, 20
Dweck, Carol, Mindset, 168

echolalia, 219
Ecstasy (MDMA), 48
ego, freedom from, 157–58
egotists, 269–70
Einstein, Albert, The Einstein Papers, 61
Eliot, T. S., The Elder Statesman, 18
Emmons, Robert, 277
emotional intelligence, 122–25
emotional resilience, 109–34
 body scan exercise, 133–34
 breaking free, 112–14
 compassionate imagery, 129–30
 compassionate mind training, 128–29
 dealing with difficult emotions, 114–16
 exercises, 114–16, 121–22, 129–30,
  133–34
 healing power, 125–27
 mindfulness and psychotherapy,
  130–32
 negative emotions, 110–12, 116–18
 self-compassion mantra, 121–22
 suppression, 116–18
 wholeness, 118–21
enjoyment, conscious, 279
exercise (physical), and health, 177–78
exercises:
 accepting our bodies, 178–80
 appreciating yourself, 274
 changing self-critical talk, 53–55
 compassionate body scan, 133–34
 compassionate imagery, 129–30
 difficult emotions, 114–16
 forgiveness, 200–201
 gratitude journal, 278–79
 hugging practice, 49–50

interconnectedness, 75–76
letter writing, 16–17
loving-kindness, 203–6
mindfully working with pain, 95
mindfulness in daily life, 100–102
motivation, 167, 171–73
noting practice, 89–90
parenting, 210, 215–17
pleasure walk, 253–54
procrastination, 171–73
relationships, 224–25
releasing sexual shame, 239–41
savoring the moment, 280
self-compassion break, 234–35
self-compassion journal, 103–4
self-compassion mantra, 121–22
self-evaluation, 22–23
silver lining, 265–66
taking care of caregivers, 193–94
"time-in," 215–17
transforming negativity, 249
trickster, 156–57
two-chair dialogue, 35–37
your reactions to yourself and your life,
    13–15
expectations, too high, 29, 168, 268

failure, fear of, 172–73
fears:
    of failure, 172–73
    of letting go, 268–69
    and self-fulfilling prophecy, 29–30
    of self-indulgence, 160
feelings, 52
    of being special, 3–4
    painful, 83–85
    suppression of, 116–18
    of unworthiness, 63
feminist movement, 189
fight-or-flight response, 110
flaws, ignoring, 5
floccinaucinihilipilification, 24
forgiveness, 195
    author's story, 196–99
    exercise, 200–201
Frederickson, Barbara, *Positivity*,
    251, 254

gay men, authenticity of, 238
Germer, Christopher, 130–32
    and Mindful Self-Compassion, 132,
        133, 202
    *The Mindful Path to Self-Compassion*, 131
Ghoste (shaman), 263–64
Gibran, Kahlil, *The Prophet*, 245
Gilbert, Paul, *The Compassionate Mind*,
    128–30
goals, 168–71
    learning, 168, 170
    performance, 168–69, 170
    too high, 29, 168, 268
Goleman, Daniel, 122
Gore, Al, *An Inconvenient Truth*, 29
Gottman, John, 225–26
gratitude, 277–79
    journal exercise, 278–79
    and savoring, 279–81
Greenberg, Leslie, 35
group identity, 68

Hahn, Thich Nhat, 72–73, 272
Hanson, Rick, *The Buddha's Brain*, 111
happiness:
    and appreciation, 276–77
    savoring, 279–81, 282
    search for, 173–74
    and self-esteem, 141
Harlow, Harry, 44–45
Harris, Eric, 144
Hasdai Ibn Shaprut, 187
healing power, 54–55, 125–27
heart:
    loving-kindness in, 201–3
    openheartedness, 246–48
    touching, 41
hedonic treadmill, 150
Hesse, Herman, 109
Hilton, Paris, 143
Hobbes, Thomas, 29
Holocaust, 68
hookups, 237
*Horse Boy, The* (Rupert), 261–65
hugging practice, 49–50
human experience, celebrating, 256–57
humanity, common. *See* common humanity

Ibn Shaprut, Hasdai, 187
Implicit Association Test (IAT), 142
inadequacy, feelings of, 81
infatuation stage, 131
interbeing, 72–73, 272
interconnectedness, 72–75
    exercise, 75–76
irritability, 182–83
isolation, 62–63

Jack, Dana Crowley, *Silencing the
    Self,* 189
James, William, 138
Jesus of Nazareth, 74
journal:
    gratitude, 278–79
    self-compassion, 103–4
joy, sympathetic, 270–71, 272
judgment, 73–74
Jung, Carl, 257

Kabat-Zinn, Jon:
    MBSR, 99, 132
    *Wherever You Go, There You Are,* 80
Keillor, Garrison, 19
Keller, Helen, 250
Kernberg, Otto, 144
Kilbourne, Jean, 236
kindness. *See* self-kindness
Klebold, Dylan, 144
Kohut, Heinz, 64
Ku Klux Klan, 67

"Lake Wobegon effect," 19
la Rochefoucauld, Duc François de, 282
learning, 168–71
letter writing, 16–17
letting go, 268–69
Levin, Diane, and Jean Kilbourne, *So Sexy,
    So Soon,* 236
loneliness, 64
love, 221–42
    and motivation, 165–67
    and romance, 221–24
    and sex, 235–39
    sexual healing, 241–42
    *See also* relationships

loving-kindness, 201–3
    exercise, 203–6
Lyubomirsky, Sonia, *The How of Happiness,*
    276–77

Magic Circle game, 146
mantra, self-compassion, 121–22
Maslow, Abraham, 63–64
MDMA (Ecstasy), 48
*Mean Girls* (film), 21
meta-awareness, 86
Mindful Awareness Parenting (MAP), 213–14
mindfulness, 41, 80–106, 271
    of awareness, 85–88
    consciousness, 88–89
    in daily life, 100–102
    definition of, 80
    as doorway to self-compassion, 102
    journal, 103–4
    learning, 98–100
    of negative thoughts, 112–13
    noting practice, 89–90
    of painful feelings, 83–85
    and psychotherapy, 130–32
    responding vs. reacting, 90–93
    and self-appreciation, 273
    of suffering, 80–83, 93–94, 119–20
    of things beyond our control, 96–98
Mindfulness-Based Stress Reduction
    (MBSR), 99, 132, 133
Mindful Self-Compassion (MSC), 132,
    133, 202
Mongolia, author's family in, 259–65
monkeys, attachment systems of, 44
motivation, 159–83
    criticism vs., 160–65
    exercises, 167, 171–73
    and happiness, 173–74
    and love, 165–67
    and personal growth, 168–71
    and procrastination, 163–65, 171–73
    self-improvement, 180–82
    and standards of beauty, 175–78
    what we really want, 167

narcissism, 141–45
    and anger, 143

malignant, 144
Narcissistic Personality Inventory, 142, 147
needs, 52
negative emotions, 110–12
  "black goo" mind, 110, 112, 113
  breaking free of, 112–14
  open-mindedness vs., 250–53
  as physical sensation, 112–13
  suppression of, 116–18
  transforming, 249
neurotransmitters, 48
Nicholson, Jack, 211
Nimmons, David, *The Soul Beneath the Skin,* 238
noting exercise, 89–90

obesity, 176–77
observation, 52
Oklahoma City bombing, 192
openheartedness, 246–48
open-mindedness, 250–53
others:
  caregivers, 192–94
  compassion fatigue, 192–93
  compassion for, 9–10, 187–206, 271
  forgiveness of, 195–201
  loving-kindness to, 201–3
  need to feel better than, 19–21
  in perspective, 190–92
overeating, 176–77
overidentification, 83–85
oxytocin, 47–48, 114

pain:
  escape from, 124–25
  mindful working with, 95
  resisting, 93–94
painful feelings, 83–85
parenting, 207–20
  of adolescents, 217–18
  author's story, 218–20
  correcting your child, 211–13
  exercises, 210, 215–17
  imperfect, 208–9, 210
  Mindful Awareness Parenting, 213–14
  "time-in," 215–17
  of young children, 213–15

parents:
  bonds with, 45
  role of, 25–26, 28
  as secure base, 45
Pearce, Joseph Chilton, 207
perfectionism, 70–71
personal growth, 168–71
perspective, 190–92
pleasure walk, 253–54
positive emotions, 251, 254
  celebrating the human experience, 256–57
positive psychology, 255–56
positive traits, appreciation of, 268–70
post-traumatic stress disorder (PTSD), 124
Powell, Anthony, 23
power, feelings of, 28, 180–81
powerlessness, 73
praise, 145–48, 268
prejudice, 67–68
problem-solving, 81
procrastination, 163–65, 171–73
  and fear of failure, 172–73
  of unpleasant tasks, 171–72
Psalms, Book of, 277
psychology, positive, 255–56
psychotherapy, and mindfulness, 130–32

Quayle, Dan, 191

reactions, exercise, 13–15
relationships:
  author's story, 230–34
  bedroom, 235–39
  choosing partners, 30–31
  dynamics of, 225–28
  exercise, 224–25
  hookups, 237
  patterns of, 224–25
  romantic, 221–24
  and self-compassion, 228–30
  and self-esteem, 228–29
religion, and gratitude, 277
requests, 52
responding, 90–93
road rage, 94
Rogers, Carl, *On Becoming a Person,* 159

romance, 221–24
Rosenberg, Marshall, *Nonviolent Communication,* 51–52
Rosenberg Self-Esteem Scale, 145–46
rumination, 111–12

Salzberg, Sharon:
    *Lovingkindness,* 7
    *The Force of Kindness,* 3
San tribesmen (Bushmen), 259, 264
savoring, 279–81, 282
schools, grade inflation in, 147
school shooters, 144
self-absorption, 63
self-aggrandizement, 24
self-appreciation, 267–83
    and common humanity, 272–73
    exercises, 274, 278–79, 280
    gift of, 281–82
    and gratitude, 277–79
    and happiness, 276–77
    and kindness, 272
    and mindfulness, 273
    of our good side, 268–70
    roots of, 271–73
    and savoring, 279–81
    and self-compassion, 282–83
    self-definition, 275
    self-esteem vs., 274–76
    sympathetic joy, 270–71
    of what's good in our lives, 276–77
self-blame, 81
self-clarity, 180–82
self-compassion:
    author's discovery of, 6–8
    backdraft stage, 131
    break (exercise), 234–35
    common humanity in, 41, 61–79, 271
    definitions of, 10–13
    discovering, 3–4
    distortion vs., 4–6
    doorways to, 102–3
    and emotional intelligence, 122–25
    gift of, 60
    healing power of, 125–27
    infatuation stage, 131
    journal, 103–4

letter writing as instrument of, 16–17
    mantra, 121–22
    mindfulness in, 41, 80–106, 271
    and openheartedness, 246–48
    and open-mindedness, 250–53
    and our bodies, 174–78
    and positive psychology, 255–56
    and relationships, 228–30
    and self-appreciation, 282–83
    self-esteem vs., 152–56
    self-kindness in, 41, 42–60, 271
    and sex, 238, 240
    stages of, 131
    taking a break, 234–35
    true acceptance, 132
self-concept, 28, 151, 275
self-criticism, 7, 24–25, 28–29, 160–61
    author's history of, 31–33
    changing your talk of, 53–55
    effects on brain, 48–49
    leading to suicide, 33, 34
    as self-care, 34–35
self-definition, 275
    letting go of, 75–76
self-efficacy beliefs, 162–63
self-esteem, 135–58
    California Task Force on, 136
    confusing the map for the territory, 151–52
    contingent, 148–50
    definitions of, 138–40
    freedom from ego, 157–58
    and happiness, 141
    hedonic treadmill, 150
    and indiscriminate praise, 145–48
    mirror image of, 140–41
    and narcissism, 141–45
    perceived, 139
    and relationships, 228–29
    Rosenberg Scale, 145–46
    self-appreciation vs., 274–76
    self-compassion vs., 152–56
self-evaluation exercise, 22–23
self-fulfilling prophecy, 29–30
self-handicapping, 163
self-harm, 33
self-improvement, 180–82

self-indulgence, 12
    fear of, 160
self-judgment, costs of, 5–6, 11
self-kindness, 41, 42–60, 271
    active, 42
    attachment system, 43–46
    caregiving system, 43–49
    definition of, 42
    as doorway to self-compassion, 102
    effects on brain, 48–49
    gentle caress of, 50–52
    healing power of, 54–55
    journal, 104
    path to, 42–43
    and self-appreciation, 272
    and suffering, 120
    and sympathy, 42
self-pity, 12
self-protection, 26
self-psychology model, 64
self-reflection, 151
Seligman, Martin, 255
serenity prayer, 96
sex life, 235–39
sexual authenticity, 238
sexual healing, author's story,
    241–42
sexual shame, releasing, 239–41
silver lining, exercise, 265–66
social identity theory, 67
specific action tendencies, 250
standards, set too high, 29, 168, 268
Stepford Wives, The (film), 189
Stepp, Laura Sessions, Unhooked, 237
stiff-upper-lip tradition, 11
Stosny, Steven, Love Without Hurt, 181
stress, 123–24
submissive behavior, 24
suffering:
    amelioration of, 10
    loving-kindness exercise, 203–6
    mindfulness of, 80–83, 93–94,
        119–20
    uses for, 12

suicide, 33–34
Sullivan, Liam Kyle, 71
suppression, 116–18
Swann, Bill, 30
sympathetic joy, 270–71, 272
sympathy, 42

Tajfel, Henri, 67–68
terrorism, 67
Thich Nhat Hahn, 72–73, 272
"This too shall pass," 124
threat, detection of, 48
"time-in," 215–17
Tolle, Eckhart, A New Earth, 135
Tomoo (Mongolian boy), 262–63
trickster, 156–57
true acceptance, 132
Tulga (guide), 261–62
Twain, Mark, 218
twelve-step programs, 96
Twenge, Jean:
    Generation Me, 146, 147
    The Narcissism Epidemic, 147–48
two-chair dialogue, 35–37

unworthiness, feelings of, 63
us against them, 67–69

vulnerability, 181

walking, for pleasure, 253–54
weight, 176–77
wholeness, journey to, 118–21
Wilde, Oscar, 221
Williamson, Marianne, A Return to Love,
    267
Winfrey, Oprah, 178
wisdom, discriminating, 74
Wiseman, Rosalind, Queen Bees and
    Wannabes, 21

young children, parenting, 213–15
Young, Shinzen, 93
yo-yo dieting, 177